T0307976

Civil War

CAMPAIGNS
in the
HEARTLAND

STEVEN E. WOODWORTH
AND CHARLES D. GREAR
SERIES EDITORS

The Confederate Heartland

Ohio

Indiana

Illinois

Cincinnati

West Virginia

Louisville

Lexington

Frankfort

Missouri

Kentucky

Perryville

Cumberland River

Virginia

Cairo

Nashville

Knoxville

North Carolina

Forts Henry and Donelson

Tennessee

Franklin-Spring Hill

Stones River

Arkansas

Shiloh

Chattanooga

South Carolina

Memphis

Corinth

Iuka

Tennessee River

Chickamauga

Resaca-Adairsville

Dallas-Pickett's Mill

Kennesaw Mountain-Peachtree Creek

Atlanta

Ezra Church

Jonesboro

Mississippi River

Tallahatchie River

Yazoo River

Fort Pemberton

Alabama

Chickasaw Bayou

Meridian

Montgomery

Savannah

Vicksburg

Jackson

Grand Gulf

Champion's Hill

Georgia

Port Gibson

Mississippi

Mobile

Louisiana

Florida

New Orleans

Gulf of Mexico

Charles D. Grear

The

VICKSBURG
—— *Campaign* ——

MARCH 29–MAY 18, 1863

Edited by Steven E. Woodworth
and Charles D. Grear

Southern Illinois University Press
Carbondale

16 15 14 13   4 3 2 1

Library of Congress Cataloging-in-Publication Data
The Vicksburg Campaign, March 27–May 18, 1863 / edited by
Steven E. Woodworth and Charles D. Grear.
  pages cm. — (Civil War campaigns in the heartland)
Includes bibliographical references and index.
ISBN-13: 978-0-8093-3269-4 (cloth : alk. paper)
ISBN-10: 0-8093-3269-8 (cloth : alk. paper)
ISBN-13: 978-0-8093-3270-0 (ebook)
ISBN-10: 0-8093-3270-1 (ebook)
1. Vicksburg (Miss.)—History—Siege, 1863. 2. Mississippi—
History—Civil War, 1861–1865—Campaigns. 3. United
States—History—Civil War, 1861–1865—Campaigns.
I. Woodworth, Steven E. II. Grear, Charles D., [date]
E475.27.V615 2013
973.7'344—dc23   2013001623

Printed on recycled paper. ♻
The paper used in this publication meets the minimum
requirements of American National Standard for Information
Sciences—Permanence of Paper for Printed Library Materials,
ANSI Z39.48-1992. ♾1992.

To my son, Jackson David Grear
I look forward to the day when I can take him to Vicksburg and
other significant sites in the United States' wonderful history.

To my daughters—Anna, Elizabeth, and Mary Woodworth

CONTENTS

ILLUSTRATIONS

ACKNOWLEDGMENTS

Many people have helped us develop this book. We, the editors, owe our deepest gratitude to all the contributors. Their cooperation and dedication to this book made it a joy to work on—more importantly, it would not exist without them. Thank you all. Southern Illinois University Press editor Sylvia Frank Rodrigue deserves special recognition for all her efforts. Sylvia goes beyond what is expected of any editor and is the driving force behind this project. We would also like to thank the rest of the SIU Press staff for their help in the development of every step of this volume. Lastly, we would like to express our deepest appreciation to our families for their constant support. They inspire us in all our endeavors.

The Vicksburg Campaign

MARCH 29–MAY 18, 1863

INTRODUCTION

It lasted only seven and a half weeks, but the maneuver segment of the Vicksburg Campaign reversed the verdict of the previous six months' operations on the Mississippi, all but sealed the doom of the Gibraltar of the Confederacy and its defending army, secured the reputation of Ulysses S. Grant as one of history's greatest generals, and paved the way to eventual Confederate defeat. From a situation of deadlock in which Confederate general John C. Pemberton believed that he had won and that Grant was about to retreat, Grant loosed a fluid campaign of rapid maneuver and lightning strikes that stunned his opponent and left Confederate forces in Mississippi demoralized and cornered. The campaign astonished Grant's own lieutenants as much as it did his foes. Only Grant and the rank-and-file of his Army of the Tennessee seemed to have expected nothing but victory from the outset.

Union forces had first appeared in the neighborhood of Vicksburg in May 1862. U.S. Navy warships under Flag Officer David Farragut reached the town, having come up the Mississippi from the Gulf of Mexico after capturing New Orleans. Farragut cruised up and down the river in the vicinity of Vicksburg for several weeks and made contact with a flotilla of Union gunboats that had fought their way past every Confederate stronghold on the Mississippi above Vicksburg. The concentration of naval power was impressive, but the gunboats and sloops-of-war could not take the town themselves and did not have enough troops with them to storm it. As the summer wore on, the depth of the river decreased, and Farragut had to take his deep-water ships back downstream.

Late that autumn, Grant made his own first attempt on Vicksburg. Beginning in late November, he marched his army southward from bases in West Tennessee into Mississippi along the line of the Mississippi Central Railroad. Grant hoped his advance would goad his opposite number, Lieutenant General John C. Pemberton, into giving battle. Once Grant had defeated Pemberton in the field, the whole state of Mississippi might lie open to him. Pemberton, however, declined battle, retreating steadily southward, deeper into the state. Not wanting to extend his own supply line too far, Grant modified his plan. While he would continue a slow advance in northern Mississippi, holding Pemberton's attention, his most trusted subordinate, William T. Sherman, would take his division back to Memphis, combine it with other Union forces assembling there, and head down the Mississippi in steamboats with an expedition of some thirty thousand men. He would land east of the Mississippi just above Vicksburg, with its bristling bluff-top batteries, and would move directly against the Confederate stronghold. Caught between two powerful Union forces, Pemberton would be in a hopeless plight. If he maintained his front against Grant, Sherman would take Vicksburg in his rear and then presumably move inland to Jackson to cut his line of supply. If on the other hand, he turned to confront Sherman, Grant would pounce on his army's rear and flanks, turning its withdrawal into a panic rout.

Events did not take that course. Pemberton dispatched his cavalry under Major General Earl Van Dorn to strike at Grant's supply line in northern Mississippi. In the finest performance of his otherwise disappointing war, Van Dorn on December 20, 1862, captured and destroyed the Union depot at Holly Springs, Mississippi, severing Grant's supply line. Compounding the situation, Brigadier General Nathan Bedford Forrest tore up the connecting Mobile & Ohio Railroad at Jackson, Tennessee, the day before. By living off the land, Grant was able to extricate his army from the interior of the state without starvation, but his campaign along the Mississippi Central was unequivocally over. Pemberton was free to turn south against Sherman with as much of his army as might be needed to defend Vicksburg.

As it turned out, the few thousand Confederates whom Pemberton had previously left to defend the town needed no further assistance. The terrain around Vicksburg provided more than enough advantage to enable the defenders to defy many times their numbers of attackers. On December 26, Sherman's army landed a few miles above Vicksburg. A direct approach to the city led across seemingly impassible swamps to the foot of forbidding bluffs. Quick scrutiny of the ground revealed what every subsequent examination, quick or lengthy, would confirm. An attacking army could approach Vicksburg with any prospect of success only from the northeast or east, that is, from Mississippi's interior plateau. Vicksburg's special strength as a defensive bastion was that it was the northernmost point in the state of Mississippi at which the Mississippi River flowed immediately at the foot of the plateau. North of Vicksburg, all the way to the Tennessee line, 190 miles to the north, the Mississippi meandered along a more westerly course, while the western edge of the plateau angled back to the east. Between the river and the plateau lay a region shaped roughly like a football, about 60 miles at its widest and 190 from tip to tip. Known as the Mississippi delta, it was comprised of low-lying alluvial soil laced with winding waterways that seemed in no hurry to go anywhere. It was home to some of the state's richest plantations and most trackless swamps.

Unwilling to risk the massive slaughter that might result if he attempted to run his troop-laden steamboats past the big guns of Vicksburg's batteries, Sherman had no alternative but to land above the town, and that meant he would have to cross at least the narrow southern end of the delta country in order to reach the plateau on which Vicksburg perched. That narrow section of delta was dominated by the multiple channels of Chickasaw Bayou and overlooked by steep bluffs atop which the Confederates had entrenched. On December 29, Sherman sent his army forward to take the bluffs, but the attackers found that the maze of bayous and backwaters funneled their advance into relatively narrow avenues where the outnumbered defenders could easily shoot them down. Nearly two thousand Federals fell in the effort. Sherman pulled his bloodied army back to its steamboats and withdrew several miles up the Mississippi.

Grant arrived a few days later and took over the expedition. Sherman recommended that he take the whole army back to its base in Memphis and then advance overland once more through Mississippi, carefully protecting the supply line. Grant demurred. Such a move would look like a retreat, and after a recent season of setbacks and disappointments across all of the fighting fronts, a retreat might prove fatally demoralizing to national morale. And so the Army of the Tennessee pitched its tents on the west bank of the Mississippi above Vicksburg and spent a wet and chilly winter in sickly camps (Civil War camps always became sickly when an army made a prolonged halt in one place) while Grant experimented with various schemes for inserting the army onto the plateau behind Vicksburg.

Reaching the plateau with an army posed a peculiar set of problems. South of Vicksburg, the Mississippi lapped the western foot of the plateau. North of Vicksburg the Yazoo River, angling down from the northeast, did the same. To get his army across either stream, Grant would have to find a way for the steamboats and the navy's gunboats to get into the stretch of river where the crossing would occur. The projects for accomplishing that purpose involved finding chains of waterways that could, with some improvements, be used either to cross the delta country and reach the Yazoo above Vicksburg or to bypass Vicksburg's batteries via the bayous of Louisiana and enter the Mississippi River below the town.

All the schemes failed, and by the early spring of 1863, Pemberton was convinced that Grant was about to give up the idea of taking Vicksburg and retreat back to Memphis. He and his fellow Confederates were in a celebratory mood. With a major assist from the terrain of the lower Mississippi Valley, they believed they had bested the Union's previously most successful general.

Meanwhile, Grant was convinced that the only way to achieve his purpose was, as he had suspected all along, to take bold and direct action. He would ask his colleague Rear Admiral David D. Porter, commanding the navy's gunboats, to dash past the Vicksburg batteries by night, hoping to keep losses to a minimum. Then, in an even more daring move, he would have several of the army's leased, unarmed transport steamboats do the same a few nights later. Meanwhile his army would pick its away among the Louisiana bayous and backwaters, down the west bank of the Mississippi, to link up with the gunboats and transports and cross the river somewhere below Vicksburg. Thus the scene was set for the seven weeks' campaign that would stagger the Confederacy and open the way to final Union victory.

The first step in Grant's bold plan called for the navy to run its gunboats past the powerful Vicksburg batteries, and in this the general found a valuable collaborator in Porter, who did not hesitate to agree to the dangerous undertaking. He personally led a squadron of his most powerful gunboats past the heavy guns of the Confederate stronghold on the night of April 16, 1863. Gary D. Joiner's chapter in this book deals with the successful Grant-Porter relationship and the navy's role in helping to secure the success of the Vicksburg Campaign.

Charles D. Grear's chapter examines the most famous of the measures Grant took in order to confuse and distract Pemberton during first phase of the campaign. From April 17 through May 2, Colonel Benjamin H. Grierson led his cavalry brigade on a raid that traversed almost the entire state of Mississippi from north to south. Grear presents not only the raid's striking success within Grant's plan of campaign but also the great attention it has enjoyed over the years in popular culture.

Jason M. Frawley's chapter examines Grant's march down the west bank of the Mississippi, the all-important river crossing, and the Battle of Port Gibson, Mississippi the following day, as a division-sized Confederate force under Brigadier General John Bowen made use of the rugged topography of the western part of the plateau to delay Grant's march for several hours. In the end, though, even with the assistance of favorable terrain Bowen's tactical skill could not overcome the operational virtuosity by which Grant had assured himself an overwhelming superiority in numbers on the battlefield.

After the victory at Port Gibson, Grant chose not to advance due north against Vicksburg over the rugged terrain near the edge of the plateau but instead moved northeastward so as to gain the advantage of advancing on

Vicksburg from the east after cutting off the city's supply line. Pemberton held his field army in readiness and eyed Grant warily from a position just east of Vicksburg. Meanwhile, in Jackson, Mississippi, forty-five miles to the east, Brigadier General John Gregg advanced with the division-sized Confederate garrison stationed in the state capital and on May 12 fought a sharp engagement with one corps of Grant's army near the town of Raymond. Once again Grant's forces had the advantage in numbers actually on the battlefield, despite the fact that the Confederates had more troops in Mississippi at that time than he did. The battle of Raymond is the subject of Parker Hills's chapter in this book.

After his troops' triumph at Raymond, Grant determined to strike Jackson before turning toward Vicksburg, removing the state capital as a potential base of Confederate operations in his rear. His orders sent two corps of the Army of the Tennessee marching rapidly toward the city, where they arrived on the morning of May 14 and took possession after a short, sharp fight, Grant's third battlefield victory in the campaign. What was to be the first of three Union occupations of Jackson followed. Both are the topic of Steven E. Woodworth's chapter.

Arriving at Jackson only hours before Grant's troops—and fleeing the city together with the retreating garrison—was Confederate general Joseph E. Johnston. Jefferson Davis had assigned Johnston the preceding November to command over Pemberton's army as well as that of Braxton Bragg in Middle Tennessee, coordinating operations and shifting troops as necessary. Johnston had immediately denounced the assignment as conceptually wrong and unworkable. Thereafter he had on almost every occasion conducted his command contrary to Davis's wishes. That spring Davis had ordered Johnston to take over immediate command of Bragg's army, but Johnston had refused to do so. Once Grant's campaign of maneuver against Vicksburg was well underway and clearly posed a threat to Confederate interests in the state, Davis ordered Johnston to go to Mississippi and direct Pemberton's troops and any other Confederate forces in the state so as to save Vicksburg. Johnston obeyed the order at least to the point of traveling to Mississippi, where he arrived just in time for the fall of Jackson. How Johnston conducted his role in the Vicksburg Campaign from that point forward is the topic of John R. Lundberg's chapter in this volume.

With Jackson rendered for the time being incapable of further Confederate use as a base of supplies and operations, Grant finally turned directly toward Vicksburg, and on May 16 he clashed with Pemberton's main field army at Champion Hill in what became the climactic action of the campaign. Having been examined by several fairly recent books, including an excellent work by one of the contributors to this volume, the battle itself is not the subject of an individual chapter in the present work.[1]

One of Grant's chief problems at the battle does, however, come in for a chapter. Major General John A. McClernand held his corps out of the fighting at Champion Hill, apparently out of pique at an unwelcome order Grant had given him that morning, and made the battle a much closer run contest than it ought to have been. McClernand was a hindrance to Grant throughout the Vicksburg Campaign. An influential Illinois Democratic politician who loudly proclaimed himself a born soldier and hoped that military glory would catapult him to the presidency when the war was over, McClernand schemed continually to get an independent command. In recent years, some historians have attempted to rehabilitate McClernand's reputation. In keeping with that view, Michael B. Ballard, in his chapter of this work, presents a sympathetic view of McClernand's role in the Vicksburg Campaign.

On the other hand, one of the factors that aided Grant throughout the campaign—from his river-crossing to his advance from Jackson to Champion Hill—was his possession and use of superior intelligence as to where his enemy was and what he was doing. Former slaves, loyal white Mississippians, and Union spies combined to provide Grant with this major force-multiplier. William B. Feis addresses this facet of the campaign in his chapter of this book.

After the Union victory at Champion Hill, Pemberton retreated toward Vicksburg with his remaining force and attempted to hold a bridgehead over the Big Black River. Grant pursued aggressively, and the result was the following day's Battle of Big Black River Bridge, the subject of Timothy B. Smith's chapter in this book.

Throughout the march down the west bank of the river in Louisiana and then through the interior of Mississippi to Jackson and then back to Vicksburg, Union troops encountered more or less unfriendly Confederate civilians. Steven Nathaniel Dossman's chapter in this volume examines the way those two groups interacted with each other at a time when the war was evolving rapidly from mild amiability toward a less friendly treatment of enemy civilians. His study shows how the campaign was on the cutting edge of Union thought about the usefulness of firm measures against a rebellious populace.

The maneuver portion of the Vicksburg Campaign was the operational masterpiece of the Civil War and demonstrated many aspects of the fundamental principles of warfare. In the final essay of this volume, Paul Schmelzer analyzes Grant's conduct of the campaign from the point of view of the nearly timeless principles of warfare distilled by the almost contemporary

Prussian military strategist Carl von Clausewitz. Though read by none of the participants of the Civil War, Clausewitz is today viewed as having sifted out a number of universal principles that are studied by modern commanders. As Schmelzer demonstrates, Grant too had discovered some of the same principles, and nowhere was his mastery of the art of command or his deft skill in handling the political nuances of the war more strikingly displayed than in the seven weeks of aggressive maneuvering that decided the fate of Vicksburg.

Note

1. Timothy B. Smith, *Champion Hill: Decisive Battle for Vicksburg* (El Dorado Hills, CA: Savas Beatie, 2006).

RUNNING THE GAUNTLET
THE EFFECTIVENESS OF COMBINED FORCES
IN THE VICKSBURG CAMPAIGN

Gary D. Joiner

Vicksburg, Mississippi, was considered by both the Union and Confederate high commands to be the key to ultimate control of the Mississippi River and its tributaries. Until the seemingly impregnable fortress fell into Union hands, Federal control of the great river would be all but impossible. The Confederate Gibraltar proved to be a very difficult prize to capture. The Union army realized early in the war that the vast reaches of the Mississippi River valley, which comprised the only true transportation system in Middle America, could not be conquered by traditional means and that the Union forces in the West must have the cooperation of the navy. The army possessed its own transports but had no means of protecting its boats. Therefore the navy was ordered to serve under the army on inland waterways in the West until late 1862. The Navy Department initially agreed. But when the War Department, under intense pressure from the army, commanded naval officers to serve under army generals, it aroused the deep-seated mistrust between these two services, with their huge differences in command style. Ultimately, a bond was forged between them in combined arms that exceeded anything prior to the western campaigns. The resentment and rivalry between the army and navy were cast aside after theater commanders settled into their jobs. Major Generals Ulysses S. Grant and William T. Sherman and Acting Rear Admiral David Dixon Porter worked well with each other, once mutual trust was established.[1] They became friends and confidants.

The Federal government built entirely new types of warships to operate on the relatively shallow waters of the narrow inland rivers. The brown water gunboats of the Western Gunboat Flotilla had either captured or assisted in the capture of every Rebel fortification above Vicksburg. Making the best use of these vessels, particularly discovering their strengths and weaknesses, was

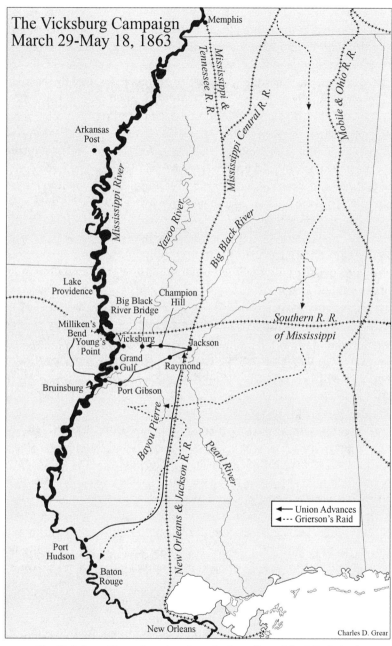

The Vicksburg Campaign
March 29–May 18, 1863

Memphis

Arkansas
Post

Mississippi River

Mississippi & Tennessee R. R.

Mississippi Central R. R.

Mobile & Ohio R. R.

Yazoo River

Big Black River

Lake
Providence

Big Black
River Bridge

Champion
Hill

*Southern R. R.
of Mississippi*

Milliken's
Bend

Young's
Point

Vicksburg

Jackson

Grand
Gulf

Raymond

Bruinsburg

Port Gibson

Bayou Pierre

New Orleans & Jackson R. R.

Pearl River

| Union Advances |
| ◄--- Grierson's Raid |

Port
Hudson

Baton
Rouge

New Orleans

Charles D. Grear

The Vicksburg Campaign played out in the valley of the Mississippi
River, as Union general Ulysses S. Grant deftly maneuvered around the
Confederate stronghold at Vicksburg to strike at its line of communication
at Jackson and then approach the Rebel bastion from the rear.

an ongoing process. The navy believed its new ironclads were invincible. It found otherwise at the Battle of Fort Donelson, in Tennessee, and with the loss of the *Cairo* in the Yazoo swamp. The Union army and navy seized one stronghold after another for most of 1862 and success had come easily, with few exceptions, until autumn. The strategies and tactics used by the inland fleet evolved rapidly.

The U.S. Navy captured New Orleans in late April 1862. The blue ocean-going steam screw sloops of Flag Officer David G. Farragut quickly steamed up the Mississippi and took Baton Rouge. They seized Natchez and attempted to gain the surrender of Vicksburg but were denied the prize. The Confederates had fortified the intimidating bluffs at Vicksburg, and Union naval vessels were unprepared to fight an engagement in which the shore batteries could rain destruction upon them while their own guns could not elevate sufficiently to counter the threat. The lack of available land forces to assist in an attack doomed the venture from the beginning. Some of Farragut's vessels were pinned down by fire from the newly constructed fortifications at Grand Gulf, Mississippi, and Port Hudson, Louisiana. It would be up to the newly formed Mississippi Squadron of brown water gunboats to help take the Rebel fortress.

The guns at Vicksburg were numerous and of large caliber. They extended from the water's edge to the heights, sometimes approaching 290 feet above the river. The Union observers could not identify all of the gun positions, nor could their ships fire accurately at the majority of them. Grant, Sherman, and Porter devised several schemes, collectively called the Bayou Experiments, attempting to bypass this major threat.

The Bayou Experiments were all failures to various degrees, but most were unquestionably disasters. Grant, Sherman, and Porter reconsidered their options, and the list was very short. Grant could move all of the forces back to Memphis and try an overland march, as he had earlier attempted. The commanders agreed that this would be seen as a retreat from Mississippi rather than a repositioning of troops and might cost Grant the command of his army. This idea was dropped quickly. Another possibility was to move three corps of Grant's Army of the Tennessee south on the Louisiana side. The regiments were already spread out from Lake Providence to Young's Point, a distance of over sixty miles. As winter gave way to spring in 1863, the incessant rain showers kept the ground soggy in the delta. The few good roads in eastern Louisiana were, at best, ribbons of mud.[2] Only the levees holding back the Mississippi and sometimes the roads that ran alongside them offered any hope for moving the Army of the Tennessee.

Likely places to cross the Mississippi far below Vicksburg were at New Carthage, near Newellton, or Hard Times Plantation, near St. Joseph, both in Tensas Parish. New Carthage was across the river and upstream from the Confederate fortifications at Grand Gulf. To carry out any plan would require the Mississippi Squadron to be in force between Vicksburg and Port Hudson. That meant doing what had been heretofore avoided and little discussed: sending the squadron past the gauntlet of the vaunted Vicksburg batteries. The admiral, who entertained the notion that Vicksburg might halt the Union advance, regained his confidence in the presence of his friends Grant and Sherman. Grant was very complimentary of Porter in his *Personal Memoirs*, stating, "The co-operation of the navy was absolutely essential to the success (even to the contemplation) of such an enterprise. I had no more authority to command Porter than he had to command me."[3]

Porter divided the squadron into two flotillas. One was to run the batteries, while the other was to remain above Vicksburg and support a deception operation to draw off some of the Vicksburg defenders from Grant's amphibious assault. The first group would reduce the Grand Gulf fortifications before Grant's infantry attempted to cross the Mississippi. The latter task alone was monumental and could not be adequately planned before the fate of the flotilla was known. Grant asked his agents to collect yawls and barges in St. Louis and Chicago to transport men across the great river.[4] This was done in distant cities for two reasons. First, the distance from the operation would help to protect their purpose. Second, these two cities were probably the only sites north of Memphis where craft in such large numbers might be collected.

Porter personally volunteered to prepare all vessels, both navy and army, and Grant gladly accepted the proposal. The admiral placed his combined fleet on the Louisiana side, above the mouth of the Yazoo, where the dense tree growth hid the boats from spies. He strengthened the ironclad gunboats with additional chains around the pilothouses, draping them over the sides to help deflect the largest caliber shells fired by the Vicksburg batteries. Large logs were strapped together and run along the waterlines to deflect any torpedoes or mines. Porter had already lost one of his precious City Class ironclads, the *Cairo*, in the Yazoo River to a torpedo the previous December. He placed planks atop the wooden decks and added cotton bales and wet bales of hay around the vitals of each vessel to absorb shot and shells.[5] All gun ports were closed until the need to fire was absolute. All internal lights were to be extinguished. Finally, Porter ordered the exhausts diverted into the wheelhouses to reduce the popping noises of the engines. This experiment had worked on the ironclad *Carondelet* as it conducted a similar passage the year before at Island No. 10.[6] With sounds baffled, internal lights extinguished, and propulsion kept just a notch above steerageway, the squadron's movements would hopefully disappear in the inky darkness.[7]

Close attention was paid to the army transports as well. Porter's men packed and stacked bales of cotton and hay several layers deep between the guards and boilers from the boiler deck to the deck above. Sacks of grain were packed tightly in front of the boilers and all around the guards on each boat. The army would need the hay and grain once it reached the assault position, and the roads were too boggy to support the weight of laden wagons.[8] Over a period of several days, Porter set coal barges adrift in the river to supply some of the vessels trapped below and to see if the Confederate batteries would allow them to pass. They made it each time. During the days preceding the attempt, the admiral ordered his shops at the mouth of the Yazoo River to come to life, repairing damage from the previous activities in the Yazoo swamp. When all the gunboats were deemed ready for service, Porter added one additional touch. He ordered that all his "Pook Turtle" City Class ironclads, the massive *Benton*, and the great ram *Lafayette*, all receive completely new paint. All hulls were painted black and cabins painted buff, reminiscent of Admiral Lord Nelson's flagship HMS *Victory*.[9]

Lessons learned in prior operations were applied to the first group's plan of movement. A vessel or coal barge would be lashed to each ironclad, as was done in the attacks on Fort Donelson, Island No. 10, and Farragut's passage at Port Hudson. Leading the single-file column was the largest of the ironclads, the *Benton*, Porter's flagship, commanded by Lieutenant Commander James A. Greer. Lashed to this vessel was the tug *Ivy*. Next in line was the long, rounded casemate ironclad *Lafayette*, commanded by Captain Henry Walke. This side-wheeler ironclad had the lightly armored tinclad *General Sterling Price* attached to its starboard side and a coal barge to the port side. A coal barge with ten thousand bushels of coal aboard was attached to each of the following ironclads: the *Louisville*, under Lieutenant Commander E. K. Owen; *Mound City*, under Lieutenant Byron Wilson; *Pittsburg*, under Acting Volunteer Lieutenant William R. Hoel; and *Carondelet*, under Lieutenant Commander J. McLeod Murphy. Next came three army transports packed with needed supplies for Grant's army, followed by the side-wheeler ironclad *Tuscumbia*, under Lieutenant Commander James W. Shirk. The *Tuscumbia*'s task was to prevent the transport captains from turning and running once the batteries began to fire upon them.

The importance of this mission was not lost on the army. General Grant, his wife Julia, their son, and his senior staff all watched the spectacle from a transport upstream, out of range of the big Confederate guns but in clear view of the coming action. General Sherman briefly became a naval commander, albeit of a tiny force. He commanded four rowboats placed across the river near the lower end of one of his doomed navigation canal projects.

They would rescue sailors if any of the survivors from a stricken vessel made it that far.[10] Union soldiers climbed trees or watched from protected places on the riverbank on the Louisiana side.[11] If this mission failed, Grant's entire strategy would collapse and with it, perhaps, his career.

The passage began at 9:15 P.M. on April 16 with little moonlight and the vessels making just enough steam to keep the wheels turning. This allowed the river current to move them along, just as had occurred with the unmanned coal barges' previous runs. General Grant's staff officer Charles Dana wrote that a mass of "black things detached itself from the shore," as the gunboats shoved off, keeping about two-hundred-yard intervals.[12] The night passage did not allow the riverboat pilots to see eddies on the surface that would affect navigation. They dead-reckoned and hoped for the best. To keep the lashed-together boats from ramming each other, the ironclads cast off their moorings about fifteen minutes apart. Admiral Porter watched from the pilothouse of the *Benton*. After the ponderous gunboat rounded DeSoto Point, he told the pilot, "the rebels seem to keep a very poor watch."[13] Porter hoped that the batteries would not notice his vessels until the flotilla was well underway, but Confederate scouts spotted the massive dark shapes moving in the night. The *Benton* was plagued from the beginning by eddies and all but refused to point her bow downstream. This delayed the procession for an hour. It also allowed the Confederates more time to pick out the darker shapes moving along the almost equally dark river.[14]

The Confederates torched dry wood and several abandoned houses on the Louisiana side to backlight the gunboats. The largest structure set ablaze was the railroad station.[15] Once the Louisiana shore glowed intensely, the Confederates lit tar barrels along the Vicksburg shoreline. Porter later described the effect as "illuminating the river and showing every object as plainly as if it was daylight."[16] As if portended by Farragut's passage at Port Hudson, where the elegant ocean-going sloops were backlit to make perfect targets, at Vicksburg, the results were even more intense. The pitch wood fires from the west bank cast a thick pall of smoke near them, punctuated only by the bright yellow and orange flashes as the guns fired. As the slow, majestic procession moved south, it was perfectly silhouetted for the Confederate gunners. The firing from the Vicksburg batteries began about 10:55 P.M. and continued for about an hour and fifteen minutes.[17] The batteries fired on the gunboats with varying accuracy from seemingly every gun on the bluffs, from the waterline batteries up to the heights of Fort Hill, and down to Warrenton on the southern end of the defense line. Acting Ensign Elias Smith, commanding the rifled guns aboard the *Lafayette*, told the *New York Times* that during the run, the shore batteries poured out a "perfect tornado of shot and shell."

He further speculated that the Confederates fired between five hundred and one thousand guns, but that only one in ten struck the squadron's vessels.[18] Porter's ironclads returned fire, and soon the sky around Vicksburg glowed like the yellow fires of Hell. The smoke from the combined guns and the fires from the Louisiana shore thickened and created low-hanging, choking, sulphurous clouds. Muzzle blasts, explosions, and the tar fires illuminated the dense clouds of smoke like heat lightning.[19] Smith stated that once the *Lafayette*'s gun ports were opened and the big naval guns were run out into firing position, "a good view could be had through the ports, of the rebel batteries, which now flashed like a thunder-storm along the river as far as the eye could see."[20]

A ball was held in Vicksburg that evening, and, as the alarms went out about the Yankee fleet on the move, the chivalrous Confederate officers wasted six minutes bidding the ladies adieu in the macabre orange glow of burning tar and cotton before they went to their units. The ladies and gentlemen of Vicksburg ran or rode in their carriages to the best places to view the coming glorious sinking of the hated gunboats.[21] The Sky Parlor on one of the highest bluffs was a popular spot for watching the show, as were the grounds and upper floors of the courthouse.

The coal barges made the passage difficult. Some of the vessels traced circles in the current as they tried to gather steam.[22] As the pilots gained control, the boats maneuvered close to the Mississippi side and pounded the shore batteries, doing a great deal of damage to the lower batteries. The Confederates in turn were able to fire point-blank into some of the ironclads with every conceivable caliber of shell. The *Benton* fared well in the passage, but the boats behind it were less fortunate. The *Lafayette*, tied to the *General Sterling Price*, was greatly slowed by the added weight and the off-center propulsion of both vessels. The *Price* was hit and heavily damaged by friendly fire from the *Louisville*, forcing its captain, Lieutenant Commander Selim Woodworth, to cut the gunboat free from the ironclad.[23] Eddies in the river continued to interfere with the larger vessels. As the *Lafayette* maneuvered downstream, the pilot could not correct for the fickle currents. The great ironclad ram found itself about one hundred yards in front of the Vicksburg wharves with its bow facing the city.[24] The *Lafayette* and several of the other gunboats cut the coal barges free to allow the vessels to maneuver.

About one mile from rounding DeSoto Point, the transport *Henry Clay* broke from the column and attempted to flee upstream to safety. The *Tuscumbia* turned to prevent this cowardly act. The *Tuscumbia* forced the steam packet around, presumably by threatening to fire its own guns into the unarmed vessel. As the *Clay* attempted to resume its place within the column, a Confederate shell exploded in the cotton barricades, stacked to protect the boat's engines and boilers. The cotton barricade immediately caught fire and burned fiercely. A second shell tore into the *Clay*'s hull.[25] The crew abandoned ship, and the captain followed after two additional rounds slammed into the transport. The shore gunners paid particular attention to the *Clay*, hoping that it might scatter the procession. The *Henry Clay* became an uncontrolled drifting inferno. The needless diversion of blasting the transport helped other vessels pass the gauntlet relatively unscathed. The *Tuscumbia* grounded, and, as it tried to extricate itself, the vessel plowed into the *Forest Queen*. Both boats drifted downstream after taking multiple hits from the Rebel gunners.[26] The column ran the gauntlet as the *Henry Clay* trailed.

As the yellow and orange glows of Vicksburg fell behind them, the officers and crew aboard the gunboats assessed their run. Elias Smith, an articulate, enthusiastic officer, was amazed to live to tell his story. He told the *New York Times*, "We still live. . . . How we escaped the firing ordeal as well as we did is a mystery to us all. . . . Earthquakes, thunder and volcanoes, hailstones and coals of fire; New York conflagrations and Fourth of July pyrotechnics—they were nothing to it."[27]

Captain Henry Walke reported that a one-hundred-pounder, steel-pointed shot struck the crown of the *Lafayette*'s casemate armor and passed completely through it. The shell then bounced on the grating in front of the boilers before halting, and did not explode.[28] In all, nine large artillery rounds struck the *Lafayette*. Some of these penetrated the casemate armor, showering shrapnel inside the vessel. Incredibly, no one was injured, not even receiving a scratch.[29]

Acting Volunteer Lieutenant William R. Hoel, commanding the ironclad *Pittsburg*, reported that his vessel received no serious damage, although it was struck seven times. Hoel also stated that his guns returned fire with forty-three rounds of five- and ten-inch shells and a stand of grapeshot.[30]

Casualties were light, and Porter was somewhat disdainful of the Rebel batteries' prowess when he reported to Secretary of the Navy Gideon Welles on April 19 that he suffered no dead, one or two badly wounded, and twelve total casualties, most of whom were walking wounded. As for the Rebel gunners, he wrote, "The shot the enemy fired was of the heaviest caliber, and some of excellent pattern; they came on board, but did no material damage beyond smashing the bulwarks."[31]

Grant was so enthusiastic about the successful run that he asked Porter to send more of these transports past the batteries. A few days later, on the night of April 22, an almost defenseless flotilla of five sternwheelers, one sidewheeler, and twelve barges made a second successful attempt. Due to a lack of cotton bales, the boats used barrels of cured beef to protect the engines and boilers. The boats and barges carried six hundred thousand rations for the 13th Corps.[32] The only boat lost was the *Tigress*, Grant's flag boat at the Battle of Shiloh. The Confederates' over-reliance on the use of batteries along and on the bluffs was evident in this second passage. More heavy guns near river level would have been more effective against the river fleet.

Porter's next task was to silence the batteries at Grand Gulf. He was very confident that his gunboats could accomplish the task since the bluffs were not nearly as high as those at Vicksburg, and he believed he had adequate resources to do this. Grant assembled his army on and around Hard Times Plantation, waiting for Porter to finish off the only obstacle in his way before he committed to the amphibious assault. Porter was ready on April 29, and his challenge to the batteries began at 8:15 A.M. The Grand Gulf complex consisted of two forts, Fort Cobun on the north and Fort Wade on the south. Covered ways and rifle pits connected these bastions.

The flotilla worked in two groups. The *Pittsburg* led, with the other City Class ironclads *Louisville, Carondelet,* and *Mound City,* following in that order, single file. They began firing, first pummeling Fort Cobun before lei-surely steaming south to pound Fort Wade. After passing the southern fort, this group maintained battle order as it circled back to blast Fort Wade again. Behind the first group was the second contingent led by the *Benton*, with the ironclads *Tuscumbia* and *Lafayette* following single file. This group trailed the wakes of the first and assaulted Fort Cobun.[33] The forts and the ironclads exchanged heavy shelling, with Fort Wade taking the most telling hits. The southern anchor was almost silenced. As the ironclads focused on Fort Wade, a gun from Cobun struck the *Benton* with Porter still aboard. The round entered the pilothouse, crashed through the deck, and exploded inside, destroying the ironclad's massive wheel. The *Benton* circled out of control and grounded where the Rebel gunners could not reach it.[34] The ironclad's carpenters then went to work repairing the paddlewheel. The *Benton* rejoined the fight and assisted the *Pittsburg* in pounding the upper batteries.[35]

William R. Hoel's report of the engagement to Admiral Porter best de-scribes the intensity of the action:

> U.S.S. Pittsburgh[36]
> Off Bayou Pierre
> May 1, 1863

> Sir: I have the honor to report that on April 29 in accordance with instructions received from you, I proceeded with this vessel to engage the enemy's batteries at Grand Gulf at 8:10 A.M. Although

struck by the enemy's shot thirty-five times during the engagement and severely cut up by them she is in no way disabled.

While engaging the enemy, four hundred and twenty-nine rounds were fired, principally from her bow and starboard broadside batteries consisting of shot, shell, shrapnel, grape and canister. At 1:30 P.M. in obedience to order, I (by signal from the LOUISVILLE) withdrew my vessel from the engagement.

I regret to have to report the following casualties: Killed—6, Wounded—13. The same night while passing below the batteries and engaging them, I fired twenty-one rounds. The vessel received but two shot, doing no serious damage, casualties none.

I am respectfully,
Your obedient servant
Wm. R. Hoel, Actg. Vol. Lt.

As Fort Wade's firing withered and finally halted, the ironclads focused on Fort Cobun. The gunboats could not break the fort's large walls or silence its guns. Both sides maintained steady fire for five hours until Cobun's guns reduced their fire rate as their ammunition ran low; however, Porter became convinced that he could not reduce the works without a land assault, and Grant agreed. The flotilla moved upstream to Hard Times by 2:30 P.M.[37] It had been a long day with little to show for it. The *Benton* suffered twenty-four casualties. The *Tuscumbia* was seriously damaged. The navy had accepted the vessel for service under heavy political pressure. The ironclad's armor was inadequate against large-bore artillery pieces. Much like its near sisters, the *Indianola* and *Chillicothe*, it was unable to deflect shells in an assault, proving it to have been poorly designed. It would spend most the remainder of the war on the ways, being repaired or patched. Porter described it as a "poor ship in a hot engagement."[38]

Grant and Porter decided that another approach must be taken. A runaway slave told the army commander that a place called Bruinsburg, thirteen miles below Grand Gulf, had a road that led inland. This was a good choice because the beachhead was very close to Hard Times Plantation.[39] The plan was altered, and with the protection of the gunboats, the largest amphibious assault prior to the North African landings in World War II was carried out the spring of 1863.[40] Grant landed unopposed beginning April 30, and although the Rebels did not yet know it, Vicksburg was doomed to fall.

Two operational feints kept the Confederates busy while the grand ferrying operation unfolded. In what has been called the greatest cavalry raid of the war, Colonel Benjamin Grierson led three regiments of horse soldiers starting with seventeen hundred troopers at the beginning of the operation. They ventured six hundred miles deep into Rebel-held territory from La Grange, Tennessee, down the eastern side of Mississippi, and across the state, ending in Baton Rouge. This raid drew away cavalry and infantry units that could and should have warned the Confederate command of Grant's landing.[41]

Of more immediate concern to Vicksburg was another feint. Grant ordered Sherman to make a "demonstration" at Haynes Bluff.[42] The naval force above Vicksburg was formidable. It consisted of the ironclads *Choctaw* and *Baron De Kalb*; the timberclad *Tyler*; Porter's flagship, the large tinclad *Black Hawk*, and the tinclads *Petrel, Romeo*, and *Signal.* The force included three mortar scows and ten of Sherman's transports with ten regiments of men. The gunboats fired enough rounds at the bluffs to make the Rebels believe that the attack was real, and Sherman's men disgorged and appeared to prepare for an assault before they withdrew. The Confederates believed this was the beginning of a major attack and held troops north of Vicksburg rather than sending them south to face Grant. This gave the Union commander the time and maneuvering room he needed.

Major General Henry Halleck, the army general-in-chief in Washington, wanted Grant to wait for reinforcements under Nathaniel Banks. Banks had been expected to take Port Hudson and join their forces. Grant had no intention of waiting for Banks, and this was the correct course. Although Banks outranked Grant and could have countermanded any order he received, the inept Banks did not know when to attack, moved tentatively, and did not want to play second fiddle to the audacious Grant. Grant secured Grand Gulf to protect his connection with Porter and then made a decision that spurred his career to true greatness. With some protection from Porter's fleet, he could have moved up the roads near the Mississippi River and attempted to destroy the Rebel works at Warrenton, Mississippi. From there, he could mount an attack on Vicksburg from the south. Instead, Grant moved his three corps northeast to Jackson, capturing the Confederate state capital. Grant knew there were two Rebel armies in the vicinity, Pemberton's army in Vicksburg and another under General Joseph Johnston building somewhere north and east of Jackson.[43] Grant's decision to move away from the fortress on the bluffs baffled the Rebels. They immediately realized the maneuver cut off all aid to the city from the interior of Mississippi. With the Mississippi Squadron dominating the river, Vicksburg was tightly squeezed. After Grant took Jackson, he turned due west and attempted to break the Vicksburg defenses, which he believed were only strong in that portion facing the river. He was wrong, and the Rebels met him outside their bulwarks. About half way between Jackson and the Vicksburg defenses, the Confederates made a stand in open country, along a low ridge named Champion Hill on May 16.[44] In what appeared to be a standoff, Grant was able to turn the Rebel's flank, and the Southerners retreated back into the Vicksburg defenses. Grant and his corps commanders met and decided to attack in an attempt to implode the Confederate line. Two bloody attempts were made, the first on May 19 and the second on May 22, but both ended in repulses. The Confederates had almost a full year to strengthen their lines and had made them as strong as possible. Grant decided to settle in for a siege.

The Mississippi Squadron was not idle as Grant's army moved away from the river. Porter revisited Haynes Bluff. He wanted to secure Grant's northern flank and reduce the threat posed to his vessels by any Confederate forces still operating in the Yazoo basin. He chose the ironclads *Baron De Kalb* and *Choctaw* and the tinclads *Forest Rose, Linden, Romeo,* and *Petrel* and prepared for a strike up the Yazoo into the heart of the basin. The flotilla found the Rebel works at Haynes Bluff abandoned but intact.[45] He destroyed them on May 18, after hearing heavy firing near Vicksburg that indicated Grant was closing in from the east. Porter's force under Lieutenant Commander John G. Walker aboard the *Baron De Kalb* continued to Yazoo City, where it found three rams under construction at the naval base. Walker destroyed the *Mobile,* which was finished and ready to receive its iron plates, as well as the *Republic,* a ram with railroad rails for plating fitted to use a ram, and a third, unnamed vessel. Porter described this gunboat in his report to Gideon Welles as "a vessel on the stocks (a monster), 310 feet long and 70 feet beam. This vessel was to have been covered with 4½-inch iron plating, was to have had 6 engines, 4 side wheels, and two propellers; she would have given us much trouble."[46] Porter also reported on the naval yard that contained a saw mill, planing machines, a large machine shop, and carpenter and blacksmith shops.[47]

As Grant's hold on the Vicksburg defenses tightened, his engineers constructed extensive counterworks and extended his efforts to thwart the Rebels at every turn. He was concerned about a Rebel army to his rear, but he never lost focus on the objective at his front. Porter was able to resupply the army and conduct a constant bombardment with his mortar scows and some schooners. The admiral also assisted Grant and Sherman with missions when requested. One of these was cause for concern. On May 27, less than a week after the investment of the siege, Porter sent the *Cincinnati* down from the mouth of the Yazoo to conduct a fire mission to destroy a masked battery at the base of Fort Hill, the northern anchor of the bluff defenses. This battery prevented Sherman from executing a move against the hilltop fort. As the *Cincinnati* approached, the treacherous river currents caught the craft and spun it around. The captain attempted to use his two-gun stern battery against the shore guns, but accurate fire poured into the ironclad. One round pierced the magazine, slammed into the keel, and passed through the bottom of the hull. Water entered the stricken turtle like a geyser. Another round disintegrated the starboard tiller. The *Cincinnati* began to rotate, performing a macabre death spiral. Other plunging rounds cracked the casemates and heavily damaged the interior. The gunboat sank in nine feet of water as forty crewmen died, most of drowning. Unlike the *Cairo*, the *Cincinnati* was raised to fight again. Porter was angry over the loss of the *Cincinnati* and worried that it had jeopardized his career. To demonstrate his support for the army, he and Thomas O. Selfridge, late commander of the *Cairo*, offered to set up an artillery battery of naval guns.[48]

While Grant pounded and starved Vicksburg into submission, Porter sent assistance to General Banks at Port Hudson, who could not crack the bastion's defenses. President Lincoln believed an invasion of Texas would help draw the war to an end, so Banks concocted a mission that might redeem his military career. Porter agreed to assist Banks with this awkwardly designed foray, called the Texas Overland Expedition, although it never reached that state. Porter's vessels steamed up the Red River as far as Alexandria and up the Ouachita to Fort Beauregard, between Trinity and Harrisonburg. Banks had no idea how to gain access to Texas with Port Hudson still not under his control, so the 1863 attempt to invade Texas ended with a whimper and not a bang.[49]

Grant's attempt to starve the Vicksburg garrison into submission succeeded. General Joe Johnston's relief force never arrived, and the city's defenders became desperate. On July 2, Confederate general John C. Pemberton held a council of war with his commanders to discuss his remaining options. He met Grant between the lines on July 3, and the particulars of surrender were consummated. The Southerners laid down their arms on Independence Day, July 4. Neither side realized that, as the two commanders met on July 3, the other great high-water mark of the war was ending with Pickett's Charge at the Battle of Gettysburg. Although historians of the eastern theater of the war—and much of the public as well—regard Gettysburg as *the* pivotal battle of the Civil War, it was the Vicksburg Campaign that split the Confederacy and ended any hope of succor from the Trans-Mississippi.

Port Hudson held out, surrendering only after receiving word that Vicksburg had fallen. Banks was deprived of his battlefield victory once again. Grant moved to Tennessee and then Virginia and became the most famous Union general of the war. His solid friendship with Sherman and Porter continued. Porter and Banks would meet once more in the coming year, again in the Red River valley.

One last tragedy was acted out as part of the Vicksburg Campaign. A little more than a week after the surrender of Vicksburg, Porter sent a flotilla comprised of the ironclad *Baron De Kalb*, the naval transport *New National*, the tinclads *Kenwood* and *Signal*, and army transports with five thousand troops, up the Yazoo again to clear any residual Rebel attempts at creating a surprise. Near Yazoo City, the *Baron De Kalb* struck a Singer torpedo. This was a different design than the ones that sank the Cairo. It was detonated using either a contact plunger or via an electrical line strung from the shore to be remotely detonated. It was designed by the Singer Submarine Corporation, the same engineers that designed and built the Confederate submarine *Hunley*. The Singer torpedo was a much improved version of the crude models that previously infested the Yazoo swamp.[50]

Aboard the *Baron De Kalb,* the crew felt a disturbance under the bow and water suddenly cascaded into the hull. The boat settled quickly by the bow. Adding insult to injury, the stern settled on another torpedo that blew a second hole in the hull.[51] Unlike its sister the *Cincinnati*, the *Baron De Kalb* would not be raised to fight again.

Early in the planning stages for the Mississippi River Valley campaigns, President Abraham Lincoln told his civilian advisors and his military commanders, "See what a lot of land these fellows hold, of which Vicksburg is the key! The war can never be brought to a close until that key is in our pocket . . . We can take all the northern ports of the Confederacy, and they can defy us from Vicksburg." He added that "I am acquainted with that region and know what I am talking about, and as valuable as New Orleans will be to us, Vicksburg will be more so."[52] The president told General Winfield Scott, "The Mississippi is the backbone of the Rebellion. It is the key to the whole operation."[53]

The combined arms operation of the Union army and navy that ran the gauntlet of Fortress Vicksburg and subsequently captured this most strategic of choke points, secured the most vital river system in North America for the Union. It split the Confederacy in two, creating a rift from which the South could never recover.

Notes

1. For an extended review of Union combined operations on the Mississippi River and its tributaries, see Gary D. Joiner, *Mr. Lincoln's Brown Water Navy: The Mississippi Squadron* (Lanham, Md., 2007). Portions of this chapter appear in that work in somewhat different form.

2. Edwin C. Bearss, *The Vicksburg Campaign*, 3 vols. (Dayton, Ohio, 1985), 1: 599.

3. Ulysses S. Grant, *Personal Memoirs of U. S. Grant* (New York, 1982), 240.

4. Ibid., 241.

5. U.S. War Department, *Official Records of the Union and Confederate Navies in the War of the Rebellion*, 31 vols. (Washington, DC, 1895–1929), 24: 553–54. (Hereafter cited as *ORN*.)

6. Ibid.

7. Chester G. Hearn, *Admiral David Dixon Porter; The Civil War Years* (Annapolis, Md., 1996), 211.

8. Grant, *Personal Memoirs*, 240.

9. Richard S. West Jr. *The Second Admiral: A Life of David Dixon Porter* (New York, 1937), 220.

10. William L. Shea and Terrence J. Winschel, *Vicksburg Is the Key: The Struggle for the Mississippi River* (Lincoln, Neb., 2003), 98.

11. Ibid.

12. Earl S. Miers, *The Web of Victory: Grant at Vicksburg* (Baton Rouge, 1955), 140.

13. *ORN*, 24: 682.

14. *New York Times*, April 18, 1863.

15. David Dixon Porter, *The Naval History of the Civil War* (New York, 1886), 310.

16. Ibid.

17. Henry Walke, *Naval Scenes and Reminiscences of the Civil War in the United States, on the Southern and Western Waters during the Years 1861, 1862, and 163, with the History of That Period* (New York, 1877), 355.

18. *New York Times*, April 18, 1863.

19. Shea and Winschel, *Vicksburg Is the Key*, 98.

20. *New York Times*, April 18, 1863.

21. Shea and Winschel, *Vicksburg Is the Key*, 98.

22. Bearss, *Vicksburg Campaign*, 2: 266–68; *ORN*, 24: 555–56.

23. *ORN*, 24: 553, 556–58, 682.

24. Walke, *Naval Scenes*, 355; *New York Times*, April 18, 1863.

25. Porter, *Naval History*, 311.

26. Ibid.; *ORN*, 24: 553. Porter's version was more heroic. He reported that the *Tuscumbia* stayed behind to assist the *Forest Queen* and then towed it to safety.

27. *New York Times*, April 18, 1863.

28. Walke, *Naval Scenes*, 356.

29. *New York Times*, April 18, 1863.

30. J. W. Rutter, "Capt. William Rion Hoel: The Life of a 19th Century Riverman," *S & D Reflector* 33, no. 4 (December 1996): 26.

31. *ORN*, 24: 554.

32. Michael Ballard, *Vicksburg: The Campaign That Opened the Mississippi* (Chapel Hill, N.C., 2004), 202.

33. *ORN*, 24: 607–8, 610–11, 613, 615–23, 625–26.

34. Bearss, *Vicksburg Campaign*, 2: 311.

35. Rutter, "Captain William Rion Hoel," 26.

36. Ibid., 27. The clerk who sent the report to Admiral Porter apparently made a common error by adding the "h" to *Pittsburg*. It is also possible that the error was made at the government printing office. Bayou Pierre was a small stream that emptied into the Mississippi River near Grand Gulf.

37. *ORN*, 24: 574–75; Grant, *Personal Memoirs*, 317.

38. *ORN*, 24: 611.

39. Grant, *Personal Memoirs*, 251.

40. Personal interview with Edwin C. Bearss, October 2008.

41. This raid was the basis for John Wayne's movie *The Horse Soldiers* in 1959. The best accounts of the raid are found in Bearss, *Vicksburg Campaign*, 2: 187–236; and Dee Alexander Brown, *Grierson's Raid* (Dayton, Ohio, 1981), originally published in 1954.

42. W. T. Sherman, *Memoirs* (reprint, New York, 1990), 347; *ORN*, 24: 240–45.

43. For an excellent examination of Joseph E. Johnston during the Vicksburg Campaign, see Terrence J. Winschel, *Triumph and Defeat: The Vicksburg Campaign* (New York, 2006), 2: 115–28.

44. For the best analysis of the campaign prior to the siege of Vicksburg, see Bearss, *Vicksburg Campaign;* and Ballard, *Vicksburg*. For the most in-depth treatment of the Battle of Champion Hill, see Timothy B. Smith, *Champion Hill: Decisive Battle for Vicksburg* (New York, 2004).

45. *ORN*, 25: 5–6.

46. Ibid., 8.

47. Ibid.

48. *ORN*, 25: 56.

49. For an excellent account of this campaign, see Richard Lowe, *The Texas Overland Expedition of 1863* (Fort Worth, 1996).

50. Mark K. Ragan, *Union and Confederate Submarine Warfare in the Civil War* (Mason City, Iowa, 1999), 105, 179, 226, 233, 245.

51. Milton F. Perry, *Infernal Machines: The Story of Confederate Submarine and Mine Warfare* (Baton Rouge, 1965), 45.

52. John D. Milligan, *Gunboats down the Mississippi* (Annapolis, Md., 1965), xxii.

53. Ibid.

2

"THROUGH THE HEART OF REBEL COUNTRY"
THE HISTORY AND MEMORY OF GRIERSON'S RAID

Charles D. Grear

At dawn on April 17, 1863, the men of Colonel Benjamin Henry Grierson's cavalry brigade broke camp in Tennessee not knowing they were about to embark on the most daring Union raid of the Civil War. Fulfilling their part in the 1863 Vicksburg Campaign, the horsemen traversed Mississippi and Louisiana for sixteen days, wreaking havoc on Confederate logistics while Grierson dumbfounded Rebel leaders as to his intentions and whereabouts. What became known as Grierson's Raid "through the heart of Rebel country"[1] has remained a cultural icon down to the current generation. Despite the complexity and significance of the 1863 Vicksburg Campaign, only Grierson's Raid truly entered the lexicon of popular history and the memory of Americans, becoming the most remembered and celebrated Union cavalry raid of the Civil War.[2]

Though only a small part of the campaign, Grierson's Raid played a pivotal role in the capture of the Gibraltar of the South. Major General Ulysses S. Grant's plan to outmaneuver and overwhelm Confederate forces in western Mississippi was complex. He deployed three main forces, two to attack enemy positions at Grand Gulf and Port Gibson, and a third under Major General William Tecumseh Sherman feigning an attack north of Vicksburg at Snyder's Bluff. Additionally, Grant organized two mounted forays. With the cooperation of Major General William S. Rosecrans, Abel Streight's five regiments of mounted infantry rode through northeastern Mississippi, Alabama, and into Georgia on mules to siphon off the bulk of Confederate cavalry from northern Mississippi and to sever the Western & Atlantic Railroad, hampering General Braxton Bragg from reinforcing and resupplying Vicksburg. Streight's other objective was to draw off the formidable Brigadier General Nathan Bedford Forrest, who had been a thorn in Grant's side in his previous attempts to capture Vicksburg. Despite the success of pulling

Confederate cavalry to Georgia, Streight's men eventually tired and were captured by Forrest.[3]

The second foray, Grierson's Raid, garnered the most attention, achieved more immediate success, and embedded its image in the American popular memory. Grant and his lieutenants devised another cavalry raid to create yet another diversion for Lieutenant General John C. Pemberton while isolating Confederate forces defending Vicksburg. Specifically, a brigade of cavalry would ride south from La Grange, Tennessee, into Mississippi. The raiders would ride between the state's two major north–south railroads, the Mississippi Central and the Mobile & Ohio, cutting both lines while severing the main east–west arterial rail line, the Southern Railroad, at Newton Station, Mississippi. Additionally, Grant ordered them to disrupt Confederate communication lines along the railways by cutting telegraph wires and wrecking telegraph offices in addition to the general destruction of military supplies discovered during their trek. Once the cavalrymen fulfilled the main objectives, they were to loop back through Alabama to the safety of friendly lines.[4]

Leading the raid was Colonel Benjamin Henry Grierson, a former music instructor from Illinois who disliked horses after of an accident as a child nearly killed him. His command was a brigade composed of the 6th and 7th Illinois and 2nd Iowa Cavalry regiments, a total of seventeen hundred men. Grierson and his raiders broke camp early on the morning of April 17, 1863, with enough rations for five days and forty rounds of ammunition each. Travelling light, the aggressive Federal horse-soldiers quickly learned how to acquire sustenance for the sixteen days they rode through the heart of Dixie. By the second day, they were already in Mississippi capturing and destroying property. Encamped at Pontotoc, Mississippi, on April 20, Grierson decided to cull out 175 men not fit to continue and sent them back to La Grange with the captured property and prisoners. Dubbed the "Quinine Brigade," after the noted antimalarial drug used since the seventeenth century, the returnees received instructions from Grierson to leave "the impression that the whole command had returned" to deceive the enemy into thinking that the raid was only to collect supplies. Grierson's stratagem worked, confusing the Confederates long enough to give him a ten-hour head start.[5]

Freed of slow troops and the weight of captured Confederates and their supplies, Grierson quickly moved south and continued his deceptions. The following day, the Illinoisan made a still larger detachment, this time the entire 2nd Iowa. Under the command of Grierson's most trusted subordinate, Colonel Edward Hatch, the regiment was to operate semi-independently of the main body. Grierson's instructions were clear and simple: circle east toward the Mobile & Ohio Railroad of Mississippi "and destroy the road and

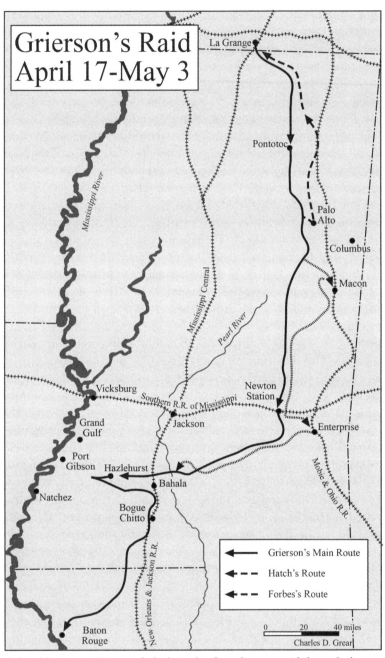

Grierson's Raid
April 17–May 3

La Grange

Pontotoc

Palo
Alto

Columbus

Macon

Mississippi River

Mississippi Central

Pearl River

Vicksburg

Newton
Station

Southern R.R. of Mississippi

Grand
Gulf

Jackson

Enterprise

Port
Gibson

Hazlehurst

Mobile & Ohio R.R.

Natchez

Bahala

Bogue
Chitto

New Orleans & Jackson R.R.

Grierson's Main Route

Hatch's Route

Forbes's Route

Baton
Rouge

0   20   40 miles

Charles D. Grear

Colonel Benjamin Grierson led a brigade of cavalry on a raid through the entire length of the state of Mississippi, distracting Confederate commanding general John C. Pemberton as Grant began to maneuver around Vicksburg.

wires," then continue the destruction as far south as Macon, if possible, before heading east to Columbus and eventually back to La Grange. In short, create as much destruction and attention as possible. Hatch did not reach Macon, because Confederate state troops caught up with the detachment at Palo Alto where a quick skirmish ensued holding the Rebels at bay.[6] Hatch moved deliberately, drawing more attention to divert enemy forces away from Grierson while successfully heading back to La Grange, in the process giving Grierson's main column "some thirty-six hours start [free] of all incumbrances."[7]

Grierson dispatched several other diversions throughout the course of the raid. Another notable one was Company B of the 7th Illinois under the command of Captain Henry Forbes. The Prairie Staters made several feints toward significant towns such as Macon and Enterprise, convincing Confederate leaders that Grierson was still in northern Mississippi rather than raiding the length of the state. Forbes and his company eventually reunited with the main column ten days later along the banks of Strong River. By this point in the raid, Grierson could move south virtually at will while Confederates pursued the three main diversions.[8]

Though Grierson held the element of surprise because most Confederate forces were looking northward, he was still blind to what lay ahead. Still believing in the martial abilities and strength of the Confederate army, the Union mounted arm needed to scout ahead undetected for enemy movements and accessibility of roads and other supplies. Grierson deployed a small group of volunteers dressed in irregular Confederate uniforms, the sort of piecemeal collections of clothing worn by partisan soldiers. Dubbed the "Butternut Guerillas" for the color of their clothes, these men reported back to Grierson vital information about the nearby roads, towns, and Confederate troops. Leading the guerillas was Sergeant Richard Surby, a railroad man who had extensively traveled the South, knew the terrain and customs, and could effectively mimic the Southern drawl in speech. These traits proved beneficial time and again, and the Rebels never discovered the identity of Surby and his men. If they had, the Confederates would undoubtedly—and quite legally—have executed the Butternut Guerillas as spies.[9]

With Confederates scrambling across northern Mississippi looking for the blue raiders and the butternut spies reporting enemy activities while spreading disinformation, Grierson easily reached his main objective on April 24—Newton Station. More than two hundred miles inside enemy lines and one hundred miles due east of Vicksburg, the Union cavaliers could now sever the Southern Railroad of Mississippi, central Mississippi's only east–west trunk line and the logistical artery of the Confederate army that protected the Gibraltar of the South.

Luck and timing were on the side of the northern horsemen at Newton Station. Not only did they destroy the tracks and telegraph lines connecting Vicksburg to points east but captured and razed two engines, thirty-eight railcars full of commissary stores, machinery, and several thousand shells. Within the town, Grierson's raiders captured and paroled over a hundred Confederate soldiers and destroyed commissary and quartermaster stores, along with five hundred stands of arms. Now Vicksburg received a significant handicap with the destruction of the summer supplies aboard the westbound train. These actions also delayed future supplies and reinforcements during those critical days while the South replaced the tracks and repaired a destroyed bridge half mile west of the town.[10]

Grierson did not tarry but ordered his men to mount and ride south of town. Before his men left Newton Station news of the event reached Pemberton's headquarters 65 miles to the west in Jackson, sending him into a fury and distracting him from "the formidable invasion preparing under my eyes."[11] Pemberton was clearly frustrated with the situation. Conflicting reports of Grierson's whereabouts had been flooding into his headquarters along with the continual reports of potential threats from Grant to both northern and southern Mississippi. Grierson's Raid was a masterful stroke by Grant. Pemberton became fixated on the Union raiders and began ordering cavalry from posts throughout Mississippi and Louisiana to thwart this menace in his backyard. To enhance the hunt for Grierson still more, he had several infantry regiments mounted and sent after the elusive Union raiders. The Confederate commander, stinging from the destruction of Newton Station and his inability to stop this small group of horsemen, nearly denuded the state of cavalry in pursuit of the raiders, leaving the potential points of Grant's invasion largely unwatched.[12]

Intelligence gathered by scouts at Newton Station alerted the Union force that Pemberton had positioned troops to intercept him if he chose to return to La Grange. Realizing he could not return through Mississippi and since looping through Alabama was too long and dangerous, Grierson contemplated marching to Grand Gulf to aid Grant and potentially flank the Confederate defenses.

Destruction of government stores and railroads continued as the force raced toward Grand Gulf. The Illinoisans quickly captured Hazelhurst, a small railroad town southwest of Jackson, and discovered a stash of six thousand artillery shells slated for shipment to Grand Gulf and Port Gibson. Grierson's men hastily tore up the tracks of the New Orleans, Jackson, & Great Northern Railroad and set fire to the railroad cars containing the shells. Fire spread uncontrollably to adjacent buildings after some of the shells exploded, threatening to burn down the town. Union soldiers worked alongside citizens and saved the town from complete destruction.[13]

Once the men cleared Hazelhurst, Grierson sent out a detachment to misdirect the Confederates. Four companies under the command of Captain George Trafton, with the Butternut Guerillas serving as scouts, left to strike the New Orleans, Jackson, & Great Northern Railroad again just south of Hazelhurst at Bahala. During Trafton's absence, Grierson stopped at a plantation outside of Union Church to replenish food supplies for both men and horses. Instead of rest, Grierson's men experienced combat as a Confederate detachment of Wirt Adams's Mississippi cavalry unsuccessfully attacked Union pickets. Though not a formidable attack, the foray raised concern in Grierson's mind since Adams's squadrons were the first trained formations the raiders had encountered and they were now far behind enemy lines. A few hours later, Trafton's detachment appeared in camp with news of his success at Bahala and the presence of Adams's men and other Confederate reinforcements heading toward the raiders from multiple directions. Pursued from many directions and unsure of Grant's success crossing the Mississippi, Grierson realized that it was in his men's best interest to reach Union-held Baton Rouge. The colonel's decision, though the safest, provided the epic conclusion to the raid. Instead of a simple strike into enemy territory, the raid penetrated deeper into the Confederacy, cutting a swath of destruction completely through it.[14]

Grierson hurried his men back onto the road, but not before leaking false plans to a Confederate civilian about attacking Natchez. The southerner quickly informed Adams, who waited for the Union cavalry at Fayette, away from Grierson's path. The raiders continued their destruction of the railroad toward the south, from Bogue Chitto Station to the town of Summit, burning depots, thirty-five freight cars, and all the commissary supplies they found. Though useful to Grant's strategy, this destruction assured that Adams could not use the railroads to catch up to the marauders. Now his greatest concern would be to outrun local Confederate cavalry and infantry blocking the path to Baton Rouge.[15]

Grierson concluded the marathon raid by sending out scouts to hold bridges for the main column. During the final sprint to friendly lines the cavalrymen fought four skirmishes, the most significant at the crossing of the Tickfaw River where one man was killed and four wounded including Surby, the leader of the Butternut Guerillas. Another clash occurred at the Confederate camp on the Comite River, the last major obstacle and just thirty miles from Baton Rouge. All the hard riding, fifteen days total, and fighting for four days straight, ended with the raiders covering the last seventy-six miles in just twenty-eight hours. It all took its toll on the men. With men and horses utterly exhausted, Grierson decided it was safe enough to stop at a house just four miles from Union lines. Most men fell fast asleep near where they stopped.[16]

News of Grierson's success first reached Union lines by accident. Early in the morning of May 2, one of the colonel's orderlies fell asleep in the saddle, letting his horse wander from the main column past the house to Union picket lines outside of Baton Rouge. Weary-eyed and wearing a uniform dirty beyond recognition, the orderly had trouble convincing the soldiers of the Army of the Gulf that he was a member of 6th Illinois Cavalry. Unaware of the raid and fearing a trap, Major General Christopher C. Augur, commander of Banks's land forces ordered two companies to investigate the suspicious visitor's story. Upon reaching Grierson's camp, with some tense moments of distrust, the squadron's commander confirmed their identities and sent a dispatch back to Augur in Baton Rouge announcing the arrival of a brigade of Grant's cavalry. Unfortunately for Grierson and his men, Augur averred that a parade was necessary despite the fatigued men and horses. The colonel obliged the general and the tired raiders slowly paraded through the town square lined by local citizens and soldiers gazing at the spectacle of men with mud-caked uniforms and filthy mounts. Grierson men then proceeded to the Mississippi River to water their horses and camped two miles south of town. Taking only time to care for the equines, the men again fell fast asleep, most without pausing to eat a meal served by the 116th New York and 48th Massachusetts Infantry. The much-deserved rest came after riding six hundred miles in sixteen days, inflicting over a hundred casualties, bringing out two hundred prisoners and paroling a thousand more, ruining sixty miles of railroad and telegraph wire, capturing or destroying three thousand stands of arms, and commandeering over one thousand horses and mules with only three men killed, seven wounded, five left behind enemy lines, and nine missing. Most importantly, Grierson estimated that approximately thirty-eight thousand Confederate troops received orders to capture his small raiding force from all parts of Mississippi and Louisiana. Though this number appears inflated, even just a fraction of this total would have been enough to help Grant's plan to capture Vicksburg. Grierson's success proved greater than anyone at the time could have imagined and transformed the image and use of Union cavalry.[17]

The story of Grierson's Raid has all the traits of a time-tested tale: a reluctant hero, sensational feats, conflict, peril at every turn, bravery, endurance, and, most important, it created a significant plot twist by proving the Confederacy was nothing "more than the utter hollowness of the rebellion."[18]

Even Grierson himself wrote, "Much of the country through which we passed was almost entirely destitute of forage and provisions. . . . Many of the inhabitants must undoubtedly suffer for want of the necessities of life."[19] Stories based on events that reveal the true nature of an opponent once thought to be dominant tend to transcend time and appeal to many interests. Historians can view the raid as a microcosm of the war itself, seeing Grierson and his raiders as David against the once imposing Goliath of the Confederacy that is exposed as weak by news of the successful raid. American culture celebrates stories of underdogs beating all odds and changing how we view the world: in this case, the Civil War.

News of the successful raid reached the masses days after Grierson arrived in Baton Rouge. Cutoff from telegraphic communications, initially an incomplete story of a cavalry raid spread only along the Mississippi River, then to Chicago in reports drafted by men in Hatch's 2nd Iowa Cavalry, and from there to Milwaukee by May 5, then Philadelphia seven days later. The full story first began to spread on May 10 when a dispatch with details of Grierson's exploits left New Orleans and arrived in New York seven days later; a full two weeks after the Union parade through the streets of Baton Rouge. Reports of the raid graced the front page of both major New York newspapers, the *Times* and the *Herald*. The newspapers reported many details, including a list of all the officers in Grierson's brigade. The *Herald* published verbatim the words of the Baton Rouge correspondent who reveled in the success while pouring salt into southern wounds by declaring, "The cavalry raids of the enemy sink into insignificance after this exploit: [J. E. B.] Stuart is nowhere; he may now hide his head from very shame at having been outdone in the kind of warfare he has so long gloried in." The North had finally found its first true cavalry hero.[20]

The timing was perfect to capture the imagination of northerners. Union armies had made very little progress in the months leading up to the raid. Grant had failed to make any significant strides capturing Vicksburg, while in the eastern theater, the bloodletting of the Army of the Potomac at Fredericksburg on December 13, 1862, and the embarrassing defeat at Chancellorsville from April 30 to May 6, 1863 left the North uncertain about the progress of the war. Unionists held onto this bright spot of the war amid the darkness. This relevance is exemplified in the lithograph of Grierson on the front cover of *Harper's Weekly*, the leading magazine in the United States, along with a map depicting the raiders' route and an image of their parade through Baton Rouge. Featured prominently in the issue was a detailed story of the raid itself and a biography of the colonel. News stories about the raid continued to be published into early June when news of Grant's siege of

Vicksburg and General Robert E. Lee's invasion of the North finally enticed the attention of northern editors.[21]

Southern newspapers, on the other hand, reviled the raiders. A writer named "Cesar" wrote about his experience with the Union cavalrymen. He claimed to have been taken as a prisoner by Grierson's men and assured of the safety of his person and property, only to be robbed before his release. At the town of Hazlehurst, he proclaimed that Union soldiers "robbed every store in the town, took whatever pleased their fancy, and called upon the negroes and rabble to 'help themselves to whatever they d——d pleased.'"[22] Grierson did consult slaves for Confederate troop strengths and movements. Also, some of the Iowans confirm entering the stores for Confederate papers and taking property in Pontotoc. Cesar elaborated later in his report, describing the brutal slaying of any citizen that ran away and a slave that refused to accompany them. The Iowans tell a similar but opposite story of a dead slave, but it was nowhere near Hazlehurst since they had already returned to Tennessee. According to the Hawkeyes they came upon a plantation and discovered a slave killed for refusing to leave his wife and children behind to accompany his fleeing master. Upset, the owner killed his servant, leaving the body exposed. The following day the raiders arrived, buried the body, and burned down the plantation house. Lastly, the southern writer stated that Grierson's men intentionally set fire to Hazlehurst, burning "the only means of subsistence of many women and children." It appears that Cesar took stories he had heard before his capture and incorporated them into his written account at Hazlehurst to sensationalize the raid. He further demonized the cavalrymen by portraying them as thieves who stole from innocent women and children; an age-old technique practiced by the media and government to garner sympathy for their cause. Similar accusations would be leveled against Sherman when he invaded Georgia a year later using similar harsh tactics of living off the land.[23]

Though Grierson received much attention immediately after the raid, larger events overshadowed his dramatic feat. The fall of Vicksburg, victory at Gettysburg, and the eventual surrender of the Confederacy took precedence in the written accounts in the years following the conflict. The only major publication of the raid was a lengthy and heavily illustrated article in the *Harper's New Monthly Magazine* February 1865 edition. Though the end of the war appeared in sight, the conflict had slowed, especially in the eastern theater, with Grant laying siege to Petersburg for more than eight months by the time of publication. Sherman was marching through South Carolina but the newspapers could only run so many headlines of victories without pitched battle before the public tired. Under a running series titled "Heroic Deeds of

Heroic Men," the magazine maintained the public's morale and support for the conflict. The author not only stirred up public sentiment but connected the raid to the contemporary purpose of the war, emancipation. Slaves not only aided Grierson in the raid, but many followed him into Baton Rouge. Cementing this image the author portrayed Grierson as Moses leading slaves "like the children of Israel, from their old oppressors." Besides this article, Grierson's Raid received little attention from anyone outside of the actual event. According to historian Carol Reardon, this was a common practice during the 1880s and 1890s when veterans focused solely on their individual achievements, essentially fighting the war again but only for their own side. For example, in the series *Battles and Leaders of the Civil War,* Union officers mentioned the raid only as a footnote, and Confederates used the incident to support their own factions in the postwar squabbles between officers over who was to blame for this or that defeat. Unfortunately, Confederates focused solely on the reactions of their own officers and forgot to give credit to the true source of the success, Grierson.[24]

Nevertheless, the raid did not fall into obscurity in the aftermath of the war. Like other veterans, both North and South, Grierson's raiders recorded their accounts for general posterity. Some of the principal raiders joined the rush to record and publish their firsthand interpretations of the most memorable event in the 1863 Vicksburg Campaign. In 1865, Sergeant Richard Surby, the leader of the Butternut Guerillas, published the first, full-length account of the raid. Writing from a journal he kept during the war and with help from other members of the expedition, especially in dealing with the 2nd Iowa's return trip, Surby chronicled the raid with little in the way of interpretation of, or context for, the event. The captivating narrative and personal account from a pivotal member of the force garnered some attention in a sea of books published by other veterans of the war and proved itself worthy of reprinting in 2008, long after Grierson had gained notoriety for his postbellum career. Surby published a shorter book in 1897 that focused more exclusively on his participation with the Butternut Guerillas.[25]

Another officer, Captain Stephen A. Forbes, wrote his account of the raid from an address he gave to the Illinois State Historical Society. Inspired by the death of his brother Henry, who led the detached company that spent the bulk of the raid independent of the main column, Stephen provided a more detailed account of the event. With more resources available to him such as the multivolume *War of the Rebellion: Official Records of the Union and Confederate Armies* and Surby's books, Forbes was the first to take a more scholarly approach but was still able to keep a lively memory of the raid available, not necessarily for the masses but as a matter of state and family

pride. By the early twentieth century, Grierson's Raid was no longer as celebrated throughout the North but was still locally remembered in Illinois.
Occasionally it appeared among the trivial facts of the war in the columns
of such papers as the *San Jose (Calif.) Evening News*, where a June 27, 1903,
article dealt with the Battle of Palo Alto (Mississippi) in the "A Fortieth Anniversary War Story."[26]

Not all early accounts of the raid came from the men who rode in it. A
curious narrative came from Benjamin Henry Jesse Francis Shepard, better
known by his pen name Francis Grierson. A distant cousin of the colonel,
son of his first cousin Emily Grierson Shepard, Francis was born in England before residing in Illinois for several years. Like the colonel, he was
a musician; unlike Grierson, he toured the world and was recognized as a
renowned writer. In 1909 he published his most celebrated book, *The Valley
of Shadows*. Still considering himself European, Francis provided readers an
outsider's view of the author's experiences and thoughts about antebellum
Illinois. Included in his reminisces are encounters with John C. Frémont,
Stephen A. Douglas, and Abraham Lincoln. Seemingly out of place is an
entire chapter devoted to Grierson's Raid. Though it adds nothing new to the
story, it brought the raid international attention with Shepard's followers in
European literary circles.[27]

Southerners, on the other hand, had little interest in remembering the
raid. Confederate veterans recognized the importance of Grierson's exploit
for Union victory, but the sting of defeat discouraged them from speaking
of the event unless they had a story of defiance toward Grierson's men. The
complete failure to stop Grierson's Raid was an embarrassment to the Confederacy. Naturally, people tend not to discuss the failures of their military.
As might be expected, former Confederate soldiers rarely discussed in detail
their resistance to Grierson's Raid in the pages of *Confederate Veteran*, a
magazine that focused on the stories of southern soldiers, most notably their
successes. Of the numerous entries in that magazine, only three obituaries
mentioned the raid. The one for William Owen Kelly stated, "He served as
aid de camp on the staff of the commanding officer in resisting the advance
of Gen. Grierson in his famous raid through Mississippi."[28] Joseph Taliaferro
Brown's death notice provided a story that painted the Union soldiers in a
dim light. According to the obituary, at fourteen he served in the home guard
and was "captured by some Federal soldiers, but his youth and the plausible
excuse he made about being out squirrel hunting saved him not only from
being taken into custody but the gun as well."[29] The final obituary, Captain Ed
B. Ross, actually noted Grierson's Raid as "the most successful raid ever made
by the Federals" because it changed the course of the war for his company in

the 3rd Kentucky Infantry. In the months following the raid, Ross received orders to serve as mounted infantry, and despite his comrades' returning to the role of foot soldiers, Ross somehow remained in the mounted arm and eventually served under Forrest.[30]

Though Grierson's Raid received little attention, Confederate veterans took every opportunity they could to belittle the colonel with a story of defeat. Plantation owner T. M. Daniel wrote about Grierson's failed raid from Memphis, Tennessee, to West Point, Mississippi, during the Meridian Campaign. He described Grierson and his men similarly to the accounts of them that appeared in southern newspaper reports of his great Mississippi raid. While Daniel was home on leave, the raiders came calling, plundered his home, forced the slaves to cook for them, and produced "one long, lurid flame, made by the conflagration of hundreds of palatial homes, barns, and corn pens, for miles around the railroad." Despite the wanton destruction, Daniel's own house remained intact. Obviously intending to display his ability to outwit the Federal soldiers, particularly the famous Grierson, Daniel describes sneaking back into his occupied house, stealing a cooked turkey leg, and offering it to his devoted servant before leaving the property undetected.[31] Another veteran, A. Curl, of the 11th Arkansas Infantry, wrote about his defiance of Grierson during the siege of Port Hudson. Just a month after his arrival in Baton Rouge, Grierson received orders to clear Confederate cavalry from around Clinton, Louisiana. During the fighting, Curl charged eighty yards toward the Union cavalry only to realize the rest of his company had halted at a fence some distance behind him. Despite his failure to follow orders, he was still proud to participate in the defeat of the famous Union leader.[32] Finally, when men of Nathan Bedford Forrest's cavalry held a reunion in New Orleans during the summer of 1906, they measured the waning martial abilities of the "grizzled and grey" men by listing Grierson as a benchmark. Southern veterans used their roles in Grierson's defeats to highlight their success, similar to sports teams when they defeat the champions of the previous year. Their boosting is a testament to the actual respect they held toward the general.[33]

By the late 1910s, with the death of Grierson and many of the principal participants, the history and memorialization of the raid began to decline outside of Illinois, Civil War scholars, and the descendants of those who had been affected by it. As the centennial of the war approached, a new wave of scholars began writing books in preparation for the celebrations and remembrances. Grierson's monumental feat also gained attention, and memory of the event started to reemerge with the publication of *Grierson's Raid* in 1954 by D. Alexander Brown, a librarian at the University of Illinois who wrote books to supplement his meager university pay. His previous two books had examined trail drives and the United States Army's campaigns against Native Americans; he would later write the acclaimed book *Bury My Heart at Wounded Knee*. One day while browsing through the stacks of the library, he discovered the letters of Henry and Stephen Forbes, which inspired him to dig deeper into Grierson's Raid. He produced a well-researched, day-to-day account of the nearly forgotten event that is now cited in most books examining Vicksburg. Brown's book brought Grierson's Raid to the attention of most Civil War scholars and the burgeoning population of "history buffs" across the United States but not yet into the sphere of the general public's notice. Since the publication of Brown's book in 1954, authors examining the Vicksburg Campaign began highlighting the importance of the Grierson expedition.[34]

The true reemergence of Grierson's Raid into American popular memory came with Harold Sinclair's 1956 novel *The Horse Soldiers*. This fictional account is based in Grierson's epic ride through Mississippi. Though the Union names are changed, Grierson replaced with Marlowe and Forbes with Bryce, the places, timeline, and Confederate names remained true to the actual events. Sinclair's previous seven books celebrated the common American and his drive to succeed, and this theme merged well with Grierson's feat. Though Sinclair denied reading Brown's *Grierson's Raid*, he had received a contract to write *The Horse Soldiers* the year after its publication and finished the novel in only six months; not enough time to research the raid fully for his level of detail. It would be plausible to surmise that he relied heavily on Brown's book for details, but Sinclair claimed he read the book only after he finished his initial manuscript. Regardless, the *Horse Soldiers* gained traction in the American public in 1956. Unrestricted by historical methods or any need to stick with the facts, Sinclair developed the characters in depth and created dialogue. The book made numerous best-seller lists, and Sinclair became famous for a brief period of time, catching the attention of studios in Hollywood. Sinclair made some money from the royalties, but his real success came in selling the rights to Twentieth Century Fox and serving as a consultant for an epic movie based on his novel and using the same title.[35]

Twentieth Century Fox acted quickly to make the film, assigning it to the acclaimed director John Ford, famous for his cavalry trilogy with John Wayne and *The Searchers*. Once again Wayne would take the lead role in a Ford film, as the railroad engineer Colonel Marlowe (Grierson) and William Holden portraying a doctor who competes with the colonel for the affections of a young southern woman. As might be expected, the movie differs from the book, but the main premise—a perilous Union cavalry raid through

Mississippi to help Grant capture Vicksburg—is still in place. With such star power—Wayne and Holden were the highest-paid actors in the business—and Ford's status as the most prominent director, the film became a national topic of discussion. Additionally, the filming of the movie pushed back the making of another epic Wayne motion picture, *The Alamo*. Interestingly the marketing of the movie reveals the divisions that still existed between North and South. A *Dallas Morning News* article states, "Director John Ford . . . to give both sides a fair shake. Southerners will be able to walk out of the theaters with heads held high." Also: "old differences have been laid aside in the good-natured competition for the Yankee dollar." In reality, the movie balanced the Union success by depicting their main Confederate opponents, a one-armed veteran and cadets from a fictional military academy, as overwhelmed by circumstances, essentially subtly stating that the raid succeeded only because the South was devoid of man-power. The film achieved modest success and brought Grierson into the collective memory of Americans in the late 1950s.[36]

The memory of Grierson remained prominent for reasons other than his famous raid. Influenced by the civil rights movement in the 1950s and 1960s, professional historians began to focus less on military, political, and economic history and began examining social and cultural topics, including African American history. After the Civil War, despite his abhorrence of horses, Grierson received a commission in the United States Army, remaining in the cavalry. In his postbellum career, Grierson, along with Hatch, commander of the 2nd Iowa during the raid, commanded African American troops. Commonly called Buffalo Soldiers, Hatch's 9th and Grierson's 10th U.S. Cavalry Regiments fought Native Americans on the southwestern frontier. Their prominent role in organizing and leading the regiments brought them and the raid back into the historical memory of another group of Americans with the help of William H. Leckie's book *The Buffalo Soldiers*. Leckie's historical narrative examined the lives and accomplishments of black soldiers winning the American frontier and, like Sinclair's novel, became a movie. In 1997 Turner Network Television released the movie *Buffalo Soldiers* starring A-list actor Danny Glover and Bob Gunton as Grierson., The movie focused on the 10th Regiment's campaign against the outlaw Chiricahua Apache chief Victorio, culminating in the Battle of Rattlesnake Springs in far west Texas. Though historically Grierson led the campaign, in the movie he is removed from command after being wounded, leaving Glover's character, Sergeant Washington Wyatt, to complete the mission. Interestingly Grierson's actual tactics against Victorio were later studied by the U.S. Army for counterinsurgency tactics in Iraq and Afghanistan. It was later published as *In Search of an Elusive Enemy* by the Combat Studies Institute Press. Grierson's role with the 10th Regiment is also prominently displayed at Fort Davis, Texas, with his officer's home restored to the period of his command.[37]

The attention paid to his postbellum career inevitably brought students of the Civil War around to remember Grierson and his famous raid. On July 4, 1975, a group of Civil War reenactors formed the 7th Illinois Cavalry Reactivated, which the governor of Illinois officially reactivated. Two years later, with the help of the United States Cavalry Association Reactivated, they reenacted a cavalry review at Fort Sheridan, Illinois, to help educate the public on the traditions of the U.S. Cavalry. In 1989, nearly fifty reenactors, most from the 7th Illinois Cavalry Reactivated, rode and apparently drove with horse trailers the actual route of Grierson's Raid on its 125th anniversary. At Newton Station, where there is a plaque commemorating the raid, they re-created the burning of the depot, with a bonfire and not the replica built near the original location, along with reproducing some "Sherman neckties" for spectators. In true fashion they ended the raid at the same final campsite in Baton Rouge. The organization still promotes the traditions of the cavalry service and educates the public about the role of the 7th Illinois in the Civil War through reenactments and school presentations. Similarly in 1993 staff members of *Blue & Gray* magazine retraced and recorded the route of the raid along modern roads and published detailed directions in a lengthy article examining Grierson's Raid.[38]

Memory of the raid also inspired Larry D. Underwood to write a novel, *The Butternut Guerillas*, in the early 1990s. Unlike Sinclair, Underwood depicts the view from the enlisted men's saddle, most prominently that of the men put most in harm's way, the scouts. Additionally, Underwood kept as close as possible to the known facts, only taking liberties with the dialogue. Although the book did not have the same success as *The Horse Soldiers*, Underwood was able to sell out the first printing and thus help to continue the memory of the raid. The Civil War artist Mort Künstler painted "Grierson's Butternut Guerrillas," depicting the scouts converging on a train entering Newton Station. The painting was available as a print and also featured in the 1999 Künstler Civil War Calendar.[39]

The latest publication to keep the memory of the raid alive is Grierson's memoir, *A Just and Righteous Cause* (2008). Grierson, who originally titled his reminiscences "The Lights and Shadows of Life," did not intend the work to be published. More than one hundred years after the colonel completed the memoir, Bruce J. Dinges and Shirley A. Leckie (wife of William H. Leckie) edited the work and brought it to the public's attention. Though his memoir was available to researchers at the Illinois State Historical Library in

Springfield, Grierson's actual thoughts at the time of the raid could only be read in his after-action report, later published in *War of the Rebellion*. While the published memoir contains a good deal of autobiographical information, it concludes shortly after his Civil War career ended. He never started on the second half of his prominent military life.[40]

To this day, Grierson is remembered in many historical circles for his military service, especially his role in the dramatic raid during the Civil War. Contemporaries recognized the significance of his actions. Grant credited Grierson with revolutionizing the Union war effort by "set[ting] the example of what can be done in the interior of the enemy's country without any base from which to draw supplies."[41]Grierson's contribution to the Vicksburg Campaign and American history is most vividly remembered today in Jacksonville, Illinois, by the General Benjamin H. Grierson Society, which organizes an annual Winter Gala and on the third weekend in June each year celebrates Grierson's Day.[42]

Notes

1. *Harper's Weekly*, June 6, 1863.

2. Confederate William Quantrill's raid on Lawrence, Kansas, has been the most immortalized cavalry foray of the Civil War. It is remembered in scholarly books, novels, songs, a band in the 1960s, and movies, not only because of the ferocity of the event but also for the involvement of Jesse and Frank James, who made names for themselves after the war as outlaws. See Thomas Goodrich, *Bloody Dawn: The Story of the Lawrence Massacre* (Kent: Kent State University Press, 1992). See also the novel by Ralph Cotton, *While Angels Dance: The Life and Times of Jeston Nash* (Seattle: CreateSpace, 2011); song by Scissorfight, "Quantrill's Raiders" (2005); and the movies "Quantrill's Raiders" (1958) and "Riding with the Devil" (2000).

3. The most complete and modern account of Streight's Raid is examined in Robert L. Willett, *The Lightning Mule Brigade: Abel Streight's 1863 Raid into Alabama* (Carmel, Ind.: Guild Press, 1999); Edwin C. Bearss and J. Parker Hills, *Receding Tide: Vicksburg and Gettysburg, The Campaigns That Changed the Civil War* (Washington, D.C.: National Geographic, 2010), 94; Michael B. Ballard, *Vicksburg: The Campaign That Opened the Mississippi* (Chapel Hill: University of North Carolina Press, 2004), 191–92; Terrence J. Winschel, *Triumph and Defeat: The Vicksburg Campaign* (New York: Savas, 1999), 8–10. The most comprehensive account of Vicksburg recognized by scholars is the three-volume series written by Edwin Cole Bearss, *The Vicksburg Campaign* (Dayton: Morningside Press, 1985).

4. U.S. War Department, *The War of the Rebellion: A Compilation of the Official Records of the Union and Confederate Armies*, 128 vols. (Washington, D.C., 1880–1901), ser. 1, vol. 24, pt. 3: 207. (Hereinafter cited as *OR*. All references are to Series 1 unless otherwise indicated); Tom Lalicki, *Grierson's Raid: A Daring Cavalry Strike through the Heart of the Confederacy* (New York: Farrar, Straus and Giroux, 2004), 11; Earl S. Meirs, *The Web of Victory: Grant at Vicksburg* (Baton Rouge: Louisiana State University Press, 1955), 150.

—

5. *OR*, vol. 24, pt. 1: 523 (quote); Lalicki, 52; D. Alexander Brown, *Grierson's Raid: A Cavalry Adventure of the Civil War* (Champaign: University of Illinois Press, 1954), 56.

6. *OR*, vol. 24, pt. 1: 530 (quote); Brown, 71.

7. Richard W. Surby, *Grierson Raids and Hatch's Sixty-four Days March with Biographical Sketches, and the Life and Adventures of Chickasaw, the Scout* (Chicago: Rounds and James, 1865), 150–51; R. W. Surby, *Grierson's Raid: Narrative of the Chief Scout* (Washington, D.C.: McElroy, Shoppell & Andrews, 1897), 7–8.

8. S. A. Forbes, "Grierson's Cavalry Raid," *Transactions of the Illinois State Historical Society for the Year 1907* (1908): 9–18; William H. Leckie and Shirley A. Leckie, *Unlikely Warriors: General Benjamin Grierson and His Family* (Norman: University of Oklahoma Press, 1984), 90; Edward G. Longacre, *Mounted Raids of the Civil War* (Lincoln: University of Nebraska Press, 1994), 107–9.

9. The Butternut Guerillas were named for the butternut tree acorns, the cheapest alternative that many Confederate guerillas used to dye their uniforms, producing a brown/ grey color to their clothing. Surby, *Grierson Raids*, 29–30; Brown, 64; Bruce J. Dinges and Shirley A. Leckie, eds., *A Just and Righteous Cause: Benjamin H. Grierson's Civil War Memoir* (Carbondale: Southern Illinois University Press, 2008), 154.

10. Brown, 105–8; Surby, *Grierson Raids*, 46–47; Dinges and Leckie, 158; Surby, *Grierson's Raid*, 18.

11. John C. Pemberton, *Pemberton: Defender of Vicksburg* (Chapel Hill: University of North Carolina Press, 1942), 292.

12. Michael B. Ballard, *Pemberton: The General Who Lost Vicksburg* (Jackson: University Press of Mississippi, 1991), 139; Ballard, *Vicksburg*, 208; William L. Shea and Terrence J. Winschel, *Vicksburg Is the Key: The Struggle for the Mississippi River* (Lincoln: University of Nebraska Press, 2003), 93; Bruce Catton, *Grant Takes Command* (Boston: Little, Brown, 1969), 217; Michael B. Ballard, "Misused Merit: The Tragedy of John C. Pemberton," in Steven E. Woodworth, ed., *Civil War Generals in Defeat* (Lawrence: University Press of Kansas, 1999), 157; *OR*, vol. 24, pt. 3:781–86.

13. Benjamin Henry Grierson, "The Lights and Shadows of Life: Including Experiences and Remembrances of the War of the Rebellion" (1892), 318–19 (quote), Benjamin Henry Grierson Papers, Southwest Collections, Texas Tech University, Lubbock; *OR*, vol. 24, pt. 1: 526.

14. Bahala has since changed its name to Beauregard in honor of Confederate General Pierre Gustave Toutant Beauregard. Brown, 162–63, 165; *OR*, vol. 24, pt. 1: 526.

15. Grierson, 320, 324–25.

16. Surby, *Grierson Raids*, 104–10; Grierson, 330–38, 342; Brown, 212–15.

17. Though Paddy Griffith focused almost exclusively on the eastern theater in his book, he does acknowledge the importance of Grierson's Raid in the transformation of the Union cavalry. Paddy Griffith, *Battle Tactics of the Civil War* (New Haven: Yale University Press, 1989), 183; Brown, 217–19; *OR*, vol. 24, pt. 1: 528; Grierson, 339–42; Surby, *Grierson Raids*, 125–26.

18. *Harper's Weekly*, June 6, 1863; Warren E. Grabau, *Ninety-Eight Days: A Geographer's View of the Vicksburg Campaign* (Knoxville: University of Tennessee Press, 2000), 451.

19. *OR*, vol. 24, pt. 1: 529.

20. *New York Herald*, May 18, 1863 (quote); *Milwaukee Sentinel*, May 5, 1863; *Philadelphia Inquirer*, May 12, 1863; *Philadelphia Public Ledger*, May 12, 1863; Brown, 223.

—

21. *Harper's Weekly*, June 6, 1863; *Milwaukee Sentinel*, June 1, 1863.

22. *Macon (Ga.) Telegraph*, May 7, 1863; *Memphis Appeal*, May 5, 1863; *Columbus (Miss.) Republic*, n.d.

23. *Macon (Ga.) Telegraph*, May 7, 1863; *Memphis Appeal*, May 5, 1863; *Philadelphia Inquirer*, May 12, 1863; *Philadelphia Public Ledger*, May 12, 1863; *Jackson (Miss.)Appeal*, April 28, 1863; *Paulding (Miss.)Clarion*, May 1, 1863; Mark Grimsley, *The Hard Hand of War: Union Military Policy Toward Southern Civilians 1861–1865* (Cambridge: Cambridge University Press, 1995), 211–12, 219; Edward Alfred Pollard, *The Lost Cause: A Southern History of the War of the Confederates* (New York: E. B. Treat, 1866), 597–98.

24. J. S. C. Abbott, "Grierson's Raid," *Harper's New Monthly Magazine*, 30, no. 226 (1865): 281; Joseph E. Johnston, "Jefferson Davis and the Mississippi Campaign," in *Battles and Leaders of the Civil War*, ed. Robert Underwood Johnson and Clarence Clough Buel (New York: Thomas Yoseloff, 1956), 3: 477; S. H. Lockett, "The Defense of Vicksburg," ibid., 3: 485–86; Ulysses S. Grant, "The Vicksburg Campaign," ibid., 3: 499; Thomas Speed, "Cavalry Operations in the West under Rosecrans and Sherman," ibid., 4: 414–15; Ulysses S. Grant, *Memoirs and Selected Letters: Personal Memoirs of U. S. Grant* (New York: Literary Classics, 1990), 2: 326; Carol Reardon, "Writing Battle History: The Challenge of Memory," *Civil War History*, September 2007, 261; David W. Blight, *Race and Reunion: The Civil War in American History* (Cambridge, Mass.: Harvard University Press, 2001), 18, 24.

25. See note 7 above.

26. Forbes, "Grierson's Cavalry Raid," 99–130; *San Jose (Calif.) Evening News*, June 27, 1903.

27. Francis Grierson, *The Valley of Shadows: Recollections of the Lincoln Country, 1858–1863* (New York: Houghton Mifflin, 1909); Harold P. Simonson, "Francis Grierson—A Biographical Sketch and Bibliography," *Journal of Illinois State Historical State Historical Society* 54 (Summer 1961): 198–99.

28. "William Owen Kelly," *Confederate Veteran*, July 1905, 321.

29. "Joseph Taliaferro Brown, "Taliaferro," *Confederate Veteran*, June 1909, 294.

30. "Capt. Ed B. Ross," *Confederate Veteran*, April 1912, 176.

31. T. M. Daniel, "He Got His Own Turkey," *Confederate Veteran*, August 1894, 245 (quote); Michael Ballard, *The Civil War in Mississippi: Major Campaigns and Battles* (Jackson: University Press of Mississippi, 2011), 189–90; Reardon, "Writing Battle History," 261.

32. A. Curl, "The Fight at Clinton, La.," *Confederate Veteran*, March 1903, 122–23.

33. "Forrest's Cavalry at New Orleans Reunion: Extracts from Minutes of the Secretary," *Confederate Veteran*, July 1906, 299.

34. Brown, *Grierson's Raid*; Neil Longley York, *Fiction as Fact: The Horse Soldiers and Popular Memory* (Kent, Ohio: Kent State University Press, 2001), 26–27.

35. Not to be confused with the more recent book *Horse Soldiers*, which was not influenced by Grierson's Raid nor Sinclair's novel. It examines the role of the first Special Forces soldiers uprooting the Taliban in Afghanistan in the months after the 9/11 attacks. Harold Sinclair, *The Horse Soldiers* (New York: Harper & Brothers, 1956); York, *Fiction as Fact*, 54–55, 77; Doug Stanton, *Horse Soldiers: The Extraordinary Story of a Band of US Soldiers Who Rode to Victory in Afghanistan* (New York: Scribner, 2009).

36. *Dallas Morning News*, December 1, 1958 (quotes); *Dallas Morning News*, October 15, 1958; York, *Fiction as Fact*, 80–81, 102–3; Gary W. Gallagher, *Causes Won, Lost, and Forgotten: How Hollywood and Popular Art Shape What We Know about the Civil War* (Chapel Hill: University of North Carolina Press, 2008), 51.

37. Shirley Anne Leckie, William's wife, edited a collection of Grierson's wife's correspondence from the times they were on the frontier. They also collaborated on an extensive biography of Grierson and his family as well that covers both his Civil War and postbellum careers. William H. Leckie, *Buffalo Soldiers: A Narrative of the Negro Cavalry of the West* (Norman: University of Oklahoma Press, 1967); Kendall D. Gott, *In Search of an Elusive Enemy: The Victorio Campaign, 1879–1880* (Fort Leavenworth: Combat Studies Institute Press, n.d.); "Fort Davis National Historic Site," http://www.nps.gov/foda/index.htm, accessed on January 5, 2012; Shirley Anne Leckie, *The Colonel's Lady in the Frontier: The Correspondence of Alice Kirk Grierson* (Lincoln: University of Nebraska Press, 1989); Leckie and Leckie, *Unlikely Warriors*.

38. *Army Times*, June 27, 1977; Larry D. Underwood, *The Butternut Guerillas: A Story of Grierson's Raid* (Lincoln, Neb.: Dageforde Publishing, 1994), ix–x; "Resting Cavalry Horses on the March," http://www.authentic-campaigner.com/forum/archive/index.php/t-29133.html accessed on January 5, 2012; "Official Website of the 7th Illinois Volunteer Cavalry," http://www.angelfire.com/rebellion/7thillinoiscav/recruits.html accessed on January 5, 2012; Dave Roth, "Grierson's Raid April 17– May 2, 1863: A Cavalry Raid at Its Best," *Blue & Gray*, June 1993: 12–27, 48–65.

39. Underwood, *The Butternut Guerillas*; "Grierson's Butternut Guerillas," http://www.mortkunstler.com/html/art-original-masterworks.asp?action=view&ID=41&cat=132 accessed on January 5, 2012.

40. Dinges and Leckie, *A Just and Righteous Cause*; OR, vol. 24, pt. 1: 521–29.

41. John Y. Simon, ed., *The Papers of Ulysses S. Grant: May 1–December 31, 1865* (Carbondale: Southern Illinois University Press, 1988), 589.

42. "General Benjamin H. Grierson Society," http://www.griersonsociety.com/. Accessed on January 5, 2012; Leckie and Leckie, *Unlikely Warriors*, ix.

3

"IN THE ENEMY'S COUNTRY"
PORT GIBSON AND THE TURNING POINT
OF THE VICKSBURG CAMPAIGN

Jason M. Frawley

On May 1, 1863, Union and Confederate forces collided west of Port Gibson, Mississippi, in what one Confederate veteran later called "one of the hottest little battles of the [American Civil] War." As part of the Vicksburg Campaign, the battle of Port Gibson had important ramifications for both sides as well as for the future of the United States. For the Federals, the engagement represented the successful establishment of a beachhead in Mississippi and put them a step closer to conquering the citadel at Vicksburg. For the Confederates, the contest stood as the beginning of the end of their control over the most important point on the Mississippi River outside of New Orleans, Louisiana, which had already fallen into Union hands a year earlier. And for the nation and its history, the battle of Port Gibson represented the culminating event in a campaign that would prove to be the turning point of the struggle for control of the Mississippi River.[1]

By the early spring of 1863, Major General Ulysses Simpson Grant saw clearly that there was only one way for his Union Army of the Tennessee to take Vicksburg. Taking the greatest risk of his military career, he sent a message to Rear Admiral David Dixon Porter on March 29, 1863, asking him to prepare for a running of the batteries at Vicksburg.[2] What Grant proposed was to have Porter's boats move south of Vicksburg, where they would link up with the army, which would spend April marching down the Louisiana side of the Mississippi River. Once the two forces connected south of their target, Porter would ferry the army across the river, and Grant would lead his men on an assault against Vicksburg via the interior of Mississippi.[3]

History would remember it as one of America's greatest military operations, but at the time, Grant's new plan was riddled with numerous complications and extreme risks. First, there was the difficult step of getting Porter

---

43

past the shore batteries at Vicksburg. This would not be the first time Union naval forces had run past the city, but it was still a very dangerous mission that would slow Porter down in the face of the Confederates' heavy guns as he navigated past DeSoto Point, the sharp bend in the Mississippi River adjacent to Vicksburg. If things went poorly, the maneuver could very well end with the loss of naval forces vital to success in conquering and controlling the Father of Waters. Moreover, as Porter reminded Grant, once the boats were below Vicksburg, "we give up all hopes of ever getting them up again." Hence, if Grant's plan did not work, Porter's brown water navy would be committed to operating below Vicksburg, where they would be cut off from directly supporting any future endeavors north of the city.[4]

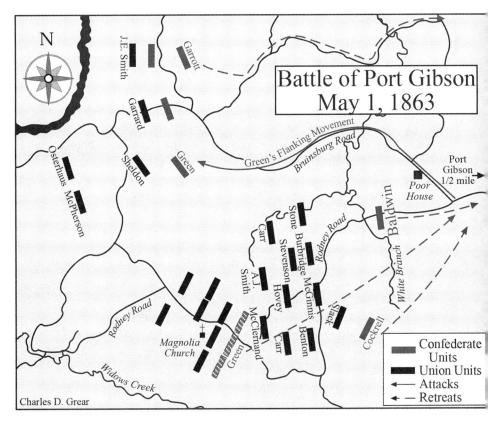

The first Confederate force to challenge Grant's army after it landed on the Mississippi shore below Vicksburg was a division commanded by Brigadier General John S. Bowen, but after several hours of fighting in rough terrain, the outnumbered Rebels had to retreat.

There was also the problem of getting the army down the west bank of the river during the spring high-water season. The only reliable way to march down the river on the Louisiana side was to rely on the winding natural levees that were surrounded by water of varying depth and sometimes not even connected to one another. Getting an army and its supplies safely to its destination along this route would not prove easy.

Finally, Grant would have to reckon with the Confederate forces in his front. To paraphrase German military philosopher Helmuth von Moltke, no plan survives contact with the enemy, and it was unlikely that the Confederates would sit by idly while Grant carried out his daring offensive. Grant would have to prepare for possible reactions from Pemberton, or he would have to develop some way of keeping the Rebels occupied while his own plans unfolded. Also, once Grant's forces were in position, they would have to launch a dangerous amphibious operation across the river into enemy-occupied Mississippi.[5]

The inherent dangers of such a crossing were substantial. In just a couple of months, President Lincoln would notably warn the commander of the eastern theater's Army of the Potomac, Major General Joseph Hooker, against crossing the Rappahannock River to get at Confederate General Robert Edward Lee's Army of Northern Virginia, writing, "In one word, I would not take any risk of being entangled upon the river, like an ox jumped half over a fence and liable to be torn by dogs front and rear, without a fair chance to gore one way or kick the other." Concerned that the army that shielded Washington, D.C., might be torn to pieces if Hooker attempted a river crossing with an enemy in his front, Lincoln advised caution. One might think the same advice should also have been applied to Grant's plan. After all, the Mississippi River and the territory through which the Army of the Tennessee would have to march were more formidable obstacles than the Rappahannock and its surrounding country; however, the major difference in this case was that Grant was not Joe Hooker, and Pemberton was no Robert E. Lee.[6]

John Pemberton was one of the more controversial figures of the Civil War. Born in Philadelphia, Pennsylvania, Pemberton graduated from the United States Military Academy at West Point in 1837 before serving with distinction in both the Second Seminole War and the Mexican American War. While his brother enlisted on the Union side and despite his having loyally served his country for many years, Pemberton elected to resign his commission in the U.S. Army and cast his lot with the Confederacy in late April 1861. Although he married into a respectable Virginia family and had conducted some of his prewar military service in the southern states, Pemberton remained a northerner by birth, and as such, he endured questions regarding his loyalty to the southern cause throughout the war. He therefore seemed an odd choice to command the Army of Vicksburg, which was charged with defending the Confederate bastion, when President Davis appointed him to the position on September 30, 1862.[7]

Odder still was Pemberton's decision upon assuming command to keep his headquarters in Jackson, Mississippi, as Grant proceeded with his efforts to capture Vicksburg. Whereas Grant regularly led his men by remaining among them, Pemberton kept his distance from the campaign's center of gravity. This distance from the Confederate citadel kept him out of touch with the strategic situation unfolding along the river. Hence, when Porter finally conducted his heroic running of the batteries in mid-April 1863 and as the Army of the Tennessee marched down the west bank of the Mississippi throughout the month, exchanging shots with Confederate cavalry and skirmishers along the way, Pemberton failed to appreciate the significance of the movements or respond appropriately. In fairness to Pemberton, he did not command the west side of the Mississippi because President Davis had imprudently decided on making the river "a departmental dividing line and creating on either side of it departments that were independent of each other," but the fault ultimately rested with the general for remaining in Jackson and never adequately grasping the situation that was developing forty miles to his west until it was too late.[8]

Aside from suffering serious shortcomings of his own and having to answer to a prickly, micro-managerial president, Pemberton's greatest problem was his opponent. Grant did not telegraph his moves by simply plodding south through Louisiana and crossing into Mississippi without taking into consideration his enemy. Rather, he planned for Pemberton and kept the Confederate general's head on a constant swivel. Ordering a series of diversionary cavalry raids into the heart of Mississippi and a joint army-navy demonstration against Snyder's Bluff part way through the operation, Grant succeeded in keeping Pemberton's focus on the areas north and east of Vicksburg. Coupling these diversions with Porter's running of the batteries and reports that Union troops were moving below Vicksburg along the west bank of the river, Pemberton was overwhelmed and remained relatively flat-footed, alerting the War Department on April 9 that the "enemy is constantly in motion in all directions. As Pemberton's foremost biographer later noted, "Grant was determined to keep Pemberton in a state of speculation," and the plan worked: Pemberton quickly became "tentative, uncertain, and slow to react."[9]

While Grant remained aggressive and despite the news that the Army of the Tennessee was on the move, Pemberton kept his headquarters in Jackson and continued to lose touch with the strategic situation along the Mississippi.

A few days after sending his exasperated message regarding Grant's bewildering movements to the War Department, Pemberton again wired his superiors, this time to inform them of his opinion that "most of Grant's forces are being withdrawn to Memphis." Confederate scouts had spotted a large number of Union boats heading north, and Pemberton believed the Federals were leaving in preparation for a major push against Confederate General Braxton Bragg's position in middle Tennessee. It turns out that Grant was merely sending some transports to assist Major General William Starke Rosecrans's Army of the Cumberland with logistical problems, and Pemberton had misinterpreted the shift of vessels to be the early stages of a general Union withdrawal from the area around Vicksburg. He could not have been more wrong.[10]

While Pemberton misread Union movements, Grant kept up the pressure and continued with his plan to attack Vicksburg's soft underbelly. Porter's boats had made it south of Vicksburg with minimal losses during two heroic runs past the city's batteries—one on April 16 and the other on April 22. Once below the city, these boats linked up with a portion of Grant's army and prepared to cross the Mississippi. The units waiting for Porter were from Major General John Alexander McClernand's Thirteenth Corps, and they had begun the difficult march through the Louisiana swamps from their camps around Milliken's Bend back on March 31. After some reconnaissance, some of which Grant personally conducted, the Federals chose Hard Times, Louisiana, as their crossing point. From there, Grant hoped to assault the Confederate position on the east side of the river at Grand Gulf, Mississippi, which could then serve as a solid beachhead from which to threaten Vicksburg.[11]

Quite fittingly, the trip to Hard Times had not been easy for McClernand's men, and the destination's apt name became synonymous with the marchers' experiences. Union soldiers had to deal not only with sporadic fighting against Confederate scouts and cavalry but also the high waters of the river and its adjoining bayous, which had done more damage than expected along the route. According to McClernand's report on the maneuver down the west bank of the Mississippi, "many obstacles were overcome, old roads were repaired, new ones made, boats constructed for the transportation of men and supplies, 20 miles of levee sleeplessly guarded day and night, and every possible precaution used to prevent the rising flood from breaking through the levee and engulfing us." Grant echoed McClernand's description of the area between Union camps to the north and Hard Times, later writing, "the roads were very bad, scarcely above water yet." When the Federals reached the vicinity of New Carthage on April 6, they found the village and surrounding countryside completely submerged, and after personally visiting

McClernand's vanguard on April 17, Grant noted that "the process of getting troops through in the way we were doing was so tedious that a better
method must be devised."[12]

Despite the hardships of the march to Hard Times, the Union troops
reflected their army commander's trademark determination and persisted to
their destination. As Grant later wrote, "the ingenuity of the 'Yankee soldier'
was equal to any emergency," including this one. Learning to take advantage
of the resources immediately available to them, the Federals commandeered
local boats, used wood from nearby homes to build their own vessels, laid
miles of corduroy road, and constructed at least five large bridges from "such
material as could be found nearby" between Milliken's Bend and Hard Times.
At one point, the men even converted an old flatboat into a gunship, which
they then used to drive off a group of stubborn Confederate defenders at
New Carthage. It was an extremely difficult march, but it was also an epic
adventure that ended with all four of McClernand's divisions gathered safely
at Hard Times on April 28. The following day, two divisions of Major General
James Birdseye McPherson's Seventeenth Corps arrived as well, bringing the
total to six Union divisions. As a result of his unwavering perseverance and
fervent commitment to overcoming obstacles, Grant finally found himself
in position to launch his proposed offensive across the Mississippi River.[13]

Three miles below Hard Times and on the opposite side of the river were
the unfinished fortifications at Grand Gulf—Fort Cobun and Fort Wade.
This was Grant's target: from Grand Gulf, he could keep his army supplied
during its invasion of the Magnolia State and assault against Vicksburg. It
was not going to be easy, however, for according to Rear Admiral Porter,
who would be in charge of the naval attack against the Confederate position, "Grand Gulf is the strongest place on the Mississippi. Had the enemy
succeeded in finishing the fortifications, no fleet could have taken them." In
fact, even Porter and the seven ironclads under his command would prove
unsuccessful in their attempt at forcing the Rebels to submit.[14]

Brigadier General John Stevens Bowen, a native of Savannah, Georgia, an
1853 graduate of West Point, and a veteran of the battle of Shiloh, had been
the Confederate commander in charge of the seemingly impregnable position at Grand Gulf since early March 1863. Bowen was among Pemberton's
most trusted subordinates, which is why he was charged with defending this
southern anchor of Vicksburg's defenses. Unfortunately for Bowen, being
one of Pemberton's most trusted lieutenants apparently did not count for
much, for during the Federals' march down the west bank of the river, Bowen
had endeavored to keep Pemberton apprised of the seriousness of the situation. On April 8, Bowen even suggested using his entire force to launch a

preemptive attack across the Mississippi to thwart the Union invaders. When Pemberton responded to the plan with uncertainty, Bowen opted instead to send two Missouri regiments and a section of artillery across the river into the Louisiana swamps under the command of their suitably named colonel, Francis Marion Cockrell, with orders to contact the enemy and send back accurate reports on Federal movements. When Porter succeeded in running the batteries at Vicksburg in mid-April, Bowen recalled Cockrell for fear that he might be cut off from the main force in Mississippi, but while in Louisiana, the colonel's Missourians proved diligent in funneling good information back to Bowen, who then made sure it reached Pemberton.[15]

Despite the high-quality intelligence Bowen consistently passed to his commander, Pemberton dismissed the early warnings. When he informed the War Department in early April about these reports regarding McClernand's movements along the Mississippi, Pemberton, who was still operating out of Jackson, dismissively remarked, "Much doubt it." Once again, Pemberton had demonstrated his inability to grasp the importance of the strategic situation developing around Vicksburg.[16]

With Union forces now in position to threaten the all-important fortifications at Grand Gulf, it was left to Bowen and his relatively small force to stonewall the Federals. Aware of the looming threat at Hard Times, Bowen fired off a series of messages to his commander on April 28 in the hopes that Pemberton would finally comprehend the seriousness of the Union threat. First, he alerted Pemberton, "Reports indicate an immense force opposite me." Still not fully appreciating Bowen's predicament, Pemberton asked, "Have you force enough to hold your position? If not, give me the smallest additional force with which you can." Bowen's response was direct: "I advise that every man and gun that can be spared from other points be sent here." A showdown at Grand Gulf was imminent.[17]

The battle of Grand Gulf commenced at 8:00 A.M. on April 29, 1863, and it stands as one of the greatest ship-to-shore engagements of the Civil War. Earlier that morning, some ten thousand Union soldiers from McClernand's Thirteenth Corps piled onto Porter's transports and took up positions behind Coffee Point, a Louisiana peninsula formed by a bend in the Mississippi River just north of Grand Gulf. As Grant reported a few days after the attack, these men stood ready to "carry the place by storm the moment the batteries bearing on the river were silenced." While they waited for their chance to land and take the Confederate fortifications, seven of Porter's ironclads unleashed a lethal, five-and-a-half-hour barrage against Bowen's defenses. Bowen's shore batteries responded with a brutal attack of their own, and the sounds of the heavy guns thundered across the Mississippi valley.[18]

Unfortunately for the Federals, the Confederate guns sat atop hundred-foot bluffs, and according to Grant, "From the great elevation the enemy's batteries had, it proved impracticable to silence them from the river." Porter's forces succeeded in neutralizing Fort Wade, but suffering serious damage to a number of their boats and unable to subdue the Rebels holding Fort Cobun, the Federals aborted the attack at 1:30 P.M. According to Porter's after-action report, "we never fairly succeeded in stopping [the enemy's] fire but for a short while. It is remarkable that we did not disable his guns, but though we knocked the parapets much to pieces, the guns were apparently uninjured." After meeting with Porter aboard his badly damaged flagship, the U.S.S. *Benton*, Grant decided on a different plan for getting across the river. The assault had ended in failure and cost the Union navy seventy-five casualties, including a slightly wounded Porter, who had been hit in the head by a piece of broken shell.[19]

In the face of the vigorous Federal bombardment, Bowen put up a stubborn defense and bought Pemberton and the rest of Mississippi valuable time. According to Porter, the Confederates fought "with a desperation I have never yet witnessed." Still working to keep his commander informed throughout the struggle, Bowen sent some early messages to Pemberton that seemed to belie Porter's assumption that the Confederate guns had withstood the Union onslaught. In his reports to headquarters, Bowen reported that "the batteries, especially the lower ones, are badly torn to pieces." When the cannonade finally ended, Bowen claimed, the Federals had "fired about 3,000 shot and shell" and killed three men while wounding twelve to fifteen others. Among the dead was Colonel William Wade, Grand Gulf's chief of artillery and "one of the bravest and best" men in Bowen's command. Expressing relief at the report that Grand Gulf was only battered and not broken, Pemberton sent a message of thanks to Bowen and his troops, and he also informed Bowen, "Yesterday I warmly recommended you for a major-generalcy. I shall renew it." Shortly thereafter, the telegraph lines connecting Grand Gulf with Jackson went dead, and Pemberton, now blind to events along the river, sent out messages speculating that either the Federals had landed in Mississippi or the lines had been cut by Union cavalry operating in the state's interior.[20]

Following the failed attempt to capture Grand Gulf, Grant kept up the pressure. After considering the possibility of landing his men and launching a frontal attack against the position, an enterprise he later admitted would have been "impossible" in the face of the Confederate guns remaining on the high bluffs, Grant decided to bypass the fortifications altogether and sought a safer crossing point farther down the river. At dusk, Porter's gunboats laid down a covering fire against Grand Gulf that lasted until 10:00 P.M. Protected by the Union shelling of the bluffs and concealed by darkening skies, the transports successfully ran past the batteries before being followed by the ironclads. Meanwhile, Grant's troops marched five miles south to Disharoon's Plantation, where they reunited with Porter's boats and once again endeavored to cross the Mississippi River.[21]

Upon reaching the new crossing point, Porter expressed regret about the day's action. He even seemed to question Grant's wisdom in ordering the attack at Grand Gulf, writing, "We are now in a position to make a landing where the general pleases. I should have preferred this latter course in the first instance; it would have saved many lives and many hard knocks." April 29 had been a long, deadly day for Porter's men, and in spite of his regrets regarding the loss of life, the admiral demonstrated determination in supporting Grant's continued offensive: "We land the army in the morning on the other side, and march on Vicksburg. . . . The squadron has been six hours and a half today under a hot and well-directed fire, and is ready to commence at daylight in the morning." Like Grant, Porter would not let a single hard day's fighting deter him; dawn would bring new opportunities.[22]

Now that the lead elements of the Army of the Tennessee were below Grand Gulf, the next logical landing point on the east side of the river seemed to be Rodney, Mississippi, a small hamlet nearly eleven miles below Disharoon's Plantation. Grant knew that a road led inland from Rodney to a junction of roads at a place called Port Gibson. If he could succeed in establishing his army at Port Gibson, he could not only turn Bowen's position at Grand Gulf but also threaten any number of Confederate points in Mississippi, including Vicksburg and Jackson. Grant also understood that it would be necessary not only to take Port Gibson but also to secure the bridges across Bayou Pierre, a small river that cut across the state before emptying into the Mississippi River. He later commented on this necessity in his memoirs, writing, "crossing a stream in the presence of an enemy is always difficult." Apparently, in his old age, Grant had forgotten that before he could move across the so-called stream at Bayou Pierre, he first had to ferry his entire army across the mighty Mississippi.[23]

Given its strategic location, Port Gibson became Grant's focus, and it turned out he would not have to ferry his army all the way to Rodney before moving against his new target. On the evening on April 29, a small group of Union cavalrymen slipped across the river into Mississippi, where they kidnapped a black man and brought him to Grant's headquarters in Louisiana. Despite the nature of his arrival, this contraband provided Grant with invaluable information. Having lived in the area his entire life, the informant explained to Grant that a suitable place to land his army could be found much closer than Rodney. He suggested the landing at Bruinsburg, a farming community located just south of Bayou Pierre. Landing at Bruinsburg, which was only five miles downstream, would not only cut the Federals' trip in half but also afford them a dry road that cut between the bluffs before ultimately connecting with the Rodney–Port Gibson Road. Most important of all, especially given the recent hard fighting at Forts Cobun and Wade, the man reported that there were no Confederate forces south of Grand Gulf. It appeared that this time, Grant's efforts to get his army onto Mississippi soil would be uncontested.[24]

At 8:00 A.M. on the morning of April 30, the men of McClernand's Thirteenth Corps became the first soldiers to leave Disharoon's Plantation and head for Bruinsburg. After packing as many soldiers as he could onto all available boats, Grant joined Porter on the squadron's flagship and inaugurated what at least two historians of the campaign have called "the greatest amphibious operation in American history up to that time." It was a nervous trip. The *Benton* led the way, and looming before Grant, Porter, and the other men onboard the flagship were Mississippi's imposing bluffs. According to First Sergeant Robert H. Martin of Company I, 46th Indiana Infantry, Grant, who likely wondered about the accuracy of the contraband's information regarding the absence of Confederates in the region, "watched the shore closely through his glass" as the Federals approached the shore. Martin and the other men of the 46th mimicked their commander's behavior: "Being in the front, we had our eyes open for anything that might show up." Perhaps sensing the concerns in his men and remembering the lesson that his enemies always had as much to fear from him as he had from them, Grant signaled a regimental band to play "The Red, White, and Blue." In response to the rousing tune, the tension dissolved, and the men let out a string of cheers that echoed across the muddy waters of the Mississippi, announcing their crossing to anyone within earshot.[25]

Fortunately for the Federals, the contraband's information proved accurate, and what could have been a bloody amphibious assault against strongly defended Confederate bluffs turned out to be little more than a glorified river crossing. As units from McClernand's corps filed off the boats, which immediately returned to Disharoon's Plantation and continued to ferry more men and equipment over to Mississippi, the soldiers found Bruinsburg largely deserted. According to Corporal Michael A. Sweetman of Company K, 114th Ohio, "Bruinsburg then had no inhabitants, and not even a house, a few old sheds and three or four straggling fig trees showing that perhaps at one time some person or persons here had a home." The first troops to disembark—members of the 24th and 46th Indiana Infantry Regiments—did detain a local farmer lest he warn the Confederates about their arrival, but otherwise, Bruinsburg proved a safe area for Grant's army to assemble before heading inland.[26]

By noon, the entire Thirteenth Corps—all seventeen thousand men—was ashore. Grant later reflected on how relieved he was to be in Mississippi with McClernand's corps securing the new foothold and on the importance of the landing:

> When this was effected I felt a degree of relief scarcely ever equalled since. Vicksburg was not taken yet it is true, nor were its defenders demoralized by any of our previous moves. I was now in the enemy's country, with a vast river and the stronghold of Vicksburg between me and my base of supplies. But I was on dry ground on the same side of the river with the enemy. All the campaigns, labors, hardships and exposures from the month of December previous to this time that had been made and endured, were for the accomplishment of this one object.

The Vicksburg Campaign was finally starting to turn, but Grant would need to solidify his recent gains and establish himself firmly in Mississippi with a military victory, the fruits of which he had not tasted in over a year.[27]

While Grant may have expressed excitement at finally being "in the enemy's country" when writing his postwar memoir, any actual relief he felt in 1863 quickly vanished when he learned that McClernand had neglected to provide his men with the requisite three-day rations as they prepared to cross the Mississippi the night before. Grant had finally made it into enemy territory, but before he could carry out his blitz through the Magnolia State, his men had to waste four vital hours waiting for the navy to ferry their rations across the river from Disharoon's Plantation. It was a blunder that could very well have cost the Federals the element of surprise had they been up against a more perceptive Confederate commander; but Pemberton, who had finally moved his headquarters to Vicksburg on May 1 so that he could better communicate with the forces combating the Army of the Tennessee, failed to capitalize on McClernand's mistake or to make good use of the time Bowen had bought him at Grand Gulf. His decision to move to the campaign's center of gravity came too late.[28]

With rations in hand, Brigadier General Eugene Asa Carr's Fourteenth Division of McClernand's corps led the Union column away from the river and toward the bluffs at 4:00 P.M. McClernand, who had botched the landing and nearly cost the Federals' their momentum by forgetting those rations, had a lot to atone for. After reaching the bluffs, which were three miles west of the landing, and setting up his temporary headquarters at Windsor Plantation, he made an important decision: "Deeming it important to surprise the enemy if he should be found in the neighborhood of Port Gibson, and if possible, to prevent him from destroying the bridges over Bayou Pierre on the road leading to Grand Gulf and to Jackson, I determined to push on by a forced march that night as far as practicable." After giving his men a brief rest, the march resumed at 5:30 P.M.[29]

Concerned that some of Bowen's forces from Grand Gulf may already be defending the Bruinsburg Road, which ran due east of the landing and served as the most direct route to Port Gibson, McClernand had Carr's division lead the Thirteenth Corps south to Bethel Church. From there, Carr turned northeast onto the Rodney–Port Gibson Road in an effort to guide the Thirteenth Corps around any Confederates operating south of Bayou Pierre. Colonel Charles L. Harris's 2nd Brigade, composed of the 11th Wisconsin and the 21st, 22nd, and 23rd Iowa Infantry Regiments, served as the vanguard with Colonel Samuel Merrill's 21st regiment leading the way. In organizing his regiment to spearhead the Union march, Merrill deployed Companies A and B as skirmishers, with Companies D and F and a gun from the 1st Iowa Battery in close support.[30]

As the Federals made their way toward Port Gibson, the skies quickly darkened. Marching under the twilight skies of Mississippi, First Sergeant Charles A. Hobbs of Company B, 99th Illinois Infantry Regiment, observed, "The moon is shining above us and the road is romantic in the extreme. The artillery wagons rattle forward and the heavy tramp of many men gives a dull but impressive sound." Hobbs also commented on the rugged terrain across which the Federals were marching: "In many places the road seems to end abruptly, but [when] we come to the place we find it turning at right angles, passing through narrow valleys, sometimes through hills, and presenting the best opportunity to the Rebels for defense if they had but known our purpose." Grant, too, would note the difficult geography, writing, "The country in this part of Mississippi stands on edge, as it were, the roads running along the ridges except when they occasionally pass from one ridge to another. Where there are no clearings the sides of the hills are covered with a very heavy growth of timber and with undergrowth, and the ravines are filled with vines and canebrakes, almost impenetrable. This makes it easy for an inferior force to delay, if not defeat, a far superior one." This terrain would play a significant role in the coming battle, for while the numbers may have favored the Federals, the topography favored the defense. Grant and his army would again have to overcome a significant obstacle in their quest for victory.[31]

Finding it difficult to navigate the harsh terrain in the dark, Colonel Merrill, still in the lead, pulled his skirmishers back and appointed a sixteen-man force under the command of Lieutenant Colonel Cornelius W. Dunlap to push ahead until they met the enemy. Dunlap soon found himself joined by Colonel William M. Stone, who had taken over command of the Second Brigade after Colonel Harris fell ill with severe stomach cramps. Guided by a contraband—perhaps the same man who had suggested Bruinsburg as the landing point for Grant's army—this patrol cut its way across the tangled topography of western Mississippi with orders to "reach Port Gibson at as early an hour as possible, and occupy the several bridges across Bayou Pierre at that place."[32]

The march was intense, and navigating the terrain in the dark kept the men on edge. Around 11:00 P.M., Merrill's troops took a brief rest in a narrow valley along the road. As Lieutenant William Charleton of the 11th Wisconsin Infantry Regiment rested against a tree, he and his comrades were suddenly "startled by a loud yelling away to the rear." Fearing that the Rebels were upon them, some of the men took cover on the sides of the road and opened fire on what turned out to be an orderly's runaway horse. According to Charleton, the episode "gave us a good waking up, and prepared us for what was soon to follow; and I have always looked upon the circumstance since as a Godsend to us." After the excitement subsided, Dunlap's scouting party and the other members of Stone's brigade continued in the direction of Port Gibson. The Confederates quietly awaited their arrival.[33]

Following the Union running of the Grand Gulf batteries back on April 29, General Bowen had not wasted time responding to the threat he knew would be coming from below Bayou Pierre. Early on April 30, Bowen ordered Brigadier General Martin Edwin Green to take 450–500 men from his brigade to cover the two main roads leading into Port Gibson from the direction of the Mississippi River. Arriving in Port Gibson at 3:00 A.M., Green took command of the 15th and 21st Arkansas Infantry Regiments as well as the 12th Arkansas Sharpshooter Battalion. Finding that the men were incorrectly deployed on the road leading south to Natchez, Mississippi, Green reset them on the Rodney Road about three miles west of Port Gibson, along a ridge near Magnolia Church. During the day, Green received a visit from General Bowen, who vetted the decision to set up a defensive line at Magnolia Church, with reinforcements in the form of the 6th Mississippi Infantry Regiment as well as the four guns of the Hudson Battery, also known as the Pettus Flying Artillery. When establishing his defensive positions around Magnolia Church, Green anchored his line with Colonel Robert Lowry's 6th Mississippi on the right and Colonel Jordan E. Cravens's

21st Arkansas on the left. He then positioned Lieutenant William D. Tisdale and four men from the 12th Arkansas Sharpshooters six hundred yards to the west at the A. K. Shaifer House, which sat at the intersection of the Rodney Road and an old farm road that ran north to the Bruinsburg Road. Green then ordered his men to "sleep on their arms and be ready for action at a moment['s] warning."[34]

At 10:00 P.M., Brigadier General Edward D. Tracy's haggard brigade of fifteen hundred Alabamians and the six guns of the Botetourt Virginia Artillery joined Green's force, bringing the total number of Confederates in the region to around twenty-five hundred. After finally coming to grips with the Federal movements against Bowen, Pemberton had started sending his lieutenant some sorely needed reinforcements. Tracy's men were exhausted, having been on the march from their camps around Warrenton, Mississippi, for the last twenty-seven hours, but there was no time for rest. Learning from a scout that Union troops had been spotted on the Bruinsburg Road, information that at the time was incorrect as the Federals were only advancing along the Rodney Road, Green quickly dispatched Tracy's entire brigade to defend against the phantom force. With both roads covered, the Confederates settled in for the night, many of them anxiously awaiting an intense fight come dawn.[35]

Unable to sleep through the night, General Green opted to ride forward to the A. K. Shaifer House at 12:30 A.M. on May 1, 1863, to insure that his lookouts remained alert. When he arrived, he found the women of the house packing a wagon and preparing to seek safety in Port Gibson. The arrival of the Arkansans justly worried them, and despite Green's declarations that the Federals would not arrive before daylight, the women kept up their frantic pace. Twenty minutes later, their panic was validated when gunfire suddenly erupted from the darkness. Some of the Confederate scouts had spotted the sixteen-man Union patrol under Lieutenant Dunlap and decided to take a few shots at the Federals. When Dunlap's men reciprocated with a salvo of their own, lead balls not only struck the Shaifer House but also crashed into the ladies' wagon and its contents. The first shots in the battle of Port Gibson—"one of the hottest little battles of the war"—had been fired. Ordering Lieutenant Tisdale and his force of four to delay the Union advance, Green returned to Magnolia Church to galvanize his main line of defense. The Shaifer women, meanwhile, leapt into their wagon and made a quick escape in the direction of Port Gibson.[36]

Following the exchange at the Shaifer House, Colonel Stone prepared to give battle. Calling the rest of Merrill's 21st Iowa into position, he ordered the men into linear formation across the Rodney Road and pushed forward.

Unable to hold their ground against an entire regiment, the four Arkansans under Tisdale withdrew to Magnolia Church, and moving slowly, Stone eventually concluded "that we had not yet reached the immediate vicinity of the enemy[']s main force." As such, he returned his men to column formation and continued the march toward Port Gibson.[37]

Back at Magnolia Church, Green had his men in position to meet the Federal advance. According to Lieutenant John S. Bell of the 12th Arkansas Sharpshooters, "We could hear the enemy forming, and it was so still we could hear every command given. Our men had orders not to fire until word was given. Soon we could see their line of skirmishers coming down the road and could hear them say there was no one here, it was only a cavalry scout." As Stone's brigade approached the Magnolia Church ridge, "they received a tremendous volley of musketry from the enemy" at a distance of about fifty yards. Shaken by the withering fire, Stone quickly ordered the entire brigade into line of battle, placed his batteries on the ridge to his rear, and prepared to test the Confederate position.[38]

In his after-action report, Stone would describe the night battle that commenced around Magnolia Church to be one of "terrific grandeur." For nearly three hours, Union and Confederate forces put on a deadly fireworks display as infantrymen and artillerymen on both sides took aim at their opponent's muzzle flashes, unable to target much else under the cover of darkness. Soldiers on both sides fell wounded or dead during the exchange. As the lethal contest continued, Stone and Green realized the futility of trying to fight a battle in the dark, where one could not accurately assess the success or failure of any given action. As such, both commanders ultimately called off their attacks and ordered their men to "lay down upon their arms to await the coming dawn."[39]

Before sunrise, more Union troops moved into position in preparation for the day's fighting. While Stone's men fought at Magnolia Church, Brigadier General William Plummer Benton's First Brigade of Carr's Fourteenth Division moved in behind them and set up at the A. K. Shaifer House to await sunrise. When McClernand visited the battlefield just before dawn, he decided that Carr's division should continue its assault against Green's forces at Magnolia Church, but he also learned "from a fugitive negro" of Tracy's Alabamians two miles to the north on the Bruinsburg Road and of their encroachment along the old farm road that connected the Rodney and Bruinsburg Roads. In order to keep those Confederates from using this route to get behind Carr, McClernand sent Brigadier General Peter Osterhaus's Ninth Division north with orders "to attack the enemy[']s right." The main thrust of McClernand's offensive would remain along the Rodney Road, but he hoped to have Osterhaus "make a diversion in favor of my right, preparatory to its attack upon the strong force understood to be in its front."[40]

As the sun climbed into the sky over the battlefield, the contest for Port Gibson continued when Carr's and Osterhaus's divisions moved against their respective targets. Deploying his two brigades on either side of the Rodney Road—Stone to the north and Benton to the south—General Carr ordered his division forward at 6:00 A.M. As the Federals pressed Green's position, the Confederates quickly found themselves overwhelmed. Within an hour, Green sent a messenger to Tracy, who was preparing to face a Union force of his own, and asked him to send reinforcements immediately. According to Tracy's second in command, Colonel Isham W. Garrott of the 20th Alabama Infantry Regiment, the request sounded quite desperate as Green contended "that if the left was not sustained the right would be cut off from all chance of retreat." Moreover, the courier informed Tracy of "Green[']s opinion that he could not sustain his position on the left fifteen minutes unless re-enforced." In response, Tracy "reluctantly" sent the 23rd Alabama and two guns from Captain John W. Johnston's Botetourt Virginia Artillery to assist Green.[41]

As Tracy's reinforcements headed to Green's relief, Osterhaus's division pressed the Alabamians' position along the farm road back toward the Bruinsburg Road. First, at 7:30 A.M., Captain Charles H. Lanphere's 7th Michigan Battery appeared on a ridge fifteen hundred yards to the Rebels' front and began exchanging shots with the remaining guns of the Botetourt Artillery. While this artillery duel continued throughout the day, Osterhaus deployed his infantry brigades along the old farm road and pressed forward. With Brigadier General Theophilus Toulmin Garrard's First Brigade in the lead and Colonel Lionel Allen Sheldon's Second Brigade in close support, the Federals charged into the ravines in a gallant offensive against Tracy's position. As both sides shifted forces around to deal with the difficult terrain, Tracy moved too close to the front to take stock of the situation and was felled by a Union sharpshooter. The bullet passed through his neck, and he was dead before he hit the ground. Edward Tracy became the first general to die in the fight for Vicksburg, leaving Colonel Garrott to command the Alabama brigade.[42]

Even with the death of Tracy, the contest for the Bruinsburg Road lasted the better part of the day as the "insurmountable obstacles of the nature of the ground and its exposure to the fire of the enemy" made it difficult for Osterhaus's men to bring their numerical superiority to bear, thus proving "the impracticability of a successful front attack." While the Federals did make progress, it was slow. Whenever the Federals gained the advantage and got within striking distance of the Confederate positions, the Rebels simply withdrew to the next available ridge and forced the Union soldiers to claw their way through deep ravines, tangled vines, and razor-sharp canebrakes. Frustrated, Osterhaus first slowed his advance before stopping altogether, solidifying his position, and awaiting reinforcements.[43]

While the fight raged on the Bruinsburg Road front, Green continued his fight against the Federals at Magnolia Church on the Rodney Road. After receiving his reinforcements from Tracy earlier that morning, Green had still been unable to hold his position against Stone's and Benton's brigades, especially after McClernand threw the remainder of his Thirteenth Corps, including Brigadier General Andrew Jackson Smith's Tenth Division and Brigadier General Alvin Peterson Hovey's Twelfth Division, into the fight. Desperate to delay the Union advance, General Bowen arrived on the field and personally attempted to rally Green's men. He failed. Overwhelmed by superior numbers and under threat of being enveloped, the Confederates broke into retreat around 10:00 A.M., only to meet more reinforcements from General Pemberton—two brigades under the command of Brigadier General William Edwin Baldwin and Colonel Francis Cockrell.[44]

While Pemberton had ordered other forces to Port Gibson, these would be the last Confederate reinforcements to reach the field in time to participate in the battle. As with Tracy's Alabamians, they would not prove to be enough to stand against the crushing number of Federals or to disrupt the Army of the Tennessee's obstinate pursuit of victory. Regardless of the odds, Confederates understood the importance of Port Gibson and Bayou Pierre, and Baldwin and Cockrell set themselves up to receive the Union onslaught about a mile and a half from Magnolia Church. Meanwhile, Green's battered brigade made its way to reinforce the beleaguered Confederate position on the Bruinsburg Road.[45]

Following the route of Green's position at Magnolia Church, General Grant arrived on the scene accompanied by Governor Richard Yates of Illinois. The two men rode among the soldiers with McClernand and celebrated their recent success. The battle, however, was not won yet. Determined to get to Port Gibson and across Bayou Pierre, Grant did not allow the festivities to continue for very long before suggesting to McClernand that he resume his advance against the Rebel forces. McClernand acquiesced, got his men back in proper formation, and ordered them to press their advantage along the Rodney Road, which suddenly turned north on its approach to Port Gibson.[46]

As the Thirteenth Corps continued along the road in the direction of Port Gibson, it ultimately met more resistance, this time from the fresh Confederate reinforcements under General Baldwin and Colonel Cockrell. While McClernand endeavored to repeat his performance at Magnolia Church by massing his force and overpowering the Confederates in his front, Bowen prepared to make the Federals pay by using the confusing terrain to his advantage. Having set up two of Colonel Cockrell's Missouri regiments in a series of ravines created by two branches of Centers Creek, which ran perpendicular to the Rodney Road, Bowen attempted to crush the Federal's right flank "and nearly succeeded." As McClernand's men marched down the Rodney Road, Cockrell's brigade unleashed a daring charge against the Union right. Unfortunately for the Confederates, the bluecoats were simply too many, and Cockrell only managed to break through one of McClernand's brigades before the Union force regrouped and drove Cockrell's men back.[47]

Even though he managed to regain the advantage, McClernand was surprised by Cockrell's offensive, which had threatened to roll up the entire Union line. Hesitant about what to do next, McClernand vacillated, allowed Cockrell's troops to retreat, and gave Bowen time to rally another attack. Sensing that McClernand's men might be spent, Bowen ordered Baldwin's fresh brigade to try the enemy's strength. At 4:00 P.M., Baldwin's forces moved forward to cover Cockrell's withdrawal and to check the Union advance along the Rodney Road. Finding the ground "too much intersected by hollows, woods, and deep ravines to admit of simultaneous action," Baldwin's brigade was split apart, and according to their commander's battle report, "companies were compelled to act independently." Such a situation made it easy for the Federals to repulse Baldwin's attack as the "sweeping fire of grape and shrapnel" and a "heavy fire of musketry" cut down Confederate soldiers. Unable to get his regiments to carry out a coordinated attack against McClernand's force, Baldwin reported his predicament to General Bowen. Bowen consequently ordered Baldwin "to relinquish the attempt." Union skirmishers did advance against Baldwin's retreating forces, but according to the Confederate commander, "Our batteries checked their advance." Unfortunately, in their desperate attempts to stop the Federals from overwhelming their position and taking prisoners, the Rebel artillerists killed and wounded several of their own men.[48]

While Confederate forces fell back along the Rodney Road, Osterhaus revived his offensive on the Union left along the Bruinsburg Road. At 2:00 P.M., portions of General McPherson's Seventeenth Corps had finally reached the battlefield and were in the vicinity of the Shaifer House. Watching the situation on both fronts, Grant decided to split Major General John Alexander Logan's Third Division between the Rodney and Bruinsburg Roads and sent Brigadier General John Eugene Smith's brigade to reinforce Osterhaus. With fresh troops to assist him, Osterhaus pushed forward at 3:00 P.M. with Smith's force on his left. While Smith assaulted the Confederate right flank, Osterhaus led his men in a series of attacks against the combined forces of Garrott and Green. Unable to stand up to the relentless offensive and despite receiving orders from Bowen to hold their position "until near sunset," the Rebels retired and began their retreat toward Bayou Pierre around 5:30 P.M.[49]

His men had fought well against an immense force of Federals, but Bowen sensed the end was at hand. At 6:00 P.M., he ordered a general retreat of all four Confederate brigades operating in the area across Bayou Pierre, thus abandoning Port Gibson to Grant's army. The battle was over. Union losses totaled 131 killed, 719 wounded, and 25 missing, whereas the Confederate defenders reported suffering 68 killed, 380 wounded, and 384 missing. Unfortunately, the Confederate records are incomplete, for there are no existing reports for the losses suffered by Tracy's or Baldwin's brigades, and the material covering Green's and Cockrell's brigades is incomplete. Though defeated, the Confederates had managed to delay the Union's premier fighting force—the Army of the Tennessee—for an entire day despite being outnumbered nearly four to one. The terrain certainly helped the Confederate defenders more often than it hurt them, though on occasion it did work to the Federals' advantage. More important than the terrain, however, was the quick thinking of the Confederate field commander. In the words of Grant, General Bowen's defense of Port Gibson was "a very bold one and well carried out." Despite Bowen's valiant attempt at resisting the Union blitz, Grant reminded the Union high command, the Army of the Tennessee "was too heavy for [Bowen], and composed of well-disciplined and hardy men, who know no defeat, and are not willing to learn what it is."[50]

Grant had his victory, and he was firmly established in Mississippi. The momentum in the campaign had finally and fully shifted in his favor. The battle of Port Gibson was not only the turning point of the contest for Vicksburg but also Grant's first victory as an army commander since the battle of Shiloh in April 1862. In achieving this victory, Grant had overcome great adversity and demonstrated his capacity as a relentless fighter, traits that would come to define him and his army for the remainder of the war. Moreover, now that he controlled the road junction at Port Gibson and the bridges across Bayou Pierre, he would have his choice of targets, the most likely being Grand Gulf, Vicksburg, or Jackson—or perhaps all three. As would come to be expected of the general, Grant did not rest on his laurels long. His greatest battlefield victories and the salvation of the Union still lay before him. The march down the Mississippi culminating in victory at Port Gibson had been a rebirth for Grant, and the general felt compelled to keep moving on.

Notes

1. T. B. Cox, "'Gen. Pettus Escapes Johnson's Island," *Confederate Veteran* 13, no. 1 (January 1905): 18.

2. U. S. War Department, *The War of the Rebellion: A Compilation of the Official Records of the Union and Confederate Armies*, 128 vol. (Washington, D.C.: Government Printing Office, 1880–1901), vol. 24, pt. 3: 151–52. (Hereinafter cited as *OR*; all references are to Series 1 unless otherwise noted.)

3. Ulysses S. Grant, *Personal Memoirs of U. S. Grant and Selected Letters, 1839-1865* (New York: Library Classics of the United States, 1990), Vol. 1, 106.

4. *OR*, vol. 24, pt. 3: 152. For more information regarding the earlier runs past the Vicksburg batteries, see Grant, 308.

5. For more on the difficulties inherent in the march down the west bank of the Mississippi River, see Steven E. Woodworth, *Nothing but Victory: The Army of the Tennessee, 1861–1865* (New York: Alfred A. Knopf, 2005), 315–16; Moltke actually wrote, "No plan of operations extends with certainty beyond the first encounter with the enemy's main strength," but it is often paraphrased as I have done. See Daniel J. Hughes, ed., *Moltke on the Art of War: Selected Writing* (New York: Presidio Press, 1995), 45–47.

6. *OR*, vol. 27, pt. 1: 31.

7. *OR*, vol. 17, pt. 1: 716–17.

8. See William L. Shea and Terrence J. Winschel, *Vicksburg Is the Key: The Struggle for the Mississippi River* (Lincoln: University of Nebraska Press, 2003), 93–94; Steven E. Woodworth, *Jefferson Davis and His Generals: The Failure of Confederate Command in the West* (Lawrence: University Press of Kansas, 1990), 124.

9. For coverage of the distractions Grant employed against Pemberton, see Shea and Winschel, 94; Terrence J. Winschel, *Vicksburg: Fall of the Confederate Gibraltar* (Abilene, Tex.: McWhiney Foundation, 1999), 49–51; Woodworth, *Jefferson Davis and His Generals*, 202–3; *OR*, vol. 24, pt. 3: 730; Michael B. Ballard, *Pemberton: The General Who Lost Vicksburg* (Jackson: University Press of Mississippi, 1991; reprint, 1999), 134.

10. *OR*, vol. 24, pt. 3: 733. See also ibid., 735; Woodworth, *Jefferson Davis and His Generals*, 202; and Shea and Winschel, 94–95.

11. *OR*, vol. 24, pt. 1:139; Grant, 307–8, 314.

12. *OR*, vol. 24, pt. 1:139–40, 489–90, 492; Grant, 309.

13. *OR*, vol. 24, pt. 1:139–40, 489–90, 492; Grant, 309. See also Woodworth, *Nothing but Victory*, 318–20, 325–26; and Brooks D. Simpson, *Ulysses S. Grant: Triumph over Adversity, 1822–1865* (Boston and New York: Houghton Mifflin, 2000).

14. U.S. War Department, *Official Records of the Union and Confederate Navies in the War of the Rebellion*, 31 vols. (Washington, D.C.: Government Printing Office, 1922), vol. 24:627. (Hereinafter cited as *ORN*.)

15. *OR*, vol. 24, pt. 3:713–14, 720, 724, 729, 730–32, 735, 754–55, 761, 770, 773–74, 792.

16. Ibid., 730. See also Ballard, *Pemberton*, 134, 140, 146, Shea and Winschel, 93–95; Phillip T. Tucker, *The Forgotten "Stonewall of the West": Major General John Stevens Bowen* (Macon, Ga.: Mercer University Press, 1997), 177.

17. *OR*, vol. 24, pt. 3: 653, 658; Tucker, 177.

18. *OR*, vol. 24, pt. 1:32; Grant, 317.

19. *OR*, vol. 24, pt. 1:48; *ORN*, vol. 24:610–11; Grant, 317.

20. *ORN*, vol. 24:611; *OR*, vol. 24, pt. 1:575–76, Pt. 3:801–2; Woodworth, *Nothing but Victory*, 335.

21. *OR*, vol. 24, pt. 1:32, 48.

22. *ORN*, vol. 24:610–11.

23. Grant, 321–22.

24. Woodworth, *Nothing but Victory*, 336; Grant, 318; Warren E. Grabau, *Ninety-Eight Days: A Geographer's View of the Vicksburg Campaign* (Knoxville: University of Tennessee Press, 2000), 144–45.

25. Edwin C. Bearss, *The Campaign for Vicksburg*, vol. 2, *Grant Strikes a Fatal Blow* (Dayton, Ohio: Morningside Press, 1986), 318, 346; Terrence J. Winschel, *Triumph and Defeat: The Vicksburg Campaign* (Mason City, Iowa: Savas, 1999), 57; Woodworth, *Nothing but Victory*, 337; Shea and Winschel, 106; Grabau, 146; Richard H. Martin, "Champion's Hill: Comrade Martin, 46th Ind., Replies to Criticisms," *National Tribune*, October 3, 1901, p. 3.

26. Michael A. Sweetman, "From Milliken's Bend to Vicksburg," *National Tribune*, August 22, 1895, p. 1; Frank Swigart, "The First Troops to Land at Bruinsburg," *National Tribune*, October 16, 1884, p. 3; Woodworth, *Nothing but Victory*, 337–38; Grabau, 146; Bearss, 318.

27. Grant, 321.

28. *OR*, vol. 24, pt. 1:143; Woodworth, *Nothing but Victory*, 338; Grabau, 146–47; Bearss, 318; Ballard, 226.

29. *OR*, vol. 24, pt. 1:143; Winschel, 58.

30. *OR*, vol. 24, pt. 1:143, 628, 631; Bearss, 320; Woodworth, *Nothing but Victory*, 339.

31. Grant, 321–23; Bearss, 319–20; Charles A. Hobbs quoted in Bearss, 345.

32. *OR*, vol. 24, pt. 1:628; Bearss, 343–45; Woodworth, *Nothing but Victory*, 339.

33. William Charleton, "Port Gibson: Who Commenced the Fight?," *National Tribune*, December 4, 1884, p. 3; *OR*, vol. 24, pt. 1:628.

34. *OR*, vol. 24, pt. 1:663, 672; Bearss, 347; Ballard, 224–25; Winschel, 62.

35. *OR*, vol. 24, pt. 1:672; Bearss, 349, 359; Winschel, 63.

36. Bearss, 353; Charleton, 3; Cox, 18.

37. *OR*, vol. 24, pt. 1:628.

38. John S. Bell quoted in Bearss, 355; *OR*, vol. 24, pt. 1:628–29, 672.

39. *OR*, vol. 24, pt. 1:629, 672–73.

40. Woodworth, *Nothing but Victory*, 341; *OR*, vol. 24, pt. 1:143. As Michael Ballard points out, "The connecting road proved to be a key tactical feature of the battlefield. The Confederates had to fight on two fronts as they had figured, but they still had to return to the road junction [near Port Gibson] to reinforce either front, while Grant's generals used the closer connecting road to reinforce each wing as needed" (229).

41. *OR*, vol. 24, pt. 1:626, 678.

42. Ibid., 143–44, 590–92; Ballard, 231; Winschel, 68–69; Shea and Winschel, 115; Bearss, 364.

43. *OR*, vol. 24, pt. 1:143–44, 585–86, 588, 590–92, 625, 658–59, 679; Woodworth, *Nothing but Victory*, 342, 345; Bearss, 365–66.

44. *OR*, vol. 24, pt. 1:144, 615–16, 620–21, 625–26, 664, 672–73; Winschel, 69–71.

45. *OR*, vol. 24, pt. 1:673; Ballard, 235–36.

46. Bearss, 385–86; *OR*, vol. 24, pt. 1:144–45.

47. *OR*, vol. 24, pt. 1:603–4, 607, 611, 613, 662, 664, 668–69; Woodworth, *Nothing but Victory*, 343–45; Bearss, 388–93; Ballard, 238–39.

48. Bearss, 393–99; Woodworth, *Nothing but Victory*, 345; *OR*, vol. 24, pt. 1:666, 676.

49. *OR*, vol. 24, pt. 1:49, 587–88, 643, 668, 670, 673, 680–81; Bearss, 366–72.

50. *OR*, vol. 24, pt. 1:33; Bearss, 405, 407; Winschel, 86.

4

ROADS TO RAYMOND

J. Parker Hills

T he first rays of sunlight filtered through the shroud-like haze that remained over the battlefield, and soon the cluttered ground appeared to
come to life as soldiers stirred from their leafy beds. Hundreds of campfires
seemed to magically spring out of the earth, and within minutes the acrid
smell of burnt gunpowder was overpowered by the pungent aroma of boiled
coffee. Sergeant James O'Bleness of the 23rd Iowa rubbed the sleep from his
eyes, sipped his scalding black brew, and then carefully settled the hot tin
cup on the damp ground beside him. While his coffee cooled, the Irishman
burrowed into his knapsack to retrieve his weathered diary. Pencil in hand,
he tersely scribbled an entry for May 2, 1863. "Commenced the fight at Port
Gibson; came out victorious; lay on the field over night." O'Bleness had no
way of knowing it, but his words resembled the no-nonsense philosophy of
his army commander, Major General Ulysses S. Grant. In Tennessee in 1862,
the taciturn Grant had said, "The art of war is simple enough; find out where
your enemy is, get at him as soon as you can, and strike him as hard as you
can, and keep moving on." In Mississippi in 1863, Grant practiced what he
preached. He moved fast, struck hard, and finished rapidly.[1]

Grant had been unable to move or strike while in Louisiana, so his first
objective of the Vicksburg Campaign was to "secure a footing upon dry
ground on the east side of the river from which the troops could operate
against Vicksburg." To achieve this footing, he deceived his opponent by
using multiple, carefully planned diversions to draw attention away from the
coup de main, or the main effort. The Confederate commander, Lieutenant
General John C. Pemberton, was repeatedly harassed by raids, demonstrations, and feints, and the result was an unopposed Federal crossing of the
Mississippi River on April 30, 1863. The next day, Grant defeated a makeshift
force of Confederates at the battle of Port Gibson when he shoved 58 cannon
and 11 brigades, or 25,270 soldiers, into battle against Brigadier General John

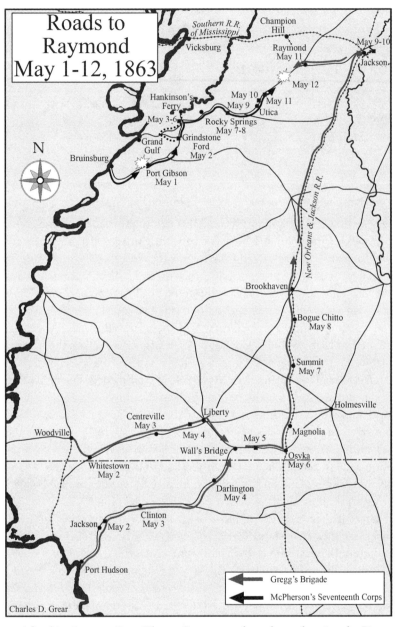

Roads to
Raymond
May 1-12, 1863

Southern R.R. of Mississippi

Champion
Hill

May 9-10

Vicksburg

Raymond
May 11

Jackson

May 12

Hankinson's
Ferry

May 10

May 9

May 11
Utica

May 3-6

Rocky Springs
May 7-8

N

Grand
Gulf

Grindstone
Ford
May 2

Bruinsburg

Port Gibson
May 1

New Orleans & Jackson R.R.

Brookhaven

Bogue Chitto
May 8

Summit
May 7

Holmesville

Centreville
May 3

Liberty

Woodville

May 4

May 5

Magnolia

Wall's Bridge

Osyka
May 6

Whitestown
May 2

Darlington
May 4

Jackson May 2

Clinton
May 3

Port Hudson

Gregg's Brigade

McPherson's Seventeenth Corps

Charles D. Grear

After his victory at Port Gibson, Grant moved northeast, keeping the Big
Black River on his left. Meanwhile, Confederate brigadier general John
Gregg marched his brigade up from positions near Port Hudson, Louisiana,
to help defend the Mississippi capital. On May 12 Gregg thought he saw an
opportunity and struck at a Union column near the town of Raymond.

Bowen's 16 guns and 4 brigades, or 5,164 men per Bowen's report. Union casualties were reported as 875, about a 3 percent casualty rate. Bowen's casualty reports totaled 832, for a 16 percent casualty rate and a loss ratio of five times that of the Federals. This disparity was the result of Grant's having not necessarily the most men, but the most men where it counted, precisely what Confederate general Nathan Bedford Forrest meant when he declared, "I would give more for fifteen minutes of bulge on the enemy than for a week of tactics." Grant had bulge at Port Gibson.²

Sergeant O'Bleness had barely finished his journal entry before the victorious Federals formed ranks and marched through Port Gibson. In his memoirs, Grant succinctly stated his next objective: "My first problem was to capture Grand Gulf to use as a base." But the Confederates had destroyed the two bridges where the centuries-old Natchez Trace crossed two rivers, Little and Big Bayou Pierre. As a result, Union pioneers were required to toil for twenty-two hours on these bridges, but at 5:30 A.M. on Sunday morning Grant moved rapidly and pushed his troops over the second water barrier, Big Bayou Pierre, using the charred but recently repaired bridge at Grindstone Ford. The column was channelized by the twelve-foot-wide span, and several hours were required for the lead division, Major General John A. Logan's division of Major General James B. McPherson's Seventeenth Corps, to cross to the open fields north of the river. Brigadier General Marcellus Crocker's division immediately followed, and by noon on May 3, the 12,500-man, six-brigade column was at Willow Springs, two miles north of Grindstone Ford and five miles northeast of Port Gibson. Here, at noon, Logan's vanguard brushed aside two Rebel regiments at the hamlet crossroads.³

Grant's capture of the Willow Springs crossroads meant that the Grand Gulf Confederate garrison, if still at Grand Gulf, was caught in a cul-de-sac formed by the Mississippi, Big Bayou Pierre, and Big Black Rivers. Grant realized this and peeled Logan's division west toward Grand Gulf to snag the prey. He then hurried Crocker's division north from Willow Springs toward Hankinson's Ferry on the Big Black to seal the only way out. Preceding Logan's infantry column on the road to Grand Gulf was a company of Ohio cavalry, and at a sharp curve four and one-half miles west of Willow Springs the troopers ran headlong into a Confederate brigade. A savvy General Bowen had positioned Missouri infantry and artillery at the bend to protect the intersection of the Grand Gulf–Willow Springs road and the Grand Gulf–Hankinson's Ferry road while he evacuated his garrison from Grand Gulf. The Northern horsemen, after rounding the curve and being treated to a peppering of Southern canister and bullets, quickly fell back toward Willow Springs. Around 2 P.M., Logan's infantry column arrived to brush aside the pesky Rebels, but all that his men found were a few stragglers from a retreating column and an intersection littered with the jetsam of war. But this intersection was key, because from this obscure junction Grand Gulf was only seven miles to the west, and Hankinson's Ferry was only nine miles to the northeast. From Hankinson's it was only sixteen miles to Vicksburg.[4]

Reports rippled down the column, and soon Grant rode to the front and glanced downward at the thousands of footprints in the dust. The fresh signs of travel toward the ferry told his experienced eyes that Grand Gulf had been evacuated only hours before. Orders were snapped to Logan to pursue the fleeing Rebels, and Colonel Manning F. Force of the 20th Ohio recalled that the troops "made a sharp turn and pushed for the ferry." Grant, however, continued straight ahead to Grand Gulf with a score of cavalrymen for protection. Governor Richard Yates of Illinois rode with Grant and recalled, "I saw guns scattered along the road, which the enemy had left in their retreat . . . I consider Vicksburg as ours in only a short time, and the Mississippi River as destined to be open from its source to its mouth." His words were prophetic. Grand Gulf was the back door to Vicksburg, and its abandonment had left that door open.[5]

Grant's entourage wound its way along the narrow road for almost seven miles, then descended the steep watershed to the Mississippi River, and arrived at Grand Gulf just before dark. There, three hundred yards to the front, they could barely discern the phantomlike forms of four of Rear Admiral David D. Porter's menacing black ironclad gunboats, *Louisville, Carondelet, Mound City,* and *Tuscumbia,* lined up along the muddy riverbank like gargantuan snapping turtles. Now that Grant was in Grand Gulf, per his agreement with General in Chief Henry W. Halleck he was to send troops south to Port Hudson "to cooperate with [Major] General [Nathaniel P.] Banks in the reduction of that place." But Grant wanted no part of such a plan and had said that, "Once at Grand Gulf I do not feel a doubt of success in the entire driving out of the enemy from the banks of the river." Grant also knew that Banks was a slow-moving political general, and he was painfully aware that the former Massachusetts governor had seniority over him. But a solution to this conundrum was produced when Grant boarded the flagship *Louisville.* It was a message from Banks, dated April 10, that said Banks's forces "could not be at Port Hudson before the 10th of May, and then with only 15,000 men." Grant seized the opportunity. "The news from Banks forced upon me a different plan of campaign from the one intended," he rationalized. "There was nothing left to be done but to go forward to a decisive victory," he later wrote. That night he fired off a message to Washington saying, "I shall not bring my troops into this place, but immediately follow the enemy . . . until

Vicksburg is in our possession." But in the bigger picture, Grant understood that a large segment of the North had grown war-weary, and that Peace Democrats, or "Copperheads," clamored for a negotiated end to the war. Years later he said, "I felt that the Union depended upon the administration, and the administration upon victory. . . . Unless we did something there was no knowing what, in its despair, the country might not do." So he made his momentous decision to move fast, strike hard, and finish rapidly.[6]

Grant later said that his message to Washington would take "some time to reach Cairo by boat, and some time for response—eight days I think." He also knew that the cautious Halleck would never agree to the bold new plan. "I remember how anxiously I counted the time I had to spare before that response could come," Grant recalled in an 1878 interview. Then he quipped, "You can do a great deal in eight days."[7]

After deciding to take Vicksburg on his own, Grant carefully made plans to establish his new supply base at Grand Gulf. While back in Louisiana on April 30, Grant had assigned one of his aides, Colonel William S. Hillyer, to be his new logistics czar with the responsibility of "superintending the transportation and supplies to the army below Grand Gulf." Now that Grant was in possession of Grand Gulf, he placed Hillyer in command of the base. Grant then sent orders to Brigadier General Jeremiah Sullivan, in command of the troops protecting the army line of communications in Louisiana, and assigned him the task of building a road from Young's Point to a point on the Mississippi River nine miles below Vicksburg. Such a road would shorten the vulnerable land transportation road from forty to ten miles. Grant then wrote to his Fifteenth Corps commander, Major General William T. Sherman, who was protecting the army's vital supply base at Milliken's Bend, near Vicksburg. Sherman was to have Major General Frank Blair's division escort 120 loaded supply wagons southward to Grand Gulf. Grant punctuated his order to Sherman by reminding him "of the overwhelming importance of celerity." He also pronounced to a skeptical Sherman that the enemy was "badly beaten, greatly demoralized, and exhausted of ammunition." Remembering the footprint-covered intersection seven miles back, Grant concluded with, "The road to Vicksburg is open. All we want now are men, ammunition, and hard bread." Since Blair's departure would practically denude Milliken's Bend of troops, Grant wrote to Major General Stephen A. Hurlbut, commander of the Sixteenth Corps in Memphis, and ordered him to send four regiments by steamboats to replace Blair's men. Finally, Grant wrote to his wife to assure her that both he and their twelve-year-old son, Fred, were fine, and to say that he felt proud of his army. All seemed to be in order, except that, despite Grant's encouragement, Sherman remained pessimistic. Sherman had written to his wife on April 29, prophesying that, "when they take Grand Gulf they have the elephant by the tail . . . my own opinion is that this whole plan of attack on Vicksburg will fail, must fail." But even with Sherman's dire predictions, in a few days Colonel Hillyer had the old town square of Grand Gulf piled high with crates containing nearly two million rations. Grant, the former logistician, was not about to "disregard his base" as was reported to Washington the next morning by tag-along Assistant Secretary of War Charles A. Dana.[8]

While Grant confidently planned at Grand Gulf, McPherson celebrated an accomplishment at Hankinson's Ferry—one that presaged the 1945 capture of the Ludendorff Bridge on the Rhine River at Remagen. That afternoon Logan's division, with Crocker's close behind, pursued the retreating Confederates to the raft bridge over the Big Black River and seized the structure before Confederate pioneers could destroy it. In the process, the 20th Ohio captured fourteen axes and a number of other implements, including Bowen's pistol belt and a brace of fine LeMat revolvers, which the Southern general had unbuckled as he both supervised and assisted his pioneers. But the bridge was the key, and the door to Vicksburg was indeed open.[9]

Late that night at Grand Gulf, Grant having attended to every conceivable detail aboard the *Louisville*, mounted up at midnight for the fourteen-mile ride to join McPherson's two divisions near the ferry. Grant's late night ride to Hankinson's must have bewildered his staff officers, for in addition to the late hour, the entourage followed a route that Colonel James H. Wilson described as a "strange and circuitous road." Just before dawn, Grant's party reached the periphery of the Seventeenth Corps camps, almost two miles south of the ferry. Wilson recalled that, "as all the houses in the neighborhood were occupied by those who got there before us, we unsaddled, spread our blankets, and threw ourselves down on the porch of a plantation house for rest. Grant was with us, tired and sleepy, but contented." Thus, the modest home of Mrs. Samuel Pipes Bagnell, perched on a ridge one mile north of Hardscrabble Crossroads, became Grant's headquarters from May 4 to May 7.[10]

Meanwhile, General Pemberton, upon learning of Grant's successful river crossing, had belatedly transferred his Jackson headquarters forty miles westward to Vicksburg on May 1. Vicksburg became his new hub of operations, and telegraphic messages flew in every direction in an attempt to concentrate Confederate units that had been scattered due to Grant's hydra-like diversions. Troops were ordered inward from as far north as Grenada, as far east as Meridian, and as far south as Port Hudson.[11]

The Port Hudson commander, Major General Franklin Gardner, was ordered to "send [Brigadier] General [John] Gregg's brigade [by rail] at once to Jackson." But first, the combat-hardened Gregg's thirty-three hundred men were to march to Osyka, Mississippi, a community located fifty miles east of Port Hudson just above the Mississippi-Louisiana state line on the New Orleans, Jackson & Great Northern Railroad.[12] Gregg's brigade at Port Hudson had been split in response to one of Grant's diversions, Colonel Benjamin H. Grierson's cavalry raid. In a failed attempt to intercept the raiders, the 7th Texas and a three-gun section of Captain Hiram Bledsoe's Missouri Battery had been sent thirty miles north to Woodville, Mississippi, while Gregg's four Tennessee regiments remained in garrison to help defend Port Hudson. Despite the scattered condition of Gregg's brigade, and the command headaches that this produced for the officers, the march order was not an unwelcome one for the rank and file. Private W. J. Davidson of the 41st Tennessee, after enduring four months of half-rations while on garrison duty at Port Hudson, wrote that the Tennesseans, "found vent in long and oft-repeated cheers" as they prepared to leave. These men had no way of knowing that the difficult path ahead of them led to Raymond, where life on earth ceased for as many as 200 of their ranks.[13]

Gregg's Tennesseans began their trek to Osyka from Port Hudson at 10 A.M. on Saturday, May 2. The weather was hot and the heavily used roads were covered with a powder of thick dust. After a few miles, the spirit of the Tennesseans morphed from elation to despair as they discovered that their poor diet during the winter had destroyed their endurance. Just as importantly, their inactive feet had softened, and many of the men foolishly threw away their shoes rather than suffer the chafing of rough leather against weeping blisters and raw dermis. Captain S. R. Simpson of the 30th Tennessee succinctly wrote in his diary, "the boys had a hard time of it." Private Davidson bitterly recalled that "we were refused water by a wealthy Louisiana woman, whose servants offered to sell it to us at twenty-five cents a canteen full; how loth we were, at that time, to drink of the dirty pools by the way-side, but had to." Thankfully, the march was only seven miles to the grounds of Mrs. Isobel K. Fluker's Asphodel Plantation, four miles south of Jackson, Louisiana. Near the Southern French Louisiana home of the widow and her twelve children, the bushed soldiers took refuge beside the refreshing waters of Karr Creek.[14]

The Texans and Missourians departed Woodville, travelled along a parallel route to the north, and had better luck on their march through Mississippi. Major K. M. Van Zandt of the 7th Texas wrote to his wife, saying, "We had a very pleasant trip before getting with our brigade. We went through a portion of the country where soldiers had never been and consequently met with much kindness at the hands of the citizens."[15]

While Gregg's two columns marched on Saturday, Pemberton received a telegram from General Joseph E. Johnston, commander of the Department of the West in Tullahoma, Tennessee, stating; "If Grant crosses, unite all your troops to beat him." Johnston had sent Pemberton virtually the same message a day earlier, but in both cases this advice was too late to be of use. Grant had already crossed the Mississippi and was moving inland while Pemberton's command was far-flung. Pemberton justifiably viewed these tardy messages as mere hindsight suggestions, and later wrote that they did not carry the "weight and force of military orders." Still, he did his best to obey Johnston, and telegraphed President Jefferson Davis in Richmond, saying, "I shall concentrate all the troops I can, but distances are great. Unless very large re-enforcements are sent here, I think Port Hudson and Grand Gulf should be evacuated, and the whole force concentrated for defense of Vicksburg and Jackson." But as far as Jackson was concerned, Pemberton was negative on his prospects for saving Mississippi's capital city, and he sent messages "to remove the state archives from Jackson." The Jackson arsenal was ordered to send the machinery to Alabama, and all ordnance and ammunition were to be sent to Vicksburg.[16]

On Sunday Gregg's Tennessee Confederates departed the grounds of Asphodel Plantation. The foot-sore column snaked its way eastward for fifteen miles, and Captain Simpson wrote that "the boys are getting along tolerably well. Some of their feet are blistered very badly." The underfed soldiers crossed the Comite River and encamped on the western edge of Clinton, Louisiana. The progress of the column to the north is unclear, but they probably marched to just east of Centreville, Mississippi.[17]

From Vicksburg, Pemberton telegraphed President Davis that Sunday, saying, "I shall concentrate all my troops this side of the Big Black. The question of subsistence and proximity to the base, and necessity of supporting Vicksburg, have determined this." In a twist of irony in Vicksburg, Pemberton decided to assume a defensive posture and surrender the initiative. This was on the same day that Grant in Grand Gulf decided to continue the offensive by moving fast and striking hard. Four decades later, British Lieutenant Colonel G. F. R. Henderson wrote, "War is between the brains and grit of the two commanders. It is thus pre-eminently the art of the man who dare take the risk." Grant simply said, "War has responsibilities that are either fatal to a commander's position or very successful."[18]

On Monday, May 4, Grant ordered his divisions in Mississippi to pause so that he could concentrate his forces, gather intelligence, and await the arrival of Sherman's divisions and the army's supply train from Louisiana. At the same time, Pemberton attempted to anticipate Grant's next move by shifting his troops to a line along the Big Black River from Hankinson's Ferry northeast to the railroad bridge. It was a game of chess with living pieces.[19]

That Monday Gregg's Tennessee column marched through Clinton, Louisiana, and tramped for fifteen more miles to the northeast. After crossing the Amite River, the soldiers were allowed to collapse into camp on Turkey Creek, twelve and one-half miles northwest of Greensburg. "The road from Clinton to camp was well lined with stragglers," wrote Captain Flavel C. Barber of the 3rd Tennessee. Private W. J. Davidson of the 41st Tennessee wrote that "our rations gave out, and the heat and the dust became almost insufferable." Presuming that the Texans and Missourians kept the same pace in the heat, their camp would have been twelve miles north of the Tennesseans on the West Fork of the Amite River near Liberty, Mississippi.[20]

In Vicksburg that Monday, Pemberton continued to work on concentrating his troops. He sent another desperate telegram to General Gardner in Port Hudson, saying, "You must come and bring with you 5,000 infantry." Even though Gregg's brigade was already en route to Jackson, Gardner was specifically ordered to augment and bring Brigadier General Samuel B. Maxey's brigade of Tennesseans and Louisianans, as well as enough cavalry to protect the flanks on the march.[21]

On Tuesday the soldiers of both sides were surprised by a sudden change in the weather. "All of a sudden it is very cold here," noted Secretary Dana. "Two days ago it was hot like summer, but now I sit in my tent in my overcoat." Taking advantage of the cool weather, Grant ordered Major General John A. McClernand, commander of this Thirteenth Corps, to send a strong reconnaissance force to the northeast, in the direction of Jackson. The mission was given to Brigadier General Peter J. Osterhaus, who took with him an infantry division and three companies of the 2nd Illinois Cavalry. McClernand reported that Osterhaus led the advance to Big Sand Creek and "threw a detachment of infantry, preceded by the 2nd Illinois Cavalry" across the creek toward Hall's Ferry on the Big Black River. "Finding a detachment of the enemy in front of the ferry," McClernand wrote, "a company of cavalry under Lieutenant [Isaiah] Stickel dashed forward and dispersed it before it had time to form, killing twelve men and capturing thirty prisoners."[22]

Grant also ordered McPherson to send a reconnaissance force commanded by Colonel George B. Boomer, which included the 5th and 10th Iowa Infantry, three companies of the 6th Missouri Cavalry, and a section of the 6th Wisconsin Battery, across the Big Black River toward Vicksburg. Grant wrote that this force was sent "with the view of leading the enemy to believe that we intended to cross the Big Black and attack the city at once." Lieutenant Colonel Ezekiel S. Sampson of the 5th Iowa reported that the mission "was entirely successful and satisfactory, without a single casualty." To support the ruse, Grant ordered demonstrations at Hankinson's Ferry to give the appearance of a river crossing operation. Lieutenant Henry O. Dwight of the 20th Ohio wrote that "all the skiffs in the country were got together and roads were cut to the water at various places." Boomer's patrol, coupled with the ruses, convinced Pemberton that Grant's *coup de main* would be directly north toward Vicksburg from Hankinson's Ferry. At the same time Osterhaus's patrol to the northeast led Pemberton to conclude that the main thrust would be shielded by an attack on the Big Black River Bridge.[23]

While the Federal reconnaissance forces probed, Grant continued his offensive scheming. He sent a request to Commander Elias K. Owen aboard the *Louisville* at Grand Gulf for two ironclads to protect Grand Gulf and two ironclads to go upriver to protect the terminus of the road he had ordered General Sullivan to construct. Grant wrote to Hillyer at Grand Gulf and ordered him to ensure all wagons were loaded "with great promptness," and to have Sherman detail an officer to supervise these affairs on the Louisiana shore. Hillyer was authorized to "issue any order" in Grant's name "that may be necessary to secure the greatest promptness" in getting the supplies across the river. He was also given the authority to, "if necessary for promptness relieve the present commissary [officer] and call on Sherman for an officer to take his place." Hillyer was emphatically informed that "every day's delay is worth two thousand men to the enemy." Finally, Grant sent orders to Hurlbut in Memphis and instructed him to send a reinforcing division to Milliken's Bend "with as little delay as possible." Considering Grant's feints to confuse the enemy and his plans to supply and reinforce his army on that Tuesday, there is truth in the Bagnell family tradition that Grant planned the next stage of his campaign while smoking a cigar over a small table in their home.[24]

On that cool Tuesday Gregg's Tennesseans continued their march northeast, hiking along the watershed ridge between the Amite and Tickfaw Rivers. They traveled the main road northeast from Clinton to Osyka and eventually turned east to cross the Tickfaw River on the rickety Wall's bridge, where only four days before the 7th Illinois Cavalry of Grierson's troopers had successfully fought with a battalion of Louisiana and Tennessee cavalrymen for possession of the crossing. After Gregg's dusty Tennesseans crossed the Tickfaw, they continued eastward and encamped in the shade of a pine grove, seven miles west of Osyka at Crawford Branch of Line Creek. The march for the day had been a seventeen-mile trudge. Captain Simpson wrote that "the night was very cool." The Texans and Missourians would not have been far behind and would have passed through Liberty and then turned southeast to Wall's bridge.[25]

By Wednesday, May 6, Grant had selected his next objective. He wrote to Halleck in Washington that he "would move as soon as three days rations are received, and send wagons back to the Gulf for more to follow." He then added an intriguing statement: "Information received from the other side leads me to believe the enemy are bringing forces from Tullahoma." Add to this Grant's statement on Tuesday to Hillyer that "every day's delay is worth two thousand men to the enemy," and it is clear that Grant knew that Rebel reinforcements were en route via rail. In his memoirs Grant recalled his next move: "The broken nature of the ground would have enabled him [Pemberton] to hold a strong defensible line from the river south of the city to the Big Black, retaining possession of the railroad back to that point. It was my plan, therefore, to get to the railroad east of Vicksburg, and approach from that direction." Grant decided to return the "gift" that Pemberton, in concert with General Braxton Bragg, had sent him the previous Christmas, when General Earl Van Dorn's cavalry incinerated Grant's railroad and forward supply depot at Holly Springs, Mississippi, while Forrest destroyed fifty miles of railroad in West Tennessee. Almost six months later Grant decided it was time for payback, and it is no secret that paybacks are hell.[26]

Grant's move to the railroad called for McClernand's Thirteenth Corps to travel the road that led from Willow Springs all the way to Raymond, though he was to halt just west of Auburn, a community located about ten miles south of Edwards Station. Sherman's Fifteenth Corps was to follow the Thirteenth, and when the Thirteenth halted, Sherman was to pass through its lines. McPherson's Seventeenth Corps was to follow different roads eastward to Utica and from there turn north. These maneuvers would place McClernand, who aggressively supported the offensive nature of this campaign, on the army's left and closest to the enemy. Sherman, who from the outset had expressed his doubts on the wisdom of the plan, was to be in the army's center with Grant. McPherson, Grant's most inexperienced corps commander, was to be on the right of the army and far from the main enemy force. Then, once the army was in place along a six-mile wide, east-west front, it was to move north to the railroad and strike the line of iron rails at three points. The targets on the railroad were to be: Edwards Station, sixteen miles east of Vicksburg; Midway Station at the Champion plantation, nineteen miles east of Vicksburg; and Bolton Station, twenty-one miles east of Vicksburg.[27]

What Grant could not have known at the time was that May 6 was a day of anguish in the White House. At 3 P.M. President Abraham Lincoln received a telegram from Major General Joseph Hooker's headquarters that confirmed the Army of the Potomac's retreat across the Rappahannock from Chancellorsville. Noah Brooks, an on-scene journalist, wrote, "Had a thunderbolt fallen upon the President he could not have been more overwhelmed . . . he walked up and down the room, saying, 'My God, my God, what will the country say! What will the country say?'" That night, in Washington's packed Willard Hotel, Brooks noted that "the Copperheads . . . sprang into new life and animation, and were dotted through the gloomy crowds with smiling faces of unsurpassed joy." The stakes of Grant's gambit had been raised by Hooker's defeat in Virginia.[28]

On that same Wednesday, Gregg's Confederate columns marched into Osyka. The Tennesseans arrived around noon, and the men were allowed to fall out and encamp a mile north of town, where they were soon joined by the column of Texans and Missourians. There the reunited brigade was most pleased to be given the afternoon off. "Our men enjoyed very much the half day of rest," wrote Captain Flavel C. Barber of the 3rd Tennessee, adding that, "the sick and the broken down and the heavy baggage were put on a train and sent up the railroad." Private Davidson recalled that the meager rations issued to the men in Osyka were "parched corn and peas, with a little rice." Late in the day Gregg received orders from Pemberton to, "Hasten rapidly to Brookhaven. Transportation will be ready there." Since Grierson had wrecked the railroad, Pemberton instructed Gregg to "Retain wagons to transport across gap." On the same day, per Pemberton's order, Gardner ordered Maxey's brigade and assorted other units out of Port Hudson to Jackson via Osyka.[29]

On Thursday, May 7, Grant moved his headquarters from Mrs. Bagnell's to the village of Rocky Springs, but he took the time to send a motivational message to his soldiers. Grant shared his confidence by saying, "A few days continuance of the same zeal and constancy will secure to this army the crowning victory over the rebellion." Grant understood what Colonel G. F. R. Henderson later wrote: "Armies are not machines, but living organisms of intense susceptibility."[30]

The Thirteenth Corps got an early start on Thursday when Brigadier General Eugene A. Carr's division began a ten and a half mile march northeastward from Willow Springs. Carr's men arrived at Big Sand Creek at 10 A.M. and went into position on the right of Osterhaus's division. Brigadier General Alvin Hovey's division marched three and a half miles from Rocky Springs to Big Sand Creek and went into position on Osterhaus's left. McClernand's fourth division, Brigadier General Andrew J. Smith's, marched eight and a half miles from Willow Springs to Little Sand Creek, effectively concentrating the corps with three divisions in advance at "Big Sandy" and Smith's reserve division two miles to the rear at "Little Sandy." In McPherson's Seventeenth Corps, Crocker's division remained at Hankinson's Ferry until Sherman could arrive. While the men waited, they continued to maintain the illusion that the attack would come from there. "Weather very cool for this season," wrote Sergeant Campbell. Logan's division, after being issued rations, was ordered to march from Hankinson's to Rocky Springs. Sergeant Osborn H. Oldroyd of the 20th Ohio noted in his diary, "We broke camp at ten o'clock A.M., and very glad of it. After a pleasant tramp . . . we reached Rocky Springs. Here we have good, cold spring water, fresh from the bosom of the hills."[31]

That same Thursday, a "fine cool day" according to Confederate captain Simpson, Gregg's reunited brigade continued its march northward toward Jackson from Osyka. After a ten-mile hike, the soldiers arrived at noon in Magnolia. Captain Barber described Magnolia as "a beautiful little town surrounded by country seats where the wealthy people of New Orleans used to spend their unhealthy seasons." The trip then took a seemingly easier turn as the troops boarded the railroad cars for the ride north. However, after a mere ten miles on the rails, the soldiers had to detrain at Summit due to the destruction of a twenty-mile stretch of track, bridges, trestlework, and water tanks by Grierson's Yankee marauders a week earlier. Still, there was a silver lining, for Private Davidson recalled that in Summit the soldiers "were most kindly treated by the ladies, who vied with each other as to who could do the most for us. They fed at least half of the brigade." Here, too, the men learned of Lee's victory at Chancellorsville. But bad news followed good when they learned of Grant's victory at Port Gibson and his subsequent capture of Grand Gulf. With this mixed news on their minds, they then fell into column and marched almost four miles north of town to encamp along the banks of Beaver Creek. But other news had not yet reached Summit. Early that morning, Major General Earl Van Dorn had been murdered. The dashing cavalier, who surprised Grant the previous December, received the ultimate surprise from a cuckolded husband in Spring Hill, Tennessee.[32]

In Vicksburg, General Pemberton telegraphed Brigadier General John Adams in Jackson on Thursday, predicting, "I have reason to believe the enemy will make a raid on Jackson at the same time they will make an attack on Big Black Bridge." Pemberton had received a report of Osterhaus's probe on Tuesday at Big Sand Creek, and he had received a report on Wednesday that Yankee troops had been seen marching northeastward on the road from Rocky Springs to Jackson. Pemberton then simply slid his prediction of Grant's strike eastward a few miles. Grant's *coup de main*, he now deduced, had shifted to a point on the railroad near the Big Black River railroad bridge, and the enemy feint had shifted east to Jackson. Pemberton was not far off in his assessment, but what he did not consider was Grant's multiple axes of advance. This oversight would cost Gregg dearly at Raymond.[33]

That afternoon Pemberton received a telegram from President Davis with the bad news that only five thousand men could be sent from the East by rail to reinforce him. But Davis tempered this news with the promise that three thousand recently exchanged soldiers from the Arkansas Post would also be sent to Mississippi. Then Davis dropped the bombshell: "To hold both Vicksburg and Port Hudson is necessary to a connection with Trans-Mississippi." Johnston had told Pemberton to concentrate his forces and beat Grant in the field, and Pemberton had attempted to obey. Now Davis ordered Pemberton to continue to hold both Port Hudson and Vicksburg by leaving his troops dispersed. Once again Pemberton tried to obey. He spread his troops, this time from Vicksburg south to Hankinson's Ferry, and from Hankinson's Ferry northeast to the Big Black River railroad bridge.[34]

On Friday, May 8, Sherman's Fifteenth Corps finally marched inland from Grand Gulf. At the Hankinson's Ferry–Willow Springs intersection seven miles east of Grand Gulf, Brigadier General James M. Tuttle's division continued east to Willow Springs while Major General Frederick Steele's division veered northeast to Hankinson's Ferry. While Sherman's men marched, the soldiers of the Thirteenth and Fifteenth Corps lounged in their camps, and gradually the army concentrated and prepared for its next move. Sergeant Allen Morgan Geer of the 20th Illinois in Logan's division at Rocky Springs wrote that Grant's order "in regard to the Port Gibson battle was read on dress parade," while teams were sent back to Grand Gulf for rations. Geer noted that orders were received for a march the next morning. Sergeant Oldroyd, in the same division, wrote that the men were ready to move but were "not ordered out." He confessed that soldiers were "generally better on the march than in camp," where, he said, they were "apt to get lazy, and grumble." But while some of the soldiers grumbled that day, Grant wrote to Halleck, advising that his advance elements were "fifteen miles from Edwards Station, on Southern Railroad. All looks well." Grant had three days' rations issued to his troops, and in the afternoon he and McClernand reviewed the three Thirteenth Corps divisions that were encamped in the wide floodplain of Big Sand Creek. According to one staff officer, "the woods reverberated" with the approving shouts of the soldiers. It's always better to use down time to raise morale than to sit idly.[35]

That same day, Gregg's brigade continued its journey. The march began at Beaver Creek, north of Summit, and paralleled the smashed railroad tracks and trestles for almost ten miles to the conflux of Gills and Boone Creeks with the Bogue Chitto River. Meanwhile, Pemberton, in accordance with President Davis's order to "hold both Vicksburg and Port Hudson," sent a telegram to Osyka for Gardner, instructing him to "Return with 2,000 troops to Port Hudson, and hold it to the last." Gardner obeyed but ordered Maxey's brigade to continue "rapidly forward" toward Jackson. Unfortunately for Gregg, these three thousand men would not arrive in time to help at Raymond.[36]

At 5 A.M. on Saturday, May 9, Crocker's division, having been relieved by Steele's division, left Hankinson's Ferry and marched five and a half miles eastward on the serpentine road to Rocky Springs. The head of the column arrived at Logan's campsite in Rocky Springs at mid-morning but did not halt. Instead, the dust-covered soldiers marched past the red-bricked Rocky Springs Methodist Church, and tromped to the northeast. A vaporous cloud of dust vented out of the deeply worn roadbed as the men marched through the town, and, as soldiers are prone to do, Logan's men lined the road and carped through the dust at their comrades as they trooped by. Still, Sergeant Oldroyd in Logan's division wrote admiringly, "O, what a grand army this is, and what a sight to fire the heart of a spectator with a speck of patriotism in his bosom. I shall never forget the scene of today, while looking back upon a mile of solid columns, marching with their old tattered flags streaming in the summer breeze." The tail of Crocker's long column finally passed through town at 12:30 P.M., and Logan's division fell in to follow in the haze raised by Crocker's six thousand marching men. Just over a mile past Rocky Springs the two divisions of the Seventeenth Corps column marched through Major General A. J. Smith's Thirteenth Corps division encamped at Little Sand Creek, and two miles farther the two divisions passed uneventfully through the other three Thirteenth Corps divisions at Big Sand Creek, with Sergeant Geer noting only that they "passed McClernand's Army Corps camped on the road." The men then hiked for almost three more miles to the village of Crossroads and turned east for another two miles to a high ridge almost seven miles west of Utica. There the lucky soldiers in the vanguard went into camp at 2 P.M., while the poor coughing souls at the end of the column did not spread their bedrolls until well after dark.[37]

Late that afternoon, word was sent to Tuttle's division in Willow Springs that the Seventeenth Corps had finally vacated Rocky Springs. Tuttle broke camp at 4 P.M., and his men endured a miserable seven-mile march over a very rough and dusty road. The division finally settled in at Rocky Springs late that night. Steele's division remained at Hankinson's Ferry to continue the appearance of a river-crossing, but this left only about four miles between Sherman's two Fifteenth Corps divisions. The men of A. J. Smith's Thirteenth Corps division waited until McPherson's two divisions had passed, and then at 3 P.M. made a leisurely two-mile march from Little Sand Creek to join the divisions of Generals Osterhaus, Alvin P. Hovey, and Eugene A. Carr at Big Sand Creek, three miles northeast of Rocky Springs. At day's end these moves placed all four of McClernand's Thirteenth Corps divisions about three miles west of McPherson's two Seventeenth Corps divisions. It was a good day for Grant, who had concentrated approximately thirty-five thousand men and twenty batteries of artillery in and around Rocky Springs. He also still had one of Sherman's and one of McPherson's divisions, or approximately ten thousand more men, across the river in Louisiana, where they guarded the line of communications and escorted the vital supply wagons. Grant's next step was to get the thirty-five thousand men in Mississippi aligned for the strike on the railroad.[38]

Fifty miles slightly to the southeast that Saturday, the men of Gregg's brigade broke camp on Gills Creek at 5 A.M. After a march of eight miles, they arrived in Brookhaven at noon and were pleased to find that railroad cars awaited them. "There we took the cars and rode to the city of Jackson," wrote a relieved Captain Simpson. During the fifty-three-mile train ride, Simpson observed, "We passed through some fine little towns and the ladies thronged the stations to see and cheer us on our way. We arrived in Jackson about six o'clock in the evening and went out beyond the city to camp, the night was cool and pleasant." Gregg made his camp that night two miles east of Jackson near the confluence of Neely Creek and the Pearl River. Here, after his brigade had been on the road for a week, he awaited orders for his next move. Major Van Zandt wrote to his wife, "How long we will remain here and where our future destination may be, I know not."[39]

That night, Major General William W. Loring, commander of one of Pemberton's five divisions, sent a proposal to Pemberton for a four-pronged offensive strike on the Army of the Tennessee, to be conducted along a twenty-one mile front that ran from Hankinson's Ferry, south of Vicksburg, to Dillon's plantation, southeast of Edwards Station. Loring asked Pemberton to "order your forces from Jackson to Raymond" to strike the Federal right, which was believed to be near Dillon's. Loring then suggested that Bowen's division attack the Federal column in its center in the vicinity of Auburn, south of Edwards Station. At the same time, Loring would take his division across the Big Black River on pontoons at Baldwin's Ferry, southwest of Edwards near Cayuga, to strike the Union left, while Major General Carter Stevenson's division, which guarded the approaches to Vicksburg from the south at Hankinson's Ferry and Hall's Ferry, would cross the Big Black River and sweep around Grant's left and into the rear of the Federal army. This converging attack from Pemberton's many units operating along a 20-mile front would have been extremely difficult to coordinate, but any offensive move was worth consideration. Pemberton never responded to Loring's suggestion.[40]

On Sunday, May 10, Grant continued to maneuver his army into position for his three-pronged strike on the Southern Railroad of Mississippi. McClernand used the Sabbath morning to issue ammunition and rations to his troops, and then at one o'clock he marched three of his divisions for six and a half miles, through the crossroads in Cayuga, and then another two miles east to Fivemile Creek, while leaving his reserve division, A. J. Smith's, at the crossroads in town. Colonel Wilson was brought forward to repair the partially destroyed bridge at Five Mile Creek, and he noted that the creek bed was "rather deep," but with "little running water." Steele's division of Sherman's corps spent Sunday morning destroying the bridges and boats at Hankinson's Ferry, and then at noon the division marched nine miles to Big Sand Creek via Rocky Springs. Tuttle's men rested in Rocky Springs that Sunday and watched as Steele's men passed through town. From Rocky Springs, Grant moved his headquarters six and a half miles northeast to Cayuga, a village that consisted of a few houses, stores, and a post office. Here were found Southern newspapers that proclaimed Robert E. Lee's victory over Joe Hooker at Chancellorsville and Bedford Forrest's capture of Abel Streight and his command near Rome, Georgia. While the news of the twin Union defeats placed greater pressure on Grant for a victory, he continued with his plans, as he knew that his opponent had spread his forces to cover a broad front. In his memoirs, Grant stated, "It would not be possible for Pemberton to attack me with all his troops at once, and I determined to throw my army between his and fight him in detail." Grant knew he still had bulge.[41]

McPherson's two divisions left their camps near Utica Crossroads that morning and plodded through the thick dust for almost seven miles to arrive at the village of Utica at noon. The men rested in town for an hour before they went back into column, turned northeast, and continued another three and a half miles on the road to Raymond. Sergeant Geer wrote in his journal that the men "suffered much from thirst, found water scarce." It was dark when the parched soldiers finally went into a dry camp on the A. B. Weeks plantation. Sergeant Campbell noted, "The country as we approach Raymond is getting less hilly and more fertile." But level terrain meant fewer watersheds, and canteen and bucket details had to be dispatched to the nearest watercourse, Tallahala Creek, just over a mile to the east. The teamsters and artillery-men knew that the first priority was to attend to their vital dray animals, as the poor, thirsty beasts required four gallons of water each day. That night McPherson dejectedly wrote to Grant, "The road is very dry and dusty. . . . There are no streams on the road and the troops have suffered some for want of water." Grant took note.[42]

In Vicksburg on that Sunday, Pemberton, possibly in response to Loring's suggestion, finally decided on an offensive move to strike the right flank—but only the right flank—of Grant's army as it moved to Raymond. Pemberton decided to poke Grant with his finger, rather than smash him with his fist. The prod was to come from Gregg's brigade in Jackson, and late Sunday night

Pemberton telegraphed Gregg in Jackson, cryptically stating, "Move your brigade promptly to Raymond, taking three days' rations, and carrying only cooking utensils and ammunition; no baggage. . . . Use Wirt Adams' cavalry at Raymond for advanced pickets." At the same time, Pemberton telegraphed his cavalry commander in Jackson, Colonel Wirt Adams. The message to Adams could not have been more vague. It ordered Adams to "Proceed at once to Edwards Depot, and take command of all the cavalry there and at Raymond, for operation against the enemy. Report to me your arrival there. Your command will remain at Raymond." Adams read and re-read this message in an unsuccessful attempt to fathom the commander's intent. Pemberton then exacerbated the situation with a second, equally foggy, order to Adams, which stated, "General Gregg is ordered to Raymond. Direct your cavalry there to scout thoroughly and keep him informed." Adams had already posted a sergeant and four troopers in Raymond, along with a captain and forty Mississippi state troops. So was Adams to "direct" his cavalry from Jackson to Raymond, or was he to "direct" those cavalrymen already in Raymond to scout for Gregg when he arrived? Strangely, both Gregg and Adams were in Jackson on the night of May 10, and Pemberton could simply have ordered Colonel Adams to report to General Gregg for instructions, thus ensuring a unified effort. But such was not the case, and a flummoxed Adams prepared to ride with his six companies of cavalry into Edwards, not to Raymond as Pemberton had intended.[43]

On Monday, May 11, per Grant's orders, McClernand's Thirteenth Corps remained in camp at Cayuga and at Five Mile Creek so that Sherman's Fifteenth Corps troops could pass through and get into position in the center of the army. Sherman, however, continued to worry and as recently as Saturday had written to Grant, asking him to "stop all troops" until the supply wagons could cross the Mississippi. He warned that the "road will be jammed sure as life" if Grant attempted "to supply 50,000 men by one single road." Grant immediately replied to Sherman, saying in no uncertain terms that "a delay would give the enemy time to reinforce and fortify . . . the advance will move today." A Grant biographer, Charles King, wrote that during these days Grant was "alive with energy and electric force." Thus, May 11 was Grant's day to share some of that vitality with his corps commanders. Grant knew that Sherman had six brigades with him, but only four batteries of artillery, and these were all smoothbore guns. So, to bolster Sherman's combat power, Grant ordered McClernand to transfer a six-gun battery of artillery to Sherman "to equalize the artillery." He also ordered McClernand to "temporarily detach" two monster 20-pounder Parrott rifles to Sherman "for the ensuing battle." Then Grant reminded Sherman that the three brigades of General

Frank Blair's Fifteenth Corps division were just across the Mississippi and were to be brought "up as soon as possible." After reassuring Sherman about combat strength, that night Grant addressed his subordinate's subsistence concerns by informing him that 200 wagons of supplies were leaving Grand Gulf that day for the front.[44]

Grant, having received McPherson's water shortage message the night before, sensed that he also had to reassure his Seventeenth Corps commander. In fact, it was not until 10 A.M. on Monday morning that McPherson's soldiers broke camp at the Weeks plantation. As they shuffled down the road, Adjutant Byers wrote that the dust "came to the shoe top. The atmosphere was yellow with it. The moving of a column far away could be traced by it. We followed it the way that Joshua's army followed the mighty cloud." The two divisions plodded through the powder for a scant mile and a half, all the while hacking from the smothering pall of dust. The column halted at noon and the men fell out and went into camp on the J. Roach plantation, only one-third mile away from the much-sought-after waters of Tallahala Creek. Due to scouting reports of enemy in the area, the men camped in line of battle on a ridge, in a position favorable for the defense. Sergeant Oldroyd wrote, "General Logan thinks we shall have a fight soon," and Sergeant Geer wrote, "strange rumors of an enemy ahead." Both water and rations were scant in the Seventeenth Corps, the march had been short, and its commander acted as if he were losing his momentum.[45]

Grant was only eight miles west of Roach's plantation in Cayuga that Monday. At 1 P.M. he sent a message to the young McPherson—a message that was masterful in its communicative skills. Grant knew that the Seventeenth Corps was falling behind the rest of the army and that time was all-important; still he gave McPherson permission to make a short march "to the next crossroads if there is water." But he also ordered the Seventeenth Corps to march "tomorrow with all activity into Raymond." Then Grant encouraged his junior corps commander by saying, "We must fight the enemy before our rations fail . . . Upon one occasion you made two days rations last seven." The thoughtfully worded message not only used the pronoun *we*, it both challenged and encouraged. It worked wonderfully.[46]

Grant must have felt extremely confident—almost cocky—that Monday in Cayuga, because he also wrote to Halleck to advise that he was "in a line nearly east and west" with his left anchored on Big Black River and his right extending toward Jackson as far east "as they can without bringing on a general engagement." He then said, "I shall communicate with Grand Gulf no more," unless it became "necessary to send a train with heavy escort." Perhaps the key to the message lay in its final words: "you may not hear from me again for several days." Grant was aware that his eight days of freedom of action had expired since he had sent the noncompliant message from Grand Gulf. In fact, that very morning in Washington, Halleck received Grant's message and immediately replied, ordering Grant to unite his forces with Banks between Vicksburg and Port Hudson "so as to attack these places separately with the combined forces." But Halleck was nine hundred miles away, and his veto did not reach the interior of Mississippi until May 17—far too late to stop Grant's juggernaut. "Boldness," wrote Carl von Clausewitz, "is the noblest of virtues, the true steel which gives the weapon its edge and brilliancy."[47]

Early that same Monday in Jackson, Gregg's men were on the march. Private Davidson recalled that "we were allowed to rest all of Sunday, but at five o'clock Monday morning we were ordered under arms without a moment's preparation, and had to start without cooked rations." Sergeant Sumner Cunningham of the 41st Tennessee recalled that the men "were no better physically than mentally to start on another forced march." As the soldiers trod through Jackson, Cunningham remembered that they did not know their destination until they "passed the depot and took the Raymond road" south of town. Private H. K. Nelson of the 41st Tennessee wrote, "Water very scarce, seldom to be had at all, and the weather was extremely hot, so there was much suffering." After a twenty-one mile march, the brigade arrived in Raymond at 4 P.M. and went into camp in a field near town. Private Davidson wrote that he "was so fortunate as to meet up with some kind ladies, who gave me something to eat and a magnificent bouquet of magnolias, and also one of onions, both of which were very acceptable." Sergeant Cunningham recalled that "The citizens met us kindly and wonderingly. Raymond was peaceful; Raymond was happy."[48]

While Gregg's infantry and artillery were en route to Raymond and Adams's cavalry was trotting to Edwards that Monday, Pemberton learned that on the previous day Sherman's men had destroyed the raft bridge and boats at Hankinson's Ferry. This information, along with reports of Yankees south of Edwards Station, confirmed the Confederate general's belief that Grant's objective was the railroad at Edwards. Pemberton made plans to shift his army to meet this threat. Bowen's division was at the Big Black River Bridge, six miles west of Edwards Station, and he was instructed to be prepared to march east to Edwards and form a blocking position on a commanding ridgeline two and a half miles south of town. Loring was to move two of his three brigades to the Big Black River Bridge behind Bowen and to be prepared to march to Bowen's support. Carter Stevenson was ordered to shift his division from south of Vicksburg to the east and anchor his left flank on Loring's right to form a line along the Big Black River. The two divisions of Major Generals Martin L. Smith and John H. Forney would remain in Vicksburg, per the instructions of President Davis to hold the city. Pemberton was convinced that the Union thrust would be a single monolithic column approaching the railroad by marching up the Telegraph Road to Edwards Station, so he sent a message to Gregg in Raymond, advising him that it was "very probable that the movement toward Jackson is in reality on the Big Black Bridge, in which case you must be prepared to attack them in rear or on flank." A second message was sent to Gregg that same day, repeating the instructions to "attack in rear or on flank," but advising that if the enemy advanced on him too strongly, "to fall back on Jackson."[49]

But Gregg had received an unpleasant surprise when he arrived in Raymond on Monday. "I found none of Colonel Adams' cavalry except a single sergeant and four men," he wrote in his report. Meanwhile, Wirt Adams arrived in Edwards and soon realized that Gregg needed help in Raymond, so he dispatched a fifty-man squadron in that direction. En route to Raymond, Adams's horsemen were fired upon by Sherman's pickets. Of course, they reported this to Gregg upon their arrival in Raymond late that night. Gregg now believed that the enemy was just where Pemberton said he would be.[50]

On Tuesday, May 12, all three Federal columns worked to complete their positioning for the strike on the railroad. That morning, in the Union right column at Roach farm, McPherson took Grant's "hurry up" message to heart. He had his 12,500-man column on the road to Raymond at 3:30 A.M., with Logan's division in the advance. Almost immediately the Federal cavalry that preceded the infantry received fire from Gregg's horsemen, and as the long column continued forward in the predawn darkness, the sound of carbine fire crackled down the line as if the soldiers were treading upon dry limbs. But the thin line of Rebel state troops was no match for the Federal cavalry battalion, and the Seventeenth Corps pushed forward for eight miles. Finally, two miles south of Fourteen Mile Creek, the belligerency of the firing caused McPherson to deploy two regiments of Logan's lead brigade on each side of the dusty road. Skirmishers were sent forward, and Logan reported that the column cautiously snaked its way northward for another one and a half miles "to a commanding position upon the summit of a hill" where it was brought to a halt. The skirmish line then descended the gentle slope and crossed the open fields toward a belt of timber bordering Fourteen Mile Creek almost three-quarters of a mile to the north. When the blue line was 100 yards from the tree line, it was violently popped with leaden balls from a line of Confederates hidden under the trees and in the underbrush. At almost the same instant, from a low hilltop one-half mile north of the creek, three Rebel cannon belched fire and smoke, and three seconds later the shells shrieked overhead. Colonel Force, on the crest of the ridge to the rear, saw the cannons fire and glanced down at his pocket watch. The time was 10 A.M. Logan ordered his troops forward, and the six guns of Captain Samuel De Golyer's 8th Michigan Battery were raced to the front in a cloud of dust. Logan wrote that the guns were "placed into position on each side of the main road and near a bridge across a ravine in which the infantry of the enemy was posted, and immediately engaged the enemy's artillery, which was posted on rising ground about 800 yards distant." The Battle of Raymond had begun.[51]

The fight at Raymond was initiated by John Gregg because shortly before dawn in Raymond, he had been handed a report that an enemy column was moving up the Utica road toward Raymond, and that his state troops had been pushed back. Since these troops were, as Gregg described, "mostly youths from the neighborhood," the veracity of their estimate of the situation was questionable. Still, it seemed that Pemberton's assessment was correct, for if the enemy advance was headed to Edwards Station, then the troops on the Utica road were almost certainly "a brigade on a marauding excursion" on the right flank of the *coup de main*. This assessment seemed to be confirmed when Gregg's own scouts, having seen only the lead Federal brigade at the head of the cloud of dust on the Utica road, reported that about twenty-five hundred or three thousand Yankees were approaching. Always ready for a fight, Gregg presumed that the reports were, as usual, a bit exaggerated, and that what he actually faced was an enemy brigade of around fifteen hundred men. So, he decided to set a trap for this lone brigade and smash it. Then, upon the arrival of promised reinforcements from Jackson, he could strike the right flank of the main column as it engaged Bowen's men south of Edwards. Gregg's troops were quickly formed and marched through Raymond, and Private Patrick M. Griffin, of the 10th and 30th Tennessee Consolidated, long remembered the ladies of the town bringing "pies, cakes, and good things," and more importantly "buckets of water and dippers." He noted that "Many a soldier blessed them as they passed down the ranks."[52]

When the brigade reached a point one and a half miles southwest of the town square, Gregg examined the situation on the ground and then made his dispositions. He sent the 7th Texas almost half a mile south to a tree line that bordered Fourteen Mile Creek. This regiment's mission was to bait the enemy into the cul-de-sac formed by the steep creek banks. The regiment was also to be the anvil in the classic hammer and anvil tactic. The pivot point of the hammer as it swung right to smash the Yankee brigade was a big 548-man regiment, the 3rd Tennessee, which was posted to the Texans' left rear and was hidden behind the trees at the creek. The striking face of the hammer had two regiments, the 50th Tennessee and the 10th and 30th Tennessee Consolidated, which were placed on Dry Grove Road to the east. Once the 3rd Tennessee pounced from behind the ridge to strike the unwary Yanks and turn their right flank, the 50th, and then the 10/30th, would hit the Yanks in their rear in an *en echelon*, or step-by-step attack. A fifth regiment, the 41st Tennessee, was held in reserve to guard against the unexpected. The First Tennessee battalion shepherded Bledsoe's three guns, which were in position on a slight hill about 850 yards north of the narrow, wooden Fourteen Mile Creek bridge. Gregg thought he had set a perfect trap.[53]

Gregg's logic cannot be faulted based upon the information provided him, but with one infantry brigade and three cannon he grabbed a tiger by the tail when he attacked a Federal cavalry battalion, six infantry brigades, and eight batteries of artillery. When the Confederates attacked they fought ferociously, but the column of bluecoats that crested the distant ridge seemed endless. The gray-clad attackers eventually became defenders when five of the six Yankee brigades and twenty-two of their forty-two cannon were brought into action. By 4 P.M. the surprisingly ferocious battle came to a conclusion when Gregg skillfully disengaged his regiments and retreated through Raymond toward Jackson. Gregg reported his casualties as 73 killed, 251 wounded, and 190 missing, for a total of 514, or about a 16 percent casualty rate. Federal casualties were reported as 66 killed, 339 wounded, and 37 missing, for a total of 442, about a 3 percent casualty rate. It was Port Gibson all over again, with a five-to-one loss ratio in favor of the Federals. Grant's skillful maneuvering had again given him bulge.[54]

Grant and Sherman listened to the guns of Raymond from their camp at Dillon's Plantation, over five miles to the west of the battleground. Grant's experienced ear told him that the forces opposing McPherson were not more than the young general's two divisions could handle, so he patiently awaited news. Around 4 P.M. he received McPherson's preliminary report, and then at sundown he received a second message in which McPherson overstated that he had defeated a force of six thousand Confederates. Regardless of the number, Grant knew that Gregg's men were headed back to Jackson, and he had once again received shadowy reports "of information that reinforcements were daily arriving at Jackson, and that General Joe Johnston was hourly expected there to take command in person." Grant also knew, from morning clashes involving McClernand's and Sherman's forces south of Edwards, that there was a considerable Confederate force to his left front. Boldly, Grant determined "to turn the whole column towards Jackson and capture that place without delay." At 9:15 P.M. he sent orders to all three corps commanders, ordering McPherson and Sherman to pivot east toward Jackson, while

McClernand was to cover the army's rear as it turned its back on Pemberton's forces. En route to Jackson, McPherson was to swing northeast to Clinton and sever Pemberton's railroad line of communications, which would include cutting the telegraph line linking Pemberton and Johnston.[55]

Perhaps Sherman, who sat beside Grant at Dillon's farm, recalled the prophecy he had proffered to Grant almost three months earlier. If Grant followed through with his plan of campaign, Sherman cautioned, he would be putting himself "into a position voluntarily which an enemy would be glad to maneuver a year" to get him into. That night it appeared as though

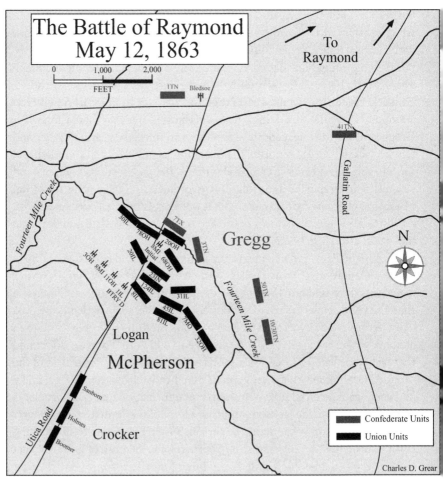

The Battle of Raymond
May 12, 1863

Outside Raymond, Gregg's Confederates clashed with the leading brigades of Major General James B. McPherson's Seventeenth Corps in the densely wooded valley of Fourteen Mile Creek.

Sherman were correct. Grant had enemy forces to his left front, and he had enemy forces to his right front, and his army was deep in hostile territory with a line of communication that had been stretched to the limit. It seemed that Grant was in deep trouble. But his warrior ethos told him differently. Years later, he unabashedly said to a reporter, "A soldier's duty is to destroy his enemy as quickly as possible." That is precisely what he decided to do at Dillon's plantation on the night of May 12, 1863. After preventing He would prevent the junction of the two enemy forces, and then he would attack them separately. Grant knew he still had bulge, and he intended to keep it.[56]

Notes

1. Steve Meyer, *Iowa Valor: A Compilation of Civil War Combat Experiences from Soldiers of the State Distinguished as Most Patriotic of the Patriotic* (Garrison, Iowa: Meyer Publishing Co., 1994), 187; John H. Brinton, *Personal Memoirs of John H. Brinton* (1914; reprint, Carbondale: Southern Illinois University Press, 1996), 239.

2. U.S. War Department, *The War of the Rebellion: A Compilation of the Official Records of the Union and Confederate Armies*, 128 vols. (Washington, D.C.: GPO, 1880–1901), series 1, vol. 24, pt. 1: 59, 259, 664, 667. (Hereinafter cited as *OR*. All references are to Series 1 unless otherwise indicated.) Headquarters, Department of the Army, *FM 100–5 Operations* (Baltimore: US Army Adjutant General Publications Center, May 1986), 128; Ulysses S. Grant, *Personal Memoirs of U.S. Grant*, 2 vols. (New York: Press of J. J. Little and Co., 1885), 1: 442, 478; Edwin C. Bearss, *The Campaign for Vicksburg*, 3 vols. (Dayton, Ohio: Morningside House, 1986), 2:405, 407, 416–17; Terrence J. Winschel, *Triumph and Defeat: The Vicksburg Campaign* (Mason City, Iowa: Savas Publishing Co., 1999), 63, 88; Katy McCaleb Headley, *Claiborne County, Mississippi: The Promised Land* (Port Gibson, Miss.: Claiborne County Historical Society, 1976), 362; John Allen Wyeth, M.D., *Life of General Nathan Bedford Forrest* (New York: Harper and Brothers, 1899), 404.

3. Grant, *Memoirs*, 1: 481; *OR*, vol. 24, pt. 1: 129, 644, 662, 677, 683, 722; Lieutenant Colonel J. H. Wilson, "A Staff Officer's Journal of the Vicksburg Campaign, April 30 to July 4, 1863," *Journal of the Military Service Institution of the United States* 43 (July–December 1908), 95; Sergeant William Pitt Chambers, *Blood and Sacrifice: The Civil War Journal of a Confederate Soldier*, ed. Richard A. Baumgartner (Huntington, W.Va.: Blue Acorn Press, 1994), 66–67; John Quincy Adams Campbell, *The Union Must Stand: The Civil War Diary of John Quincy Adams Campbell, Fifth Iowa Volunteer Infantry*, ed. Mark Grimsley and Todd D. Miller (Knoxville: University of Tennessee Press, 2000), 92; Myron B. Loop, *The Long Road Home: Ten Thousand Miles through the Confederacy with the 68th Ohio*, ed. Richard A. Baumgartner (Huntington, W.Va.: Blue Acorn Press, 2006), 75; Bearss, *Campaign for Vicksburg*, 2: 415; James Harrison Wilson, "Reminiscences of General Grant," *Century* 30, no. 6 (October 1885): 953; Terrence J. Winschel, *Triumph and Defeat: The Vicksburg Campaign* (New York: Savas Beatie, 2006), 2: 7–8.

4. Ephraim McD. Anderson, *Memoirs: Historical and Personal; including the Campaigns of the First Missouri Confederate Brigade* (Saint Louis: Times Printing Co., 1868), 301–2; *OR*, vol. 24, pt. 1: 644–45, 735.

5. Grant, *Memoirs*, 1: 490; Adam Badeau, *Military History of Ulysses S. Grant*, 3 vols. (2nd ed., New York: D. Appleton and Co., 1885), 1: 215; Manning F. Force, "Personal Recollections of the Vicksburg Campaign," *Sketches of War History, 1861–1865: Papers Read before the Ohio Commandery of the Military Order of the Loyal Legion of the United States, 1883–1886*, 6 vols. (Cincinnati: Robert Clarke & Co., 1888), 1: 297; Richard Yates, Governor of Illinois, *New York Herald*, May 23, 1863; William Freeman Vilas, "A View of the Vicksburg Campaign," Paper Read before the Madison Literary Club, October 14, 1907 (Madison: Wisconsin History Commission, August 1908), 36; Bearss, *Campaign for Vicksburg*, 2: 431; Warren E. Grabau, *Ninety-Eight Days, A Geographer's View of the Vicksburg Campaign* (Knoxville: University of Tennessee Press, 2000), 175–76; Winschel, *Triumph and Defeat*, 2:7.

6. *OR*, vol. 24, pt. 1: 25, 29, 33, 49–50; Ulysses S. Grant, *The Papers of Ulysses S. Grant*, ed. John Y. Simon, 31 vols. (Carbondale: Southern Illinois University Press, 1967–2009), 8: 155; Grant, *Memoirs*, 1: 443, 491–92; Edward D. Mansfield, *A Popular and Authentic Life of Ulysses S. Grant* (Cincinnati: R. W. Carroll & Co., 1868), 192; James G. Hollandsworth Jr., *Pretense of Glory: The Life of General Nathaniel P. Banks* (Baton Rouge: Louisiana State University Press, 1998), 35, 89, 118–19; Winschel, *Triumph and Defeat*, 157; Michael B. Ballard, *Vicksburg: The Campaign That Opened the Mississippi* (Chapel Hill: University of North Carolina Press, 2004), 247–48; Vilas, "A View of the Vicksburg Campaign," 36–37, 40–41; John Russell Young, *Around the World with General Grant*, 2 vols. (New York: American News Co., 1879), 2: 615–16; Charles A. Dana, *Recollections of the Civil War* (reprint, Lincoln: University of Nebraska Press, 1996), 48; Bearss, *Campaign for Vicksburg*, 2: 432–35; Badeau, *Military History*, 1: 217–22; William Marvel, *Lincoln's Darkest Year* (Boston: Houghton Mifflin, 2008), 335.

7. Grant, *Memoirs*, 1: 492, 524–25; *OR*, vol. 24, pt. 1: 36; Bearss, *Campaign for Vicksburg*, 2: 671–72; Young, *Around the World*, 2: 621.

8. *OR*, vol. 24, pt. 1: 84; ibid., pt. 3: 268–69, 272–75, 281–82; Grant, *Memoirs*, 1: 486–87, 494; Grant, *Grant Papers*, 8: 137, 153, 155, 159–60, 162–63, 166–67, 219; Mansfield, *A Popular and Authentic Life*, 192–96; Bearss, *Campaign for Vicksburg*, 2: 436, 447; ibid., 3: 721–25; Charles A. Dana and J. H. Wilson, *The Life of Ulysses S. Grant, General of the Armies of the United States* (Springfield, Mass.: Samuel Bowles and Co., 1868), 117; Francis Vinton Greene, *The Mississippi* (New York: Charles Scribner's Sons, 1882), 138; William T. Sherman, *Sherman's Civil War: Selected Correspondence of William T. Sherman, 1860–1865*, ed. Brooks D. Simpson and Jean V. Berlin (Chapel Hill: University of North Carolina Press, 1999), 465; Dana, *Recollections*, 48; Frederick D. Grant, "With Grant at Vicksburg," *Outlook*, July 2, 1898, 3. Fred Grant took leave from his schooling in Covington, Kentucky, and joined his father at Young's Point in March 1863.

9. *OR*, vol. 24, pt. 1: 83, 636, 645; 651; ibid., pt. 2: 204; Bearss, *Campaign for Vicksburg*, 2: 427–28; Greene, *The Mississippi*, 133–34; Osborn H. Oldroyd, *A Soldier's Story of the Siege of Vicksburg, from the Diary of Osborn H. Oldroyd, Late Sergeant, Co. E. 20th Ohio* (Springfield: H. W. Rokker, 1885), 6; Force, "Personal Recollections of the Vicksburg Campaign," 298; Loop, *The Long Road Home*, 78; Anderson, *Memoirs*, 303–305; Phillip Thomas Tucker, *The Forgotten "Stonewall" of the West": Major General John Stevens Bowen* (Macon, Ga.: Mercer University Press, 1997), 268–69.

10. James Harrison Wilson, *Under the Old Flag: Recollections of Military Operations in the War for the Union, the Spanish War, and the Boxer Rebellion*, 2 vols. (New York: D. Appleton and Co., 1912), 1: 197; and, "Reminiscences of General Grant," *Century* 30, no. 6 (October 1885): 954; Dana, *Recollections*, 48; Dana and Wilson, *Life of Grant*, 117; Greene, *The Mississippi*, 134; Bearss, *Campaign for Vicksburg*, 2: 436; Sarah Anne Ellis Dorsey, *Recollections of Henry Watkins Allen, Brigadier-General, Confederate States Army, Ex-Governor of Louisiana* (New York: M. Doolady, 1866), 403; Headley, *Claiborne County, Mississippi*, 378; *WPA Files* (Claiborne County, Miss.: 1936–39), Box 10666, Series #447, p. 20.

11. *OR*, vol. 24, pt. 1: 259; ibid., vol. 15, 1069–70; Bearss, *Campaign for Vicksburg*, 2: 405, 407, 416–417; Michael B. Ballard, *Pemberton: A Biography* (Jackson: University Press of Mississippi, 1991), 141; Winschel, *Triumph and Defeat*, 2: 13.

12. *OR*, vol. 24, pt. 3: 810; Ballard, *Vicksburg*, 256–57; Edward Cunningham, *The Port Hudson Campaign, 1862–1863* (Baton Rouge: Louisiana State University Press, 1963), 36; Lawrence Lee Hewitt, *Port Hudson: Confederate Bastion on the Mississippi* (Baton Route: Louisiana State University Press, 1987), 44–45, 122; John D. Winters, *The Civil War in Louisiana* (Baton Rouge: Louisiana State University Press, 1963), 243; Rebecca Blackwell Drake, *In Their Own Words: Soldiers Tell the Story of the Battle of Raymond* (Raymond, Miss.: Friends of Raymond, 2001), 22.

13. *OR*, vol. 24, pt. 3: 801; Bearss, *Campaign for Vicksburg*, 2: 456; K. M. Van Zandt, *Force without Fanfare*, ed. Sandra L. Myres (Fort Worth: Texas Christian University Press, 1968), 98–99; Davis Blake Carter, *Two Stars in the Southern Sky: General John Gregg C.S.A. and Mollie* (Spartanburg, S.C.: Reprint Co., 2001), 151; W. J. Davidson, "Diary of Private W. J. Davidson, Company C, Forty-First Tennessee Regiment," *The Annals of the Army of Tennessee and Early Western History*, ed. Edwin L. Drake (Nashville: Guild Bindery Press, 1878), 166; Hewitt, *Confederate Bastion*, 121–22.

14. Herschel Gower, *Pen and Sword: The Life and Journals of Randal W. McGavock* (Nashville: Tennessee Historical Commission, 1960), 85; Davidson, *The Annals of the Army of Tennessee*, 166–67; Flavel C. Barber, *Holding the Line: The Third Tennessee Infantry, 1861–1864*, ed. Robert H. Ferrell (Kent, Ohio: Kent State University Press, 1994), 116; H. K. Nelson, "Battles of Raymond and Jackson," *Confederate Veteran*, 43 vols. (Wilmington: Broadfoot, 1986), 12:12; Patrick M. Griffin, "The Famous Tenth Tennessee," *Confederate Veteran*, 13:555; Paul and Lee Malone, *Louisiana Plantation Homes* (Gretna, La.: Pelican, 1966), 20; J. Frazer Smith, A.I.A., *White Pillars: Early Life and Architecture of the Lower Mississippi Valley Country* (New York: Bramhall House, 1941), 131–32.

15. Carter, *Two Stars in the Southern Sky*, 154.

16. *OR*, vol. 24, pt. 3: 808, 815; John C. Pemberton, *Pemberton, Defender of Vicksburg* (Chapel Hill: University of North Carolina Press, 1942), 126–29; David M. Smith, *Compelled to Appear in Print: The Vicksburg Manuscript of General John C. Pemberton* (Cincinnati: Ironclad, 1999), 93–94; Bearss, *Campaign for Vicksburg*, 2: 417, 419.

17. Davidson, *The Annals of the Army of Tennessee*, 167; Barber, *Holding the Line*, 117; Nelson, "Battles of Raymond and Jackson"; Gower, *Pen and Sword*, 85; Griffin, "The Famous Tenth Tennessee."

18. *OR*, vol. 24, pt. 3: 821; Ballard, *Pemberton*, 147; Bearss, *Campaign for Vicksburg*, 2: 439; G. F. R. Henderson, *The Science of War: A Collection of Essays and Lectures, 1891–1903* (London: Longmans, Green, 1906), 45; Young, *Around the World*, 2: 615.

19. Badeau, *Military History*, 1: 224–25; Bearss, *Campaign for Vicksburg*, 2: 443; Grant, *Grant Papers*, 8: 156–59; *OR*, vol. 24, pt. 1: 50.

20. Davidson, *The Annals of the Army of Tennessee*, 167; Barber, *Holding the Line*, 117; Nelson, "Battles of Raymond and Jackson"; Gower, *Pen and Sword*, 85; Griffin, "The Famous Tenth Tennessee."

21. *OR*, vol. 24, pt. 3: 828; Bearss, *Campaign for Vicksburg*, 2: 440; ibid., 3: 1150; Hewitt, *Confederate Bastion*, 45, 106, 122.

22. Dana, *Recollections*, 48; Grant, *Memoirs*, 1: 493; *OR*, vol. 24, pt. 1: 50, 146; ibid., pt. 3: 277; Wilson, *Journal of the Military Service*, 43 95; Bearss, *Campaign for Vicksburg*, 2: 441, 443, 445; Badeau, *Military History*, 1: 224–25; Dana and Wilson, *Life of Grant*, 118; Grabau, *Ninety-Eight Days*, 197; Terrence J. Winschel, *Triumph and Defeat*, 2: 14; Albert Richardson, *Personal History of Ulysses S. Grant* (2nd ed., Hartford, Conn.: American Publishing Co., 1885), 312.

23. Grant, *Memoirs*, 1: 493; *OR*, vol. 24, pt. 1: 50, 146; Wilson, *Journal of the Military Service*, Vol. 43, 95; Oldroyd, *A Soldier's Story*, 7; Bearss, *Campaign for Vicksburg*, 2: 441, 443, 445, 446–47, 452; Badeau, *Military History*, 1: 224–25; Richardson, *Personal History*, 312; Dana and Wilson, *Life of Grant*, 118; Grabau, *Ninety-Eight Days*, 197–98; Terrence J. Winschel, *Triumph and Defeat*, 2: 14; Drake, *In Their Own Words*, 16; Meyer, *Iowa Valor*, 188; Campbell, *The Union Must Stand*, 92.

24. *OR*, vol. 24, pt. 3: 274–75; Grant, *Memoirs*, 1: 255, 494; Bearss, *Campaign for Vicksburg*, 2: 446–47; ibid., 3: 721; *WPA Files*, p. 21.

25. Barber, *Holding the Line*, 117; Gower, *Pen and Sword*, 85; R. W. Surby, *Grierson Raids, and Hatch's Sixty-Four Days March, with Biographical Sketches, also the Life and Adventures of Chickasaw, the Scout* (Chicago: Rounds and James, 1865), 103–14; Benjamin H. Grierson, *A Just and Righteous Cause: Benjamin H. Grierson's Civil War Memoir*, ed. Bruce J. Dinges and Shirley A. Leckie (Carbondale: Southern Illinois University Press, 2008), 171–73; D. Alexander Brown, *Grierson's Raid* (Dayton, Ohio: Morningside House, 1981), 198–203, 241; Bearss, *Campaign for Vicksburg*, 2: 229–30.

26. *OR*, vol. 24, pt. 1: 35; Grant, *Memoirs*, 1: 494–95; Grant, *Grant Papers*, 8: 163, 169; Badeau, *Military History*, 1: 218; Major General Grenville M. Dodge, *Personal Recollections of President Abraham Lincoln, General Ulysses S. Grant and General William T. Sherman* (Council Bluffs, Iowa: Monarch, 1914), 50–51; Winschel, *Triumph and Defeat*, 2: 13; Brooks D. Simpson, *Ulysses S. Grant: Triumph over Adversity, 1822–1865* (Boston: Houghton Mifflin, 2000), 194; Edwin C. Bearss and J. Parker Hills, *Receding Tide: Vicksburg and Gettysburg, the Campaigns that Changed the Civil War* (Washington, D.C.: National Geographic, 2010), 149.

27. Grant, *Memoirs*, 1: 496; Brevet Major Charles Dana Miller, *The Struggle for the Life of the Republic: A Civil War Narrative by Brevet Major Charles Dana Miller, 76th Ohio Volunteer Infantry*, ed. Stewart Bennett and Barbara Tillery (Kent, Ohio: Kent State University Press, 2004), 92; Bearss, *Campaign for Vicksburg*, 2: 451–52; Winschel, *Triumph and Defeat*, 2: 15–17; Bearss and Hills, *Receding Tide*, 163.

28. *OR*, vol. 25, pt. 2: 434; Noah Brooks, *Washington, D.C., in Lincoln's Time*, 3rd ed. (Chicago: Quadrangle Books, 1971), 61–62; Ernest B. Furguson, *Chancellorsville, 1863: The Souls of the Brave* (New York: Alfred A. Knopf, 1992), 319; Bearss and Hills, *Receding Tide*, 152.

---

29. *OR*, vol. 24, pt. 3: 840; ibid., vol. 15: 1076; Barber, *Holding the Line*, 117–19; Davidson, *The Annals of the Army of Tennessee*, 166–67. Captain Flavel C. Barber wrote, "The commissary had failed to provide sufficient rations and the men often went supperless to bed" (119). Private W. J. Davidson wrote that the men were "breaking down under the unaccustomed loads" (166).

30. *OR*, vol. 24, pt. 1: 35; Henderson, *Science of War*, 189.

31. Lieutenant S. C. Jones, *Reminiscences of the Twenty-Second Iowa Volunteer Infantry* (Iowa City: S. C. Jones, 1907), 32; *OR*, vol. 24, pt. 2: 134; pt. 3: 279; Captain Marcus Spiegel, *Your True Marcus: The Civil War Letters of a Jewish Colonel*, ed. Frank L. Byrne and Jean P. Soman (Kent, OH: Kent State University Press, 1985), 275; *OR*, vol. 24, pt. 1: 85, 645, 723; Bearss, *Campaign for Vicksburg*, 2: 459–60; Dana, *Recollections*, 50; Loop, *The Long Road Home*, 79; Campbell, *The Union Must Stand*, 93; Oldroyd, *A Soldier's Story*, 10.

32. Brown, *Grierson's Raid*, 182–83; *OR*, vol. 24, pt. 1: 527; Bearss, *Campaign for Vicksburg*, 2: 226; Barber, *Holding the Line*, 119; Davidson, *The Annals of the Army of Tennessee*, 167; Carter, *Two Stars in the Southern Sky*, 154; Gower, *Pen and Sword*, 85; Oldroyd, *A Soldier's Story*, 10; Victor M. Rose, *Ross' Texas Brigade: Being a Narrative of Events Connected with Its Service in the Late War between the States* (Louisville, Ky.: Courier Journal Book and Job Rooms, 1881), 99–102.

33. *OR*, vol. 24, pt. 3: 277, 835, 843; Bearss, *Campaign for Vicksburg*, 2: 445, 453, 455–56.

34. Bearss, *Campaign for Vicksburg*, 2, 455-56; *OR*, vol. 24. pt. 1: 259; ibid., pt. 3: 842.

35. Loop, *The Long Road Home*, 79; Campbell, *The Union Must Stand*, 93; Meyer, *Iowa Valor*, 188; Jones, *Reminiscences of the Twenty-Second Iowa Volunteer Infantry*, 32; Oldroyd, *A Soldier's Story*, 10–11; Geer, *The Civil War Diary of Allen Morgan Geer*, ed. Mary Ann Andersen (Bloomington, Ill.: McLean County Historical Society, 1977), 98; *OR*, vol. 24, pt. 1: 35; ibid., pt. 2: 12; Grant, *Grant Papers*, 8: 176; Ballard, *Vicksburg*, 257; Richard L. Kiper, *Major General John Alexander McClernand: Politician in Uniform* (Kent, Ohio: Kent State University Press, 1999), 234.

36. Barber, *Holding the Line*, 119; Davidson, *The Annals of the Army of Tennessee*, 167; Carter, *Two Stars in the Southern Sky*, 154; Gower, *Pen and Sword*, 85; *OR*, vol. 15: 1080; ibid., vol. 24, pt. 1: 259; ibid., pt. 3: 845; Bearss, *Campaign for Vicksburg*, 2: 456, 549. Maxey's brigade did not arrive in Hazlehurst, 30 miles south of Jackson, until May 14.

37. Oldroyd, *A Soldier's Story*, 11–12; Geer, *The Civil War Diary of Allen Morgan Geer*, 98. Crossroads is today known as Reganton. *OR*, vol. 24, pt. 1: 645, 759; ibid., pt. 3: 283, 287; Campbell, *The Union Must Stand*, 93; Badeau, *Military History*, 1: 231; Bearss, *Campaign for Vicksburg*, 2: 488; Force, "Personal Recollections of the Vicksburg Campaign," 298.

38. *OR*, vol. 24, pt. 1: 595, 636, 728; ibid., pt. 2: 12, 250; Bearss, *Campaign for Vicksburg*, 2: 463–64; Miller, *Struggle for the Life of the Republic*, 93; Badeau, *Military History*, 1: 232.

39. Gower, *Pen and Sword*, 85; Carter, *Two Stars in the Southern Sky*, 154; Barber, *Holding the Line*, 119; Davidson, *The Annals of the Army of Tennessee*, 167; *OR*, vol. 24, pt. 1: 736. The course of the Pearl River has since changed, and this site is now at Crystal Lake.

40. *OR*, vol. 24, pt. 3: 849; Bearss, *Campaign for Vicksburg*, 2: 475; Grabau, *Ninety-Eight Days*, 217.

41. Wilson, Journal of the Military Service, 43: 95–96; OR, vol. 24, pt. 1: 595; pt. 3: 284, 289; Bearss, Campaign for Vicksburg, 2: 465, 469; Wiley, The Civil War Diary of a Common Soldier, 46; Kiper, McClernand: Politician in Uniform, 235; Jones, Reminiscences of the Twenty-Second Iowa, 32–33; OR, vol. 24, pt. 1: 636, 735, 753, 759, 769, 772, 774, 779, 781; Grant, *Grant Papers*, 8: 192; OR, vol. 24, pt. 3: 289; Young, *Around the World*, 2: 615; Bearss and Hills, *Receding Tide*, 160; Grant, *Memoirs*, 1: 496; Badeau, *Military History*, 1: 232.

42. Geer, *The Civil War Diary of Allen Morgan Geer*, 98; OR, vol. 24, pt. 1: 636, 735, 772, 774, 779, 781; pt. 3: 290; Grant, *Grant Papers*, 8: 194; Bearss, *Campaign for Vicksburg*, 2: 488; Campbell, *The Union Must Stand*, 93; Loop, *The Long Road Home*, 81; Bearss and Hills, *Receding Tide*, 160.

43. Bearss and Hills, *Receding Tide*, 164; OR, vol. 24, pt. 3: 851, 853; Bearss, *Campaign for Vicksburg*, 2: 484; Grabau, *Ninety-Eight Days*, 219.

44. Grabau, *Ninety-Eight Days*, 214; Bearss, *Campaign for Vicksburg*, 2: 469; Grant, *Memoirs*, 1:492–493, 495, 542; Grant, *Grant Papers*, 8: 199; OR, vol. 24, pt. 1: 753; ibid., pt. 3: 284–86, 289–90, 296–97; General William T. Sherman, *Memoirs of General W. T. Sherman*, 2 vols. (4th ed., New York: Charles L. Webster, 1892), 1: 349; Charles King, *The True Ulysses S. Grant* (Philadelphia: J. B. Lippincott, 1914), 237; Badeau, *Military History*, 1: 228; Robert R. McCormick, *Ulysses S. Grant: The Great Soldier of America* (New York: D. Appleton-Century, 1934), 88–89. Before the transfer of artillery "to equalize the artillery" on May 11, Sherman had 6 brigades and 24 guns, McPherson had 6 brigades and 42 guns, and McClernand had 8 brigades and 52 guns.

45. Geer, *The Civil War Diary of Allen Morgan Geer*, 98; OR, vol. 24, pt. 1: 636, 728; Bearss, *Campaign for Vicksburg*, 2: 489; Major S. H. M. Byers, *With Fire and Sword* (New York: Neale Publishing, 1911), 68; Edmund Newsome, *Experience in the War of the Great Rebellion by a Soldier of the Eighty-first Regiment Illinois Volunteer Infantry* (Carbondale, Ill.: Edmund Newsome, 1880), 45; W. S. Morris, L. D. Hartwell, and J. B. Kuykendall, *History, 31st Regiment Illinois Volunteers* (2nd ed., Herrin, Ill.: Crossfire Press, 1991), 59–60; Oldroyd, *A Soldier's Story*, 13; Campbell, *The Union Must Stand*, 93; Loop, *The Long Road Home*, 81; Grabau, *Ninety-Eight Days*, 214, 222–23.

46. Grant, *Grant Papers*, 8: 200; OR, vol. 24, pt. 3: 297; Bearss, *Campaign for Vicksburg*, 2: 490.

47. OR, vol. 24, pt. 1: 35–36; Grant, *Grant Papers*, 8: 196; Badeau, *Military History*, 1: 234; Richardson, *Personal History*, 312; General Carl Von Clausewitz, *On War*, translated by Colonel J. J. Graham, 3 vols. (reprint, London: Kegan Paul, Trench, Trubner and Co., 1940), 1: 186.

48. OR, vol. 24, pt. 1: 736; Barber, *Holding the Line*, 119; Gower, *Pen and Sword*, 85; Carter, *Two Stars in the Southern Sky*, 155; Davidson, *The Annals of the Army of Tennessee*, 167; Drake, *In Their Own Words*, 23–25.

49. OR, vol. 24, pt. 3: 855–56; Bearss, *Campaign for Vicksburg*, 2: 477–78; Grabau, *Ninety-Eight Days*, 219–20.

50. Grabau, *Ninety-Eight Days*, 225; OR, vol. 24, pt. 1: 736; Bearss, *Campaign for Vicksburg*, 2: 484–85.

51. Bearss, *Campaign for Vicksburg*, 2: 490–91; *OR*, vol. 24, pt. 1: 637, 645–46, 714, 723, 735; Geer, The Civil War Diary of Allen Morgan Geer, 98; Force, "Personal Recollections of the Vicksburg Campaign," 298; Greene, *The Mississippi*, 142; Oldroyd, *A Soldier's Story*, 15; Grabau, *Ninety-Eight Days*, 222–23; Winschel, *Triumph and Defeat*, 2: 25; Bearss and Hills, *Receding Tide*, 170.

52. Bearss and Hills, *Receding Tide*, 168; *OR*, vol. 24, pt. 1: 737; Bearss, *Campaign for Vicksburg*, 2: 485–86; Griffin, "The Famous Tenth Tennessee."

53. Bearss, *Campaign for Vicksburg*, 2: 493–94; *OR*, vol. 24, pt. 1: 737; Bearss and Hills, *Receding Tide*, 168–70.

54. *OR*, vol. 24, pt. 1: 705–6, 739; Grant, *Memoirs*, 1: 497; Bearss, *Campaign for Vicksburg*, 2: 511; Bearss and Hills, *Receding Tide*, 178–79; Warren E. Grabau, *Confusion Compounded: The Pivotal Battle of Raymond, 12 May 1863*, Papers of the Blue and Gray Education Society, no. 12 (Saline, Mich.: McNaughton and Gunn, 2001), 26, 59.

55. *OR*, vol. 24, pt. 1: 50; ibid., pt. 3: 300–301; Grant, *Memoirs*, 1:499–500; Grant, *Grant Papers*, 8: 206–7; Bearss and Hills, *Receding Tide*, 179–80; Grabau, *Confusion Compounded*, 62–65.

56. Grant, *Memoirs*. 1: 542; Badeau, *Military History*, 1: 184–85; Young, *Around the World*, 2: 447.

5

THE FIRST CAPTURE AND OCCUPATION
OF JACKSON, MISSISSIPPI

Steven E. Woodworth

The surprising encounter between James B. McPherson's Seventeenth Corps and John Gregg's oversized Confederate brigade at Raymond, Mississippi, on May 12, 1863, brought the nearby capital city of Mississippi to the forefront of Grant's thinking. It was clear that Gregg's troops had marched from Jackson and must have been based there, and Grant could not escape the reflection that the town, which was in any case the rail and transportation hub of the region, might well become a base for further aggressive Confederate action. Such Rebel activity might become a severe nuisance or even threat to his rear as he faced Pemberton's field army and, later, the defenses of Vicksburg itself. Heightening Grant's concerns were reports he had recently received indicating that Confederate western theater commander Joseph E. Johnston was on his way to Jackson, along with reinforcements of unknown strength. Like most officers of the prewar United States Army, Grant was highly impressed with Johnston's intellect and skills as an officer. Grant believed Johnston in Jackson, whatever the force he might have with him, could be a much more serious threat than Pemberton and his army hovering somewhere off to the west near Edwards Station.

These reflections led Grant to the conclusion that he would have to neutralize Jackson before continuing with his campaign against Pemberton and Vicksburg. With that goal in mind, Grant on the evening of that same May 12 dispatched orders to his corps commanders changing the direction of his army's march from north to northeast and placing Jackson squarely in its sights. McPherson's Seventeenth Corps, which had been on the right front of Grant's advance, would turn toward the northeast and become the left wing of the advance on Jackson, while William T. Sherman's Fifteenth Corps, which had been in reserve, bringing up the rear in the march up from Bruinsburg, would forge ahead and move into position on McPherson's right, though out of sight, advancing on parallel roads that would lead it to the southwest side of Jackson while McPherson's corps approached the northwest side of town. John A. McClernand, whose Thirteenth Corps had been advancing on the army's left front would veer farther left, continuing north to take up a blocking position facing toward Pemberton. Grant and his staff had been riding with Sherman on May 12 and continued to do so as the army turned toward its new target.[1]

On May 13 McPherson's Seventeenth Corps marched northeast about eight miles to Clinton, Mississippi, traversing a landscape of prosperous farms and plantations. The weather was hot and dusty, as it had been for the past

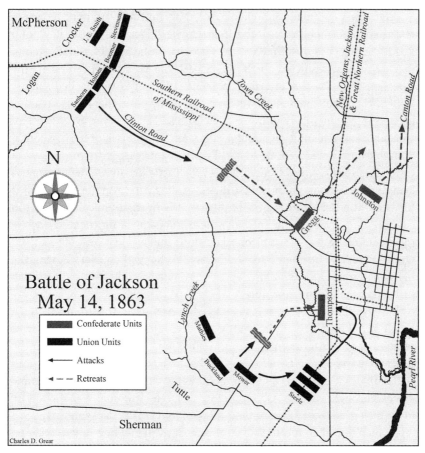

Battle of Jackson
May 14, 1863

Confederate Units
Union Units
Attacks
Retreats

Charles D. Grear

After the clash at Raymond, Grant decided to take on and neutralize Jackson before turning toward Vicksburg. At his orders William T. Sherman's Fifteenth Corps attacked the city from the south while McPherson's Seventeenth Corps stormed in from the west.

several days. Somewhat to the surprise of the Union soldiers, they encountered no significant opposition during the march. They noticed that the white inhabitants eyed their passage sullenly, the blacks hailed their coming joyfully. Clinton lay ten miles west-northwest of Jackson, on the line of the Southern Railroad of Mississippi, which connected Vicksburg with the state capital. Or it did before the blue-coats arrived. McPherson had his men tear up the railroad tracks and cut the telegraph wire that ran alongside them, cutting off Vicksburg from any sort of convenient communication with the rest of the Confederacy. Some of McPherson's men also captured dispatches that Pemberton had sent to John Gregg, who had commanded the Confederate brigade at Raymond the day before and had retreated back to Jackson afterward.[2]

Sherman's command marched to Raymond and after an hour or two of rest there, continued its march directly toward Jackson via the Raymond Road, keeping pace with McPherson, who with his head start from Raymond that morning had shifted north to approach the Mississippi capital via the Clinton Road. Late that afternoon the Fifteenth Corps approached Mississippi Springs, not the modern town of that name but rather a different one located about ten miles southwest of Jackson and about seven miles south of Clinton. Near a plantation about a mile short of Mississippi Springs, Sherman's advance guard about 5 P.M. skirmished briskly with an outpost of Confederates. Brigadier General James M. Tuttle, commanding Sherman's lead division, shook out a full regiment in skirmish formation and sent it forward. The Rebels beat a hasty retreat. The head of Sherman's column advanced into Mississippi Springs, where it encamped for the night, while the rest of Sherman's corps bivouacked along the road just west of town. On Grant's orders, Sherman and McPherson exchanged couriers during the night, with messages arranging for a coordinated simultaneous advance on Jackson the following morning.[3]

Heavy rains moved across the region that evening and continued through much of the next day, transforming the deep dust on the roads to mud at least as deep. Both Sherman's and McPherson's corps broke camp in the downpour and were on the roads again before 6:00 A.M., Grant and his staff still riding with Sherman's column. Slogging through mud and, in some places, through water as much as a foot deep, the Union foot soldiers were nevertheless exuberant about their mission for that day. Jackson had been a goal much talked about in the army since Corinth had first fallen to Union troops almost a year before. There had been many times over the intervening months that it hardly seemed likely they would ever reach the capital of Mississippi, "and now that we were but 10 miles from it," an Indiana soldier explained in a letter home, "you may believe we were in high spirits."[4]

Here and there at houses along the route of march, Mississippi women stood in their doorways, watching the rain-sodden blue-coats tramp by in the downpour. Some of the women shouted taunts at the passing soldiers, predicting they would be thrashed when they got to Jackson. Nothing could damp the northern men's spirits this day, however, not the torrential Mississippi rain and certainly not the disdain of its women. A soldier in the 8th Illinois noted that his comrades' only response was to keep marching and occasionally sing a patriotic song or two.[5]

Awaiting them in Jackson was Gregg's command, reinforced to a total of about six thousand men but still badly outnumbered by each of the Union columns now approaching the town. Also in Jackson was Johnston, who had arrived just the day before in response to a direct order from Confederate president Jefferson Davis.

Davis had assigned Johnston to oversee Confederate operations in the cis-Mississippi West the proceeding November in hopes that he would use his renowned military knowledge and skill to coordinate the activities of the Confederacy's two major armies in the region, Pemberton's command in Mississippi and General Braxton Bragg's Army of Tennessee, then encamped about thirty miles southeast of Nashville near the town of Murfreesboro. Johnston considered the arrangement flawed and had told Davis so from the outset. Davis had insisted on assigning Johnston anyway, and the Virginia general had responded with sullenness and a bare minimum of cooperation. Unable to get Johnston to use the command as he meant him to use it and yet unwilling to replace the haughty general with someone who would, Davis resorted to trying to exercise command of Confederate forces in the heartland over Johnston's shoulder, as it were, from Richmond, 500 miles from Murfreesboro and more than 800 from Vicksburg.

The results had not been happy for the Confederacy. In December 1862, when Grant and Sherman's combined inland and river-borne offensives seemed to threaten Vicksburg, Davis had insisted, against Johnston's and Bragg's advice, on ordering Bragg to send a quarter of his infantry to reinforce Pemberton. As events turned out, Pemberton did not need the extra troops, but Bragg did. His under-strength army narrowly lost the year-end Battle of Stones River, and he had to fall back forty miles to Tullahoma. That winter, bickering within the high command of the Army of Tennessee had become so intense that Davis had lost confidence in Bragg and ordered Johnston to Bragg's headquarters to relieve him. Johnston went but refused to relieve Bragg, delaying and temporizing until Davis gave up. Johnston was still at Tullahoma when the deteriorating situation in Mississippi prompted Davis on May 9 to order him to that state. On arriving in Jackson five days later

Johnston had hardly taken time to familiarize himself with the operational situation in the state before he telegraphed Secretary of War James A. Seddon in Richmond to say that with Grant's army between Jackson and Vicksburg, all was lost. "I am too late."[6]

That was classic Johnston style. It was important to him to establish in advance that the situation was hopeless and that Vicksburg could not be saved, so that he could not be blamed for whatever might go wrong. In fact, it was not too late to save Vicksburg—not quite—but with that attitude Johnston could certainly help to make it so over the course of the next few days. Whether it was too late to save Jackson was another story. Grant could be expected on May 14, but so could heavy Confederate reinforcements. Nevertheless, Johnston's first exercise of command in Mississippi was another of his trademark moves, ordering Confederate troops to pull out of the state capital. Somewhat less characteristically, Johnston decided not to depart so hastily as to abandon the valuable supplies and wagons in the town. He therefore ordered Gregg to deploy his troops so as to keep Grant's columns out of Jackson until the wagons could be loaded and could make their escape.[7]

At three o'clock on the morning of May 14, Gregg began giving the orders that would deploy his troops for the temporary defense of the Mississippi capital. He personally positioned the brigade of Colonel Peyton H. Colquitt three miles east of Jackson on the Clinton Road to counter the Union column that scouts had reported in that nearby town. He placed the brigade of Brigadier General William H. T. Walker in rear of Colquitt with orders to support him. In response to new scouting reports indicating another Union column advancing up the road from Mississippi Springs, Gregg dispatched Colonel Albert P. Thompson's 3rd Kentucky Mounted Infantry to take up a defensive position about two miles out the road in that direction. To support Thompson's badly outnumbered horsemen, Gregg detached a battalion of sharpshooters and a battery of artillery from Walker's brigade and sent them hurrying after the Kentuckians. Still worrying chiefly about the force reported to be on the way from Clinton, Gregg ordered Colonel Robert Farquharson, commanding Gregg's own large brigade, to take it out the Clinton Road and position it on Colquitt's right so as to threaten the flank of any comparably sized Union force that might move against Colquitt directly up the road toward Jackson.[8]

At about nine o'clock, marching up the road from Clinton through the driving sheets of rain behind a heavy screen of skirmishers came members of the 10th Missouri. The Missourians exchanged fire with the defending Confederates and then fell back to join their regiment as Colonel

Samuel A. Holmes's brigade, which led McPherson's column that morning, deployed into line of battle on either side of the road. Minutes later the other two brigades of Brigadier General Marcellus Crocker's division moved up and deployed on either side of Holmes, Colonel George Boomer's on his left and Colonel John Sanborn's on his right. Logan's division then moved up and came into line on the right of Crocker's, extending McPherson's line in the direction of Sherman's Fifteenth Corps to the south. This line was far too extended for Farquharson to flank.[9]

Artillery opened up on both sides, but the ongoing thunderstorm was so intense that soldiers had difficulty discerning the sound of the guns from the crash of the thunder. The Federals advanced until they were about five hundred yards from the Confederate line, and then the Union officers ordered their men to go to ground for protection from the Rebel artillery fire while the skirmishers further developed the extent of the Confederate position. The ground was muddy, but hugging it beat standing as a target for the Rebel gunners.[10]

While they waited, trouble developed near the point where Sanborn's brigade of Crocker's division joined Brigadier General John E. Smith's brigade of Logan's. Afterward several stories made the rounds among the troops as to how it had started. One account had it that a soldier of the 48th Indiana had taken advantage of the pause to rob a nearby beehive, and the bees had taken offense. An alternate version was that a stray shell fragment had ripped through the hive. It was apparently all the same to the bees, who swarmed out of their hive bent on vengeance. "Men can stand up and be shot at all day with the deadly musket," an Illinois soldier later explained, "but when a swarm of bees pounces upon a company of men in concert, it's beyond human nature to stand it." Fortunately the Confederates, if they noticed the affair, were not present in sufficient strength to take advantage of the temporary confusion in the Union lines. Some minutes later the officers managed to re-form their line, though with an indentation to give the bees a wide berth.[11]

While McPherson's troops were deploying and advancing to their position just beyond the effective range of the Confederate riflemen, Sherman's column was making contact and beginning its own deployment on the Raymond Road. So well had Sherman and McPherson coordinated their arrivals via separate roads that Gregg noted in his report the outbreak of firing on Sherman's front only "a few minutes" after his guns had opened up on McPherson's advancing Federals. Sherman reported hearing McPherson's guns at "about 10 A.M.," just before his own cavalry encountered Confederates, and John Sanborn, one of Crocker's brigade commanders, noticed the sound of Sherman's guns, a mile or two away, after the fight along the Clinton Road was well underway.[12]

Brigadier General James M. Tuttle's division was first in Sherman's column that day, and Tuttle quickly deployed it for battle with two brigades in line, one on either side of the road, and a third brigade in reserve behind them. He deployed two batteries of artillery near the road itself, between Tuttle's two lead brigades. Sherman's cannon had little difficulty silencing their Confederate counterparts, and after a fairly brief skirmish the entire Confederate line fell back into the woods behind them. Sherman's command followed but was delayed by a deep creek, crossable only via the bridge on the road. The Confederates had left the bridge intact, but it took time for Tuttle's division to file across it and then redeploy on the far side. The Federals advanced through the woods and emerged on the far side to find that the Rebels had retreated into an extensive system of fortifications that had obviously been built some time before. The breastworks stretched as far as Sherman could see to either side of the road, and their presence gave him pause.[13]

Sherman arranged Tuttle's division in preparation for an assault on the Rebel works, and Grant personally helped guide the 95th Ohio to its jumping-off point on the right end of Sherman's line. The paucity of Confederate numbers dawned on several of Sherman's officers at about the same time. Officers of the 95th sent back word that beyond a short distance from the road itself the works stood empty. Major General Frederick Steele's division was just then arriving behind Tuttle's, and Sherman dispatched it to the right to drive through the empty section of line and flank the defenders of the road. Meanwhile, Brigadier General Joseph Mower, commanding one of Tuttle's two lead brigades, rode forward to make a reconnaissance of his own. He soon came galloping back and announced to the men of his brigade, "Boys, we can take those works and not half try."[14]

The various troop movements necessary to deploy two divisions of the Seventeenth Corps and two of the Fifteenth across sodden fields while one thunderstorm after another rolled across the central Mississippi countryside took a considerable amount of time, and by the time it was done, mid-morning had passed into mid-afternoon. Sherman and McPherson may have coordinated their attacks by courier, or it may be that a lull in the rain that set in about that time, complete with a glimpse of the sun through a rift in the clouds, may have been an opportunity that both corps commanders took to launch their final assaults on Jackson. Over on the Clinton Road, where the men of Crocker's division lay prone on the sodden ground, "flattened out," as an Iowa soldier described it, to avoid the fire of the Confederate artillery still blazing away, the order to fix bayonets passed along the line, and the men obeyed while still hugging the ground. Then came the order "to charge at double-quick," and then men rose and rushed forward, yelling "like Indians."[15]

In the fields flanking the Raymond Road, Sherman rode along the line of Mower's brigade together with its commander as Mower gave his men their final orders for the attack. "Attention! Fix bayonets—Forward—Double-quick—Now, steady, boys! Keep your alignment—March!" Mower's final word was the execute order for his previous "Forward, Double-quick," and at its sound his Eagle Brigade swept forward across an open field toward the Confederate breastworks. One of Mower's regiments was the 8th Wisconsin, and alongside its national and regimental colors advanced another bearer with a similar pole on top of which, tethered to a perch, sat Abe, the live eagle who was the mascot of the regiment and the pride of the whole Eagle Brigade, spreading his wings in excitement as an enormous cheer went up from the whole Union line. Sherman, who by this time was a few yards to the rear of Tuttle's charging troops, could also hear Steele's men cheering as they swept over the empty breastworks farther to the right. The 95th Ohio encountered a similar situation in its front, charging through house yards, trampling fences, and swarming over earthen ramparts that had no defenders. Soon the rest of Sherman's troops caught sight of the 95th's flag waving behind the breastworks.[16]

Inside the city, Gregg had by that time received word that the Confederate supply wagons were on their way and that he could now afford to withdraw and abandon the Mississippi capital. He gave the order for his troops to retire and later proudly reported that they had withdrawn in good order, not driven by the enemy, but in fact some Confederate troops remained in their positions to contest the final Union advance, particularly in the immediate vicinity of the Clinton Road. The 17th Iowa, whose line straddled the road itself, took heavy casualties when a Rebel gunner fired a cannon loaded with canister into the regiment's ranks from a range of only about twenty yards. The blast felled eighteen or twenty of the charging Iowans. The 17th suffered more severely than any other Union regiment in the brief assault at Jackson. Its dead and wounded totaled 80 men, which was 27 percent of all the casualties suffered by Grant's forces at Jackson and 23 percent of the 350 men the regiment had carried into battle that day. The 17th Iowa captured the gun that had done the final execution in its ranks as well as three others, all of them still warm from firing and several of them still loaded. The Iowans turned them around and discharged them at the retreating Confederates. Then the survivors of the regiment gathered around their colors and sang, "Rally Round the Flag."[17]

Elsewhere along the lines, charging Union troops encountered differing degrees of resistance. On either end of McPherson's line, the Federals found the earthworks empty and the Rebel skirmishers scampering for the rear. Close to the Clinton Road, where the Confederate artillery was posted, the

Rebels made a brief but futile resistance. "The loud shouts along our lines told the fate of the day," wrote an Illinois officer in his diary that night. In all, the Union losses in the operations around Jackson, from the first encounter with Confederate skirmishers several miles out to the final rush over the breastworks, came to exactly 300 men killed, wounded, and missing, 265 of them in Crocker's division on the Clinton Road. Confederate losses were more than twice that many, as some of Gregg's troops apparently did not leave their breastworks soon enough or retire rapidly enough to escape Grant's charging Federals. Grant's men also captured nearly all of the cannon deployed against them in defense of Jackson, giving the lie to Gregg's rather glib report that his troops had retreated only on his command and "in excellent order." On the other hand, the fact that the Confederate wagon train was not captured does tend to bear out Gregg's claim that he had held the works as long as he needed to and had initiated the retreat of his own accord. Nevertheless the Federals had hastened the withdrawal and inflicted some punishment on the retiring Confederates.[18]

The fight outside Jackson had not amounted to much of a battle, but it had accomplished something for each side. Aided by the pouring rain and sodden ground, the Confederates had saved much-needed supplies and wagons. On the other side of the ledger, the Federals had taken eighteen cannon in the fight, and these were guns the Confederates could almost certainly have saved had they not chosen to attempt to delay Union entry into the Mississippi capital. Beyond this, the fight gave the Union troops an additional boost to their already high morale. Jackson was the second Confederate state capital to fall to the Army of the Tennessee and only the third to fall to Union forces overall. Not surprisingly, those Federals who had been engaged at Jackson viewed the capture of the town as a much more serious fight than it had actually been, and in their letters and diaries written at the time they expressed a supreme confidence that they could and would whip the Rebels every time they met. "We drove them from Jackson and took possession with great cheering," a Missouri soldier wrote to his wife. An Iowan wrote in his diary, "This brigade made a gallant charge and routed the enemy and sent them flying into Jackson." And an Illinoisan summed it up succinctly in his diary: "The rebels [were] licked, running as usual or captured."[19]

The morale boost was not absolutely necessary in an organization such at the Army of the Tennessee, which by then had extremely high morale, but it was no doubt helpful. The Seventh Division, Crocker's, played an important part in the decisive Battle of Champion Hill two days later. Its Second Brigade, under Holmes, which overran the Confederate defenses adjacent to the Clinton Road at Jackson, played a particularly crucial role at Champion

Hill in turning back a Confederate attack at a time when the tide of battle seemed to have turned against the Union. Holmes's men, along with the rest of Crocker's division, would probably have done their duty at Champion Hill even if they had strolled into Jackson unopposed two days before, but the added boost to their confidence gained by seeing the Rebels running, leaving their cannon behind, could only have strengthened their expectation that they would whip the enemy at every encounter. As one of McPherson's officers wrote after the fight at Jackson, "The only wish expressed [by the troops] is to be led into the fight."[20]

Champion Hill was still in the future, of course, as the Federals pursued the fleeing Confederates into Jackson on the afternoon of May 14 or else rested and re-grouped outside the town. While the 17th Iowa sang "Rally Round the Flag" out on the Clinton Road, several other units rushed into Jackson, and in later years their members waged long wars of words in the pages of veterans' publications as to which regiment had been first to enter and which had raised its flag above the cupola of the Mississippi state capitol. Indeed so insistent were the claims as to raise the question of whether some of the Federals might have mistaken the Jackson city hall for the state capitol.[21]

Grant and his staff rode to the State House, and Sherman soon followed. Assured that his troops had overrun the defenses on both fronts, Grant ordered a brigade of Logan's division to hasten to the east side of town and, if possible, cut off the retreat of Gregg's Confederates. It proved impossible, as Gregg's men already had too large a head start, though the Federals came near snaring them. Next, some of Grant's troops at once had to go to work to put out fires that the Confederates had lit on the way out of town for the purpose of destroying food and equipment they were leaving behind. The town of Jackson would see a fair number of fires started in it over the course of three Union occupations in the next nine months. It was ironic that the first soldiers to set fire to structures in the town were Confederate and the first soldiers to fight the fires, Union.[22]

That afternoon, Grant and Sherman visited a textile mill. Outside the plant was "an immense amount of cotton," stacked in bales. Inside, a large number of workers, mostly young women, continued working diligently at their looms, apparently oblivious of the cannonading on the outskirts of town during the middle part of the day. Perhaps the sound of the guns had blended with that of the thunderstorm. Busy with their machinery, the workers and their supervisors took no notice of the two Union generals laconically watching their labors. From the looms emerged bolt after bolt of tent cloth with the letters "C.S.A." woven into each. After watching for some time, Grant remarked quietly to Sherman that he thought the women "had done work enough." Before sending them home, Grant made sure that each operative was permitted to take with her as much of the cloth as she could carry. Then with the building empty, Union troops torched it and the stockpile of cotton outside.[23]

Back on the town's central square, opposite the State House, Grant selected the Bowman House Hotel as his headquarters and then sent word for Sherman and McPherson to meet him there to discuss the army's next moves. McPherson had recently received from a Union spy a copy (one of three) of a dispatch of the previous day from Johnston to Pemberton directing the latter to try to strike Grant near Clinton and promising the cooperation of the troops under his, Johnston's, command.[24]

Unknown either to Grant or to Pemberton, Johnston had no intention of trying to cooperate with his hapless subordinate, whom he thus hung out to dry. He would march off to the north, farther from Pemberton with every mile. Pemberton could march and fight or sit still and rot for all Johnston cared. The Virginian would be far away and thus could claim not to have been responsible for whatever happened—unless it were a victory. Like most officers of the Old Army who had known Johnston when less responsibility rested on the Virginian's shoulders, Grant overestimated him. On the other hand, Grant, knowing that Pemberton had almost certainly received at least one of the other two copies of Johnston's dispatch, had a fairly good idea of how Pemberton would act and rightly judged that the commander of the Confederate army guarding Vicksburg would, in response to Johnston's order, feel compelled to come out and fight. In preparation for that event, Grant ordered McPherson to take the Seventeenth Corps back west to join McClernand in confronting Pemberton's expected advance. This time Grant would ride with McPherson. Meanwhile, Grant assigned Sherman to stay behind at Jackson, as Sherman later put it, "to break up railroads, to destroy the arsenal, a foundery," and generally render the city at least temporarily ineffective as a base of Confederate operations.[25]

That night Grant enjoyed the luxury of the rare opportunity for a bath at the Bowman House and then slept in the same room Johnston had occupied the night before, presumably the best in the house, while the various units under his command made themselves comfortable in various locations and public buildings around the city and its environs. The 31st Illinois camped in the capitol square, while the 8th Wisconsin, the "Eagle Regiment," made its headquarters in the State House itself. Elsewhere in the building however, apparently in the assembly chamber, soldiers from various regiments held a mock legislative session "and passed an act to pay the boys off, which was done in Confederate scrip, there being any quantity of it," as an Iowa soldier wrote many years later. "If it had been worth anything," he added, "we would have been rich." As it was, however, the five-hundred- and one-thousand-dollar Confederate bills were about the right value for use in lighting a pipe. And the smokers among the soldiers found themselves well supplied, as Jackson contained large amounts of cigars and pipe tobacco.[26]

Next morning the Seventeenth Corps continued its westward march under cloudy skies but without the rain that had soaked the columns the day before. The soldiers found it a pleasant change from both the storms and the brutal heat of recent days. They marched along amid wispy bluish clouds of tobacco smoke generated as the smokers among them puffed away at their share of booty from Jackson. Grant stayed a few hours after the corps had marched, making final consultations with Sherman, and then left and caught up with McPherson on the road.[27]

While McPherson's troops marched toward their appointment with Pemberton at Champion Hill, Sherman's corps got down to the work of serious destruction. Railroad tracks were the top-priority target. Railroads entered Jackson from north, south, east, and west, and Sherman detailed troops to tear up all four lines. Brigadier General Charles L. Matthies's brigade drew the duty of destroying the Mississippi Central, the north-south line, while Brigadier General Ralph P. Buckland's received the highly important assignment of destroying the Southern Railroad of Mississippi leading west from Jackson toward Vicksburg. It was important to do the work of destruction thoroughly on the railroads, since relatively small breaks in the tracks could be quickly repaired. Thus Sherman wanted his men to tear up as much track as possible, even though McPherson's troops had already broken the tracks of the Southern Railroad of Mississippi at Clinton two days before.[28]

Buckland led his brigade out to the west of town with some misgivings about its ability to perform its important task because it had only four axes among all four regiments, and those Buckland had borrowed from one of the artillery batteries. To his delight, his men found five or six axes and about that many picks in an abandoned Confederate camp. With the Rebels thus having supplied the tools, Buckland's men got down to the work of destruction, tearing up the tracks, piling the ties, and laying the rails on top of the piles so that when the piles burned the heated rails would sag at the ends and bend in the middle. Thus they proceeded, working their way west toward Vicksburg until by evening they had disassembled four miles of track. While the track details had been busy, a foraging party Buckland sent out had collected plenty of cattle and sheep to feed the brigade that evening, though the men had no bread, of which the neighborhood seemed to offer little. The next morning Buckland had them at work on the railroad again, and by early afternoon they had reached Clinton, having wrecked a total of six miles of track between that point and Jackson.[29]

While Buckland's brigade was thus engaged, Matthies took his brigade five miles out the Mississippi Central north of Jackson and began a similar process. By day's end Matthies could report proudly that "every tie was burned and every rail bent" for a distance of three miles. That evening Matthies led his brigade back to Jackson to camp within the earthworks there, bringing as prisoners fifteen Confederate stragglers his men had picked up during the course of the day.[30]

Captain Charles Miller of the 76th Ohio recalled that his regiment was involved in tearing up the Southern Railroad of Mississippi east of town. They crossed to the east side of the Pearl River, tore up half a mile of track, piled up the ties, and made bonfires of them. On their return to Jackson, they methodically destroyed the railroad bridge over the Pearl, throwing all of the iron into the river. Meanwhile other troops burned the arsenal, depots, machine shops, banks, and remaining cotton factories in the town, along with additional stocks of baled cotton. While destroying stockpiles of Confederate weapons they made the curious discovery of a large number of spears, produced early in the war on the theory that southern valor might make such arms effective against the Yankee hirelings. They had never been issued and joined the bonfire with the more practical weapons. One estimate of the damage was $10 million.[31]

While such official acts of military destruction were taking place, other of Sherman's soldiers seem to have had time for a considerable amount of extracurricular activity. "At Jackson we had a fine old time," wrote Iowa soldier Robert Hoadley. "The Soldiers was allowed to take whatever they wanted." Hoadley was not exactly correct about that, although the difference mattered little. Ohioan Frank Wise pointed out that in fact guards had been posted on many stores to try to prevent looting, but as Wise admitted, their efforts were generally ineffective. "The boys went for every thing in the town," an Ohio soldier wrote to his wife.[32]

As Iowa soldier Henry Ankeny succinctly summed it up, "The town was sacked." Stores were opened, and soldiers helped themselves to the wares, sometimes using their newly acquired wealth of banknotes in mock payment for the goods taken, much as Lee's soldiers would be doing in Pennsylvania the following month. Like them, Sherman's men had been marching hard in enemy's country at the end of a long and tenuous supply line. They had not always been eating well, and their clothes and shoes were often in very bad shape. Not surprisingly, then, clothing and food were prime targets for the plunderers. Human vice being what it is at most times and places, whiskey and tobacco were also much-prized booty. On the last day of the occupation, Captain Miller of the 76th Ohio visited the Mississippi State Library and found "the soldiers were helping themselves to books apparently without objections being made by General Sherman"—though the general was not present. Miller picked up "a few small volumes such as I could carry conveniently," but regretted that a number of large, expensive books were simply too bulky and heavy to carry on the marches he still had to make before he made contact with his baggage again.[33]

Besides appropriating large amounts for themselves, Hoadley noted that Sherman's men distributed much to "the poorer class of inhabitants." Ankeny corroborated that report: "The poor whites and negroes of course got all they wanted."[34]

Sherman had assigned Joseph Mower's Eagle Brigade, reinforced by two companies of cavalry, to serve as provost guard and keep order in Jackson during the Union occupation. Mower and his men had few equals as fighters, but this task had apparently been too much for them, probably because they were so badly outnumbered. Mower had "maintained as much order as he could among the mass of soldiers and camp-followers that thronged the place during our short stay there," Sherman reported, "yet many acts of pillage occurred that I regret." Sherman attributed the excesses to the soldiers' having found "some bad rum" in some of the stores in town.[35]

Off-duty soldiers were not the only people causing trouble for Mower's overworked provost guards. On the eve of the Union arrival in Jackson, Confederate authorities had released all the convicts in the state penitentiary on the condition that they would then fight to defend the capital from the Yankee invaders. Instead, most of them had deserted and were roving around the town and its environs bent on mischief. Some of them apparently torched their former home, the penitentiary and then impenitently watched it burn to the ground.[36]

The soldiers' private war against Jackson extended beyond the appropriation of portable property to the destruction of buildings. Besides the burning of the factories, depots, and other obvious military-economic targets, the men claimed to have torched a significant number of additional structures, both public and private. "All their public works were burned," wrote Ankeny. Wise noted that the fires had claimed "the state house and all the large buildings," and recalled several weeks later how he and his comrades had been "burning houses down" in Jackson. Hoadley added that not only had the soldiers burned "all of the public buildins" but also "moste of the Town." In fact, the State House did not burn, and neither did the governor's mansion nor city hall. Sherman noted in his report that a Catholic church building and one hotel had been burned in actions that were "not justified by the laws of war," though the former case had been an accident. Very likely a number of houses did burn, giving Jackson a good start it on the way to its wartime nickname, well earned by the time it fell for the third time to Union forces in February 1864, as "Chimneyville." Nevertheless it is interesting to note that the soldiers themselves overestimated the amount of arson they and their comrades had committed in Jackson.[37]

Sherman recalled in his memoirs how as he was about to leave Jackson on May 16, "a very fat man" hurried up to see him, anxiously inquiring whether his hotel was also doomed to the flames. He was, he assured the general, a good, loyal Union man. Sherman drily quipped that he could tell as much from hotel's signboard, where the name "United States Hotel" had been painted over but was still faintly visible beneath the newer paint of the current name, "Confederate Hotel." In fact, Sherman remembered the hotel from before the war, having dined there when passing through Jackson by rail in happier days. No, he assured the politically flexible hotelier, he had "not the least purpose" of burning his hotel. However, as the troops were preparing to march out of the town, flames began to sprout from the building, and it subsequently burned to the ground. "I never found out exactly who set it on fire," Sherman wrote in his memoirs many years later. Captain Miller of the 76th Ohio wrote of the incident in his own memoirs, noting simply that because of the obvious change in the hotel's sign, "the boys concluded that it had better close up business under its new title and accordingly applied the torch," though it is unclear whether he meant the boys involved were members of his own regiment.[38]

Sherman paroled the several hundred Confederate prisoners his men had taken in and around Jackson, both because they would have been an encumbrance to his corps's continued march and because he had no choice but to leave behind in Jackson a number of his own and McPherson's wounded men under the care of an army surgeon. The Rebels would resume control of the town after he left, and Sherman hoped they would reciprocate the lenient treatment he had shown their prisoners by paroling the wounded Federals and their surgeon. As it turned out later, the Confederates shipped them all to Richmond as prisoners of war.[39]

On the morning of May 16, Sherman received a message from Grant, who was then at Clinton, informing him that a battle was impending somewhere to the west. The note directed Sherman to put one of his divisions on the march to join Grant as soon as possible and to follow with the other division as soon as work in Jackson could be finished. Sherman started Steele's division on its way at 10:00 A.M., and Tuttle's followed at midday.[40]

One more incident of note occurred during the final minutes of this first Union occupation of the Mississippi capital. Mower's brigade, as provost guard, was last to leave the town. About a mile out of Jackson, Colonel John N. Cromwell of the 47th Illinois turned back. Accounts vary as to his purpose, with some reporting that he wanted to give some final words of encouragement to the wounded men who were left behind to become prisoners and others that he wanted to round up the few last stragglers from his regiment and the rest of the brigade. Very possibly it was both. The popular, thirty-three-year-old officer was riding along a Jackson street when a squad of Confederate cavalry emerged from a side street just ahead. What happened next was subsequently disputed. One story had it that Cromwell surrendered and was then murdered in cold blood. According to another version, however, the Rebels summoned him to surrender, but Cromwell had turned and put the spurs to his horse, only to fall dead a moment later in a fusillade of shots from the Confederate horsemen. Cromwell had been captured in the aftermath of the September 1862 Battle of Iuka, and after his exchange and return to duty, he had told fellow officers that he would never again allow the Rebels to take him alive.[41]

The proprietor of the Bowman House, a Mr. Daniels and, like Cromwell, a Mason, was eye-witness to the event. He recounted that Cromwell had dismounted and hitched his horse in front of a saloon and then gone in to see if any of his men were still there. Shouts warned of the Rebels' approach, and Cromwell dashed out, unhitched, mounted, and started to ride off. It was then that the Confederate troopers had emerged from a side street and called on Cromwell to halt and surrender. Daniels averred that Cromwell had halted and turned toward the Rebel horsemen, as though he were about to surrender, and Daniels believed the colonel was surrendering. Only then came the fatal fusillade.[42]

After the shooting, Cromwell was carried to the Bowman House, where he died. Daniels expressed the intention of laying the colonel to rest in the municipal burying ground. Angry townsmen warned him they would have no Yankee buried in their cemetery, but Daniels insisted. At an expense of one hundred dollars he purchased a coffin and had Cromwell interred in his own family plot in the cemetery. Other Masons may have attended, and an Episcopal clergyman later claimed to have officiated. Thereafter, however, Daniels was a marked man in Jackson, the target of persecution from his neighbors. Less than two months later, they burned down his hotel, making their own contribution to their town's transformation into Chimneyville. Back in the ranks of the 47th, news of the highly popular colonel's death reached his men before the end of the Vicksburg siege, leading to mutterings about revenge in the form of burning Jackson to the ground if they ever got there again. They did get there in July but did not carry out their threats.[43]

The battle and occupation of Jackson was a two-day chapter in Grant's whirlwind inland campaign to take Vicksburg. It was not the decisive battle of the campaign, but it did contribute to Grant's ultimate success. The relatively easy capture of the capital of Mississippi raised the already very high morale of the Union troops, helping to brace them even more stoutly for the trials of the unsuccessful May 19 and 22 assaults on the Vicksburg fortifications and of the prolonged siege that followed. Union possession and subsequent neutralization of Jackson as a Confederate depot and transportation hub completed the separation of Pemberton's forces from those with Johnston or on their way from the eastern Confederacy. The thoroughness of the destruction Sherman's men wrought on the arsenals, depots, and especially the railroads of Jackson deprived the Confederacy of a convenient base from which to support attempts to relieve beleaguered Vicksburg during the six-week siege that followed.

The soldiers' treatment of civilians and their property in Jackson, though no doubt thoroughly unpleasant for the inhabitants of the Mississippi capital, was not particularly out of the ordinary in terms of what armies routinely did in enemy territory. As compared to most other wars, it was unusual in that the persons of civilians, including women, were not molested. Property of course was destroyed, sometimes in ways that may have exceeded the strict limits of the laws of war, but such violations in regard to property were not at all uncommon by this stage of the conflict. Both Federals and Confederates had burned houses in Louisiana during the previous several months when it had suited their purposes or their fancies. As compared to Lee's march through Pennsylvania the following month, the occupation of Jackson exposed civilians to somewhat more danger of having their houses burned but much less—precisely zero—risk of being kidnapped and carried off into slavery. Plundering was probably about the same in both operations.

As for what happened to Colonel Cromwell, if, as seems likely, he was shot while attempting to surrender, it was a clear-cut violation of the laws of war and may have revealed an early stage of what would later become a Confederate tendency to retaliate against Union destruction of property by the murder of Union prisoners. In any case, although the events in Jackson in May 1863 marked no dramatic departure from the previous practices, they were clearly consistent with a gradual drift into a level of conflict that was increasingly brutal and less restrained.

Notes

1. Ulysses S. Grant, *Personal Memoirs of U. S. Grant*, vol. 1 (New York, 1982), 499–500; John Y. Simon, ed., *The Papers of Ulysses S. Grant*, vol. 8 (Carbondale: Southern Illinois University Press, 1979), 204–8; Edwin C. Bearss, *The Vicksburg Campaign* (Dayton, Ohio, 1985), 512–14; Israel M. Ritter Diary, May 13, 1863, Civil War Miscellaneous Collection, U.S. Army Military History Institute, Carlisle, Pa,; William Tecumseh Sherman, *Memoirs* (New York: Library of America, 1990), 347.

2. U.S. War Department, *The War of the Rebellion: A Compilation of the Official Records of the Union and Confederate Armies*, 128 vols. (Washington, DC: GPO, 1880–1901), vol. 24, pt. 1: 50, 771, 775. (Hereafter cited as *OR*. All citations refer to series 1); Thomas N. McCleur Diary, May 13, 1863, Jackson County Historical Society, Murphysboro, Ill.; Joseph B. Williamson Diary, May 13, 1863, Illinois State Historical Library, Springfield; Edward P. Stanfield to "Dear Father," May 26, 1863, Edward P. Stanfield Papers, Indiana Historical Society, Indianapolis; Luther H. Cowan Diary, May 13, 1863, Wisconsin Historical Society, Madison; Isaac Vanderwarker Diary, May 13, 1863, Civil War Miscellaneous Collection, U.S. Army Military History Institute, Carlisle, Pa.; Campbell, John Quincy Adams Campbell, *The Union Must Stand: The Civil War Diary of John Quincy Adams Campbell, Fifth Iowa Volunteer Infantry*, ed. Mark Grimsley and Todd D. Miller (Knoxville: University of Tennessee Press, 2000), 93–94; W. S. Morris, L. D. Hartwell, and J. B. Kuykendall, *History of the 31st Regiment Illinois Volunteers* (Carbondale: Southern Illinois University Press, 1998; originally published 1902), 61–62.

3. *OR* vol. 24, pt. 1: 753, 759, 767, 769; S. C. Miles, "Capture of Jackson," *National Tribune*, July 27, 1893, p. 3; U. S. Grant, *Personal Memoirs*, 1:501; Edward P. Stanfield to "Dear Father," May 26, 1863, Edward P. Stanfield Papers, Indiana Historical Society, Indianapolis; Simon, *Papers of Grant*, 8:212; Morris, Hartwell, and Kuykendall, *History of the 31st Regiment*, 61–62; Campbell, *The Union Must Stand*, 93–94.

4. L. F. Parrish, "At Jackson," *National Tribune*, May 14, 1863, 3; Miles, "Capture of Jackson"; Frederick D. Grant, "Ulysses S. Grant: His Son's Memories of Him in the Field," *National Tribune*, January 27, 1887, 1; *OR* vol. 24, pt. 1: 50, 753; U. S. Grant, *Personal Memoirs*, 1:503–4; Sherman, *Memoirs*, 347; Simon, *Papers of Grant*, 8:212; Edward P. Stanfield to "Dear Father," May 26, 1863, Edward P. Stanfield Papers, Indiana Historical Society, Indianapolis.

5. James W. Jesse, *Civil War Diaries of James W. Jessee, 1861–1865, Company K, 8th Regiment of Illinois Volunteer Infantry*, ed. William P. LaBounty (Normal, IL: McLean County Genealogical Society, 1997) chapter 3, pp. 19–20.

6. *OR* vol. 24, pt. 1: 215.

7. Ibid., 785.

8. Ibid., 785–86.

9. Ibid., 775; Miles, "Capture of Jackson."

10. *OR* vol. 24, pt. 1: 775; Edward P. Stanfield to "Dear Father," May 26, 1863, Edward P. Stanfield Papers, Indiana Historical Society, Indianapolis; John B. Sanborn, "The Campaign against Vicksburg," *MOLLUS* 27: 130–31; Joseph J. Huston, "Who Planted the Flag at Jackson, Miss.?" *National Tribune*, February 19, 1885, 3.

11. Enoch Weiss Diary, May 14, 1863, Civil War Miscellaneous Collection, U.S. Army Military History Institute, Carlisle, Pa.; Wilber F. Crummer, *With Grant at Fort Donelson, Shiloh, and Vicksburg* (Oak Park, IL: E. C. Crummer & Co., 1915), 100–101.

12. *OR* vol. 24. pt. 1: 753, 786; Miles, "Capture of Jackson"; Sanborn, "The Campaign against Vicksburg."

13. *OR* vol. 24, pt. 1: 753.

14. Ibid., 753–54, 762; Burke, "The Ninety-fifth Ohio at Jackson, Miss.," *National Tribune*, May 1, 1884, 3; U. S. Grant, *Personal Memoirs*, 1: 505; Charles B. Clarke and Roger B. Bowman, *University Recruits: Company C, 12th Iowa Infantry Regiment, U.S.A., 1861–1866* (Elverson, PA: Mennonite Family History, 1991), 176; Byron Cloyd Bryner, *Bugle Echoes: The Story of Illinois 47th* (Springfield, IL: Phillips Bros., 1905), 79–80.

15. Miles, "Capture of Jackson"; R. W. Burt to "Dear Wife," May 23, 1863, R. W. Burt Letters, Western Historical Manuscript Collection, Ellis Library, University of Missouri, Columbia; L. F. Parrish, "At Jackson," *National Tribune*, May 14, 1863, 3.

16. Miles, "Capture of Jackson"; *OR* vol. 24, pt. 1: 754, 762; James H. Burke, "The 95th Ohio at Jackson, Miss.," *National Tribune*, May 14, 1884, 3.

17. *OR* vol. 24, pt. 1: 778, 786; Campbell, *The Union Must Stand*, 94–95; Parrish, "At Jackson."

18. Campbell, *The Union Must Stand*, 94–95; Luther H. Cowan Diary, May 14, 1863, Luther H. Cowan Papers, Wisconsin Historical Society, Madison; *OR* vol. 24, pt. 1: 751; U. S. Grant, *Personal Memoirs*, 1: 506; Stewart Bennett and Barbara Tillery, eds., *The Struggle for the Life of the Republic: A Civil War Narrative by Brevet Major Charles Dana Miller, 76th Ohio Volunteer Infantry* (Kent, Ohio: Kent State University Press, 2004), 94.

19. Bryner, *Bugle Echoes*, 79–80; Sherman, *Memoirs*, 347; R. W. Burt to "Dear Wife," May 23, 1863, R. W. Burt Letters, Western Historical Manuscript Collection, Ellis Library, University of Missouri, Columbia; Campbell, *The Union Must Stand*, 94–95; Luther H. Cowan Diary, May 14, 1863, Cowan Papers.

20. Luther H. Cowan Diary, May 14, 1863, Cowan Papers.

21. Frederick Dent Grant, "Ulysses S. Grant: His Son's Memoirs of Him in the Field," *National Tribune*, January 27, 1887, 1; C. B. Reese, "The First Troops in Jackson," *National Tribune*, March 6, 1884, 7; S. C. Miles, "Capture of Jackson," *National Tribune*, July 27, 1893, 3, and August 3, 1893, 3; Isaac Vanderwarker Diary, May 14, 1863, Isaac Vanderwarker Papers, Civil War Miscellaneous Collection, U.S. Army Military History Institute, Carlisle, Pa.; James H. Burke, "The 95th Ohio at Jackson, Miss.," *National Tribune*, May 14, 1884, 3; Campbell, *The Union Must Stand*, 95.

22. U. S. Grant, *Personal Memoirs*, 1: 506; Michael B. Ballard, *Vicksburg: The Campaign That Opened the Mississippi* (Chapel Hill: University of North Carolina Press, 2004), 278.

23. U. S. Grant, *Personal Memoirs*, 1: 507.

24. Sherman, *Memoirs*, 347; U. S. Grant, *Personal Memoirs*, 1: 507–8; F. D. Grant, "Ulysses S. Grant."

25. U. S. Grant, *Personal Memoirs*, 1:510; Sherman, *Memoirs*, 347.

26. U. S. Grant, *Personal Memoirs*, 1:506; F. D. Grant, "Ulysses S. Grant"; Bennett and Tillery, *Struggle for the Life of the Republic*, 94; John Melvin Williams, *The Eagle Regiment* (Belleville, Wisc.: Recorder Printing, 1890), 16–17; Parrish, "At Jackson."

27. Sherman, *Memoirs*, 347; Isaac Vanderwarker Diary, May 15, 1863, Vanderwarker Papers; Campbell, *The Union Must Stand*, 95; Parrish, "At Jackson," *National Tribune*, May 14, 1863, 3.

28. *OR* vol. 24, pt. 1: 759.

29. Ibid., 762–63.

30. Ibid., 770.

31. Bennett and Tillery, *Struggle for the Life of the Republic*, 94; Ballard, *Vicksburg*, 280; Williams, *The Eagle Regiment*, 16–17.

32. Robert Bruce Hoadley to "Dear Cousin," May 29, 1863, Robert Bruce Hoadley Papers, Perkins Library, Duke University; Franklin A. Wise Diary, May 15, 1863, Western Reserve Historical Society, Cleveland, Ohio; R. W. Burt to "Dear Wife," May 23, 1863, R. W. Burt Letters.

33. Henry G. Ankeny, *Kiss Josey for Me*, ed. Florence Marie Ankeny Cox (Santa Ana, Calif.: Friss-Pioneer Press, 1974), 156; Luther H. Cowan Diary, Mary 14, 1863,: Cowan Papers; Franklin A. Wise Diary, May 15, 1863, Western Reserve Historical Society, Cleveland, Ohio; Bennett and Tillery, eds., *The Struggle for the Life of the Republic*, 95.

34. Robert Bruce Hoadley to "Dear Cousin," May 29, 1863, Robert Bruce Hoadley Papers, Perkins Library, Duke University; Ankeny, *Kiss Josey for Me*, 156.

35. *OR* vol. 24, pt. 1: 754.

36. Bennett and Tillery, eds., *The Struggle for the Life of the Republic*, 94–95; Ballard, *Vicksburg* 280.

37. Ankeny, *Kiss Josey for Me*, 156; Franklin A. Wise Diary, May 16 and June 15, 1863, Western Reserve Historical Society, Cleveland, Ohio; Robert Bruce Hoadley to "Dear Cousin," May 29, 1863, Hoadley Papers; *OR* vol. 24, pt. 1, 754; Ballard, *Vicksburg*, 280.

38. Sherman, *Memoirs*, 347–48; Bennett and Tillery, *Struggle for the Life of the Republic*, 95.

39. *OR* vol. 24, pt. 1: 755.

40. Ibid., 754–55.

41. Robert J. Burdette, *Drums of the Forty-seventh* (Indianapolis: Bobbs-Merrill, 1914), 48–49; Bryner, *Bugle Echoes*, 81–82; Joe R. Vail to "Mrs. Cromwell," July 15, 1863, and Statement of Capt. John T. Bowman, Co. A, 47th Illinois, both in John Nelson Cromwell Papers, Illinois State Historical Library, Springfield

42. J. H. Hazen to Mrs. J. N. Cromwell, July 29, 1863, John Nelson Cromwell Papers, Illinois State Historical Library, Springfield.

43. Joe R. Vail to "Mrs. Cromwell," July 21, 1863; J. H. Hazen to Mrs. J. N. Cromwell, July 29, 1863. Statement of Capt. John T. Bowman, Co. A, 47th Illinois, all in John Nelson Cromwell Papers, Illinois State Historical Library; item about Cromwell in the *Peoria Daily Transcript*, June 23, 1863.

6

"I AM TOO LATE"
JOSEPH E. JOHNSTON AND THE VICKSBURG CAMPAIGN

John R. Lundberg

On the morning of May 9, 1863, a telegram arrived in Tullahoma, Tennessee, addressed to General Joseph E. Johnston. The telegram, written by Confederate secretary of war James A. Seddon, peremptorily ordered Johnston to: "Proceed at once to Mississippi and take chief command of the forces, giving to those in the field, as far as practicable, the encouragement and benefit of your personal direction." At 6:40 P.M. Johnston replied to Seddon: "I shall go immediately, although unfit for field service." With this melodramatic pronouncement, Johnston boarded a train bound for Mississippi on the morning of May 10.[1]

This exchange began the strange odyssey of General Joseph Johnston in the Vicksburg Campaign. Johnston possessed many talents as a general and a leader of men, but during the maneuvering for Vicksburg, he allowed the worst facets of his personality and short-sighted strategic goals to surface, resulting in disaster for the Confederate forces in the field. Although in command of all Confederate forces in Tennessee and Mississippi, Johnston never really took his imperative to hold the Hill City seriously due to his flawed understanding of the nature of war. He considered his troops in the field more important than holding key positions, no matter how vital. He believed in "concentration of force," to the detriment of all other factors, military and political, and he displayed from first to last his greatest weakness as a commander, a petty, selfish, and prevaricating nature.[2] In light of this attitude, Johnston remained so obsessed with his own reputation and his strategic vision for the war that he neglected his duties in Mississippi until it was almost too late. Then, when Johnston finally did travel to Mississippi, he did nothing but create confusion and chaos through his dereliction of duty. One of the great question marks of the American Civil War remains, What would have happened if Joseph Johnston had acted decisively and competently during the maneuvering for Vicksburg? Could Johnston have saved the city or materially altered Grant's unbroken string of successes? If Johnston had displayed a more proactive attitude toward his duties in Mississippi, the facts support the conclusion that he probably could have slowed down or temporarily stopped Grant's advance on Vicksburg.

Historians have divided sharply in their treatment of Johnston during the Civil War. Although most historians have come down negatively on him, there are some who, in recent years, have attempted to salvage his reputation, at least to a degree. Steven Newton, in his *Joseph E. Johnston and the Defense of Richmond*, Alan Downs in his essay "'The Responsibility Is Great': Joseph E. Johnston and the War in Virginia," and most notably, Craig Symonds in his *Joseph E. Johnston: A Civil War Biography* have all tried to rehabilitate Johnston in some way, with Symonds in particular focusing on Johnston's strategy as a case for vindication. However, none of them have tried seriously to defend Johnston's actions during the Vicksburg Campaign, and with good reason: his performance in the Vicksburg Campaign was the nadir of Johnston's service to the Confederacy. It is difficult to argue that Johnston provided any valuable service in fighting for the Gibraltar of the South, and in fact the only reasonable conclusion remains that dereliction of duty characterized all of his behavior from first to last. His actions yielded the initiative to Grant, compromised John C. Pemberton and his army, and generally resulted in chaos and dire results for the Confederacy.[3]

Johnston's actions in the Vicksburg Campaign reflected his earlier service to the Confederacy. In July 1861, he commanded the Confederate army that triumphed at the First Battle of Bull Run, but he followed this success with controversy. In the summer and fall of 1861, Johnston became embroiled in a feud with Confederate president Jefferson Davis over his rightful rank among Confederate generals. Johnston argued against Davis's interpretation of a law passed by the Confederate Congress naming him fourth, instead of first, on a list of five officers elevated to the rank of full general. This feud continually poisoned the relationship between Johnston and Davis, leading to mutual distrust and suspicion. To make matters worse, Johnston insisted on maintaining a close personal relationship with Texas senator Louis T. Wigfall, one of Davis's foremost critics. This mistrust and disagreement colored Johnston's actions in the Vicksburg Campaign.[4]

Despite this feud, Davis kept Johnston in command, and in the spring of 1862 the Virginian commanded the Confederate army facing Major General George McClellan's Union campaign up the Virginia Peninsula against the Confederate capital of Richmond. On May 31, after retreating all the way to the gates of Richmond, Johnston counterattacked McClellan in what became known as the Battle of Seven Pines. During the fighting, Johnston sustained serious wounds when a bullet struck his right shoulder and moments later a shell fragment struck the right side of his chest. These wounds broke his shoulder blade and two ribs and caused him a great deal of pain. Carried from the field, he recuperated in the home of Senator Wigfall in Richmond.[5]

Finally, on November 12, 1862, Johnston again reported for active duty, and twelve days later Davis assigned him to command the entire western department of the Confederacy, including the Army of Tennessee under Braxton Bragg in Tennessee and the forces under Lieutenant General John Pemberton in Mississippi. Johnston harbored grave doubts about the effectiveness of having the two parts of his command so widely spread apart, and he immediately began to advocate a concentration of *all* forces under his command to operate against Grant in Mississippi. Dourly, Johnston noted after the war, "This suggestion was not adopted, nor noticed."[6]

Davis ignored this request because such a concentration would open up large parts of the Confederacy to Union penetration. Davis understood the political imperative of holding as much territory as possible to maintain Confederate morale and protect vital industrial and strategic points. Johnston apparently never understood this imperative, and this lack of understanding hampered him throughout his command in the West. After this initial attempt at a proactive approach, he resigned himself merely to reacting to Davis's orders, refusing to take any independent action because he feared that without implementing his strategy he would lose Mississippi anyway, damaging his public reputation, and because if he did succeed in holding Vicksburg it would justify Davis's treatment of him.

On December 4, 1862, Johnston arrived at his new headquarters in Chattanooga, Tennessee, and for the next six months he continued to advocate a concentration of forces, complain about his assignment, and request that Davis relieve him of command. In mid-December Davis came to visit Johnston at Chattanooga, and the two visited Bragg's Army of Tennessee around Murfreesboro. At this time Pemberton, threatened by the forces of Grant and Sherman in Mississippi, requested reinforcements. Instead of trying to persuade Lieutenant General Theophilus Holmes to abandon Arkansas, Davis, against Johnston's advice, ordered Major General Carter Stevenson's Division from Tennessee to Mississippi. Johnston complained in a letter to Wigfall that this unnecessarily weakened Bragg, a strange argument considering that both Johnston and Davis remained impressed with Bragg's army, convinced that it could handle any Union threat in Tennessee. The only logical conclusion is that if Holmes could not reinforce Pemberton, Johnston was prepared to let Vicksburg go instead of sending reinforcements from Tennessee, which he apparently considered of preeminent importance.[7]

From Tennessee, Johnston and Davis departed for Vicksburg where Johnston, frustrated by Davis and Pemberton, kept urging a concentration of force and, when that failed, melodramatically offered his resignation. In a memorandum to Davis written from Vicksburg on December 22, 1862, Johnston urged a concentration of force by having Holmes reinforce Pemberton, but he argued that "No more troops can be taken from General Bragg without the danger of enabling William S. Rosecrans [Union commander of the Army of the Cumberland in Tennessee] to move into Virginia or to reinforce Grant." He continued: "I firmly believe, however, that our true system of warfare would be to concentrate the forces of the two departments on this side of the Mississippi, beat the enemy here, and then reconquer the country beyond it, which he might have gained in the mean time." Davis refused this suggestion, and before the president left Jackson, Johnston met personally with him to express his belief that his command "was little more than nominal," asking for a reassignment due to the fact that the armies in Mississippi and Tennessee had different objectives and remained too far apart to reinforce one another effectively. Davis responded by telling him that he needed Johnston to command because the western theater was too far from Richmond for Davis to manage. Johnston responded that he was not the right man for the job essentially because he had already decided that the job was impossible. Davis still refused to remove Johnston from command. In early January 1863, Davis returned to Richmond, and Johnston returned to Chattanooga, more frustrated than ever. At this point, Johnston seems to have written off Mississippi entirely and decided to concentrate on Tennessee. He would correspond with Pemberton to give him advice but declined to get personally involved with the defense of Vicksburg until peremptorily ordered to do so.[8]

Throughout February and March, Johnston continued to complain to Wigfall about his position. He apparently believed that Davis intended to undermine him and ruin his reputation, and he referred to the position in which the government had placed him as "mischievous. On March 8 Johnston wrote to Wigfall, asking the senator to impress on Secretary of War Seddon the imperative of reassigning him, hopefully to command the Army of Northern Virginia. In justification for not taking direct command in Mississippi, Johnston wrote: "The only effect, then, of my taking direction of affairs, would be my being responsible for Pemberton's generalship, instead of himself. If he entitled himself to praise, robbing him of it. If he deserves blame, bearing it for him." Through the rest of the month and into April, Johnston remained in Tullahoma attending to Bragg and his army, while receiving increasingly alarming messages from Pemberton regarding Grant's movements. On May 2, Johnston received news of the Battle of Port Gibson, and yet he did nothing but relay Pemberton's communications to Richmond. At this point, Johnston should have understood that Vicksburg faced grave danger, but he still obstinately refused to take command in Mississippi or even go there himself, despite the fact that everything remained quiet in Tennessee. Finally, on May 9 the telegram arrived from Seddon, ordering him to Mississippi.[9]

At the time, and after the war, Johnston gave several excuses for neglecting his duties in Mississippi, none of which hold up under scrutiny. Johnston claimed, in letters to Davis and Seddon on April 10 and April 28, that he had reaggravated the wounds he suffered at Seven Pines almost exactly one year earlier and therefore found himself "unfit" for field service. He gave this as the first excuse, in his postwar memoirs, as to why he did not proceed to Mississippi once he learned of Grant's activities. Johnston did suffer discomfort and pain, but he never mentioned the renewed pain in any of his personal letters to Wigfall, and only briefly mentioned the injuries, solely as an excuse, in his postwar memoirs. In addition, once he received the telegram on May 9, he made no further mention of his illness. If truly incapacitated, Johnston surely would have complained or at least mentioned his injuries to Wigfall, and he would have continued to claim illness when Seddon ordered him to Mississippi. Also telling is the fact that Johnston emphasized his illness mostly in his memoirs, after Davis had already blamed him for losing Vicksburg. Although he was in pain, it seems highly unlikely that Johnston's wounds incapacitated him enough to prevent travel. The more likely scenario is that Johnston used his discomfort as a cover for not pursuing his command in Mississippi more proactively.[10]

Johnston used Braxton Bragg as his second excuse for not traveling to Mississippi at an earlier date. On January 22, 1863, as Johnston traveled on an inspection to Mississippi, Davis urgently wired him in Mobile, instructing him to return to Chattanooga at once to investigate the situation in the Army of Tennessee, where Bragg had solicited from his officers their true feelings about him. In the wake of the Battle of Stones River, Bragg's subordinates had begun openly questioning his authority, and Bragg, deeply wounded, asked them what they thought of him. In this crisis, Davis instructed Johnston to "determine what is in the best interest of the service," even if that meant removing Bragg from command. Johnston rushed back to Tennessee and eventually reported that Bragg should retain his command. Davis and Seddon both urged Johnston to replace Bragg, but he refused, feeling it improper to relieve a fellow officer after he himself had conducted the investigation.

In any event, Johnston continued to defend Bragg even after Seddon ordered him to replace Bragg temporarily while Bragg traveled to Richmond for a "conference" with Davis. Despite this direct order, Johnston refused to order Bragg to Richmond on account of his wife's declining health. For almost a month, from early March to early April Bragg remained absent with his wife. By the time he returned to Tennessee, Johnston had begun feigning illness and refused to replace Bragg on account of the fact that he could not take "field command." After the war Johnston defended his conduct in not proceeding to Mississippi earlier with the idea that Bragg desperately needed him in Tennessee. Despite this claim, after Bragg's return Johnston merely sidelined himself, sending mundane orders and requests to the War Department regarding the commissary of the Army of Tennessee and other trivial matters.[11]

Lastly, Johnston used his orders, or his interpretation of his orders, as the crux of the reason he did not go to Mississippi. Johnston claimed that the orders of January 22, recalling him to Tennessee, had superseded his original orders placing him in command of Bragg's and Pemberton's forces. Johnston wrote after the war: "I had been prevented, by the orders of the Administration, from giving my personal attention to military affairs in Mississippi at any time since the 22nd of January. On the contrary, those orders had required my presence in Tennessee during the whole of that period." At best, Johnston fooled himself with this statement; at worst, he outright lied. The orders assigning him to command stated: "General Johnston . . . will repair in person to any part of said command whenever his presence may for the time be necessary or desirable." When Davis ordered Johnston to Tennessee in January, it in no way relieved him of responsibility for Mississippi. At most, Johnston could claim that his presence in Tennessee remained necessary only until early April when Bragg returned to the Army of Tennessee, and probably not even that long considering the fact that Rosecrans and his Union forces remained quiet in middle Tennessee during this period. It is difficult to escape the conclusion that Johnston wasted at least a month if not more dragging his feet instead of going to Pemberton's aid.[12]

By the time Johnston started out for Jackson, the military situation had deteriorated rapidly for the Confederates. On the last day of April, Grant began ferrying his forty-three-thousand-man Army of the Tennessee to the east bank of the Mississippi River at Hard Times Landing. Then he advanced into the interior of Mississippi, defeating Confederate detachments at Port Gibson on May 1 and Raymond on May 12. When Grant learned that Johnston was headed for Jackson to take command of a small army there, he decided to advance on Jackson rather than leave Johnston to operate in his rear. On May 13 Grant ordered John A. McClernand to move his corps north to the railroad near Bolton between Edwards Station and Jackson. Meanwhile McPherson and Sherman marched directly toward Jackson in a converging attack, with Sherman approaching from the southwest and McPherson from the northwest.[13]

The city of Jackson held the key to Vicksburg and indeed all of central Mississippi. In addition to its central location in the state, the city also contained the intersection of several major railroads and a number of factories and other machinery the Confederacy needed desperately. Geographically and logistically, whoever controlled Jackson would control central Mississippi. Grant had these things in mind when he turned to advance on Jackson. Capturing Jackson would make his advance toward Vicksburg that much easier. In many ways Jackson provided a potential turning point in Grant's advance on Vicksburg; if Johnston could hold the city it might free up Pemberton to strike Grant's rear; if not, Pemberton appeared doomed.

On May 13 Johnston had reached Lake Station, fifty miles east of Jackson, when he received a telegram from Pemberton detailing the desperate situation. Pemberton communicated the fact that he believed Grant was moving toward Edwards Station. He also informed Johnston that he intended to strike the Federals there, but that he had to leave behind men to guard both Vicksburg and the crossings over the Big Black River. At this point, Johnston knew that Grant could strike toward either Vicksburg or Jackson, although he obviously believed that the objective remained Vicksburg. Rushing ahead to Jackson, Johnston established his headquarters at the Bowman House and immediately called for John Gregg, who had retreated into Jackson that day with the remnants of his brigade.[14]

Gregg called on Johnston that night, and the meeting produced a great many misconceptions that confirmed Johnston's worst fears. Gregg reported that Sherman had reached the railroad at Clinton, east of Edwards Station, with four divisions, interposing himself between Johnston and Pemberton. Gregg also reported that Pemberton had concentrated his forces in the vicinity of Edwards Station in the hope of striking Grant's rear. Finally, the Texan informed Johnston that only his and Brigadier General W. H. T. Walker's brigades occupied Jackson, a force of some six thousand men against all of Grant's army, which Gregg assumed was advancing on Jackson. Although Gregg assumed a great deal in his report to Johnston, he presented it as fact, misleading Johnston. In reality, Grant was indeed descending on Jackson, but Pemberton was nowhere near Edwards Station, still having his headquarters at Bovina on the railroad west of the Big Black River. Gregg also painted an excessively negative picture of the situation in Jackson. Although only he and

Walker occupied Jackson at the time, Johnston learned shortly thereafter that Brigadier General Samuel Maxey's brigade would arrive from Port Hudson at almost any time and that Brigadier General States Rights Gist's brigade, coming from the East Coast, would also arrive momentarily. With these two additional brigades, and more on the way, Johnston would have an army of at least twelve thousand, more than enough men, even with the poorly placed and constructed fortifications around Jackson, to hold the Mississippi capital for some time. Nevertheless, Johnston had apparently already decided that Vicksburg could not be held, and after his briefing with Gregg, he wired Richmond: "I arrived this evening, finding the enemy's force between this place and General Pemberton, cutting off the communication. I am too late." Many historians have blamed Gregg for misleading Johnston, but Johnston became aware of the true situation on his own even after his conversation with Gregg. Once again Johnston's desire to protect his reputation had cost the Confederacy.[15]

Judging from his communication with Richmond, Johnston had apparently decided to abandon Jackson as soon as he arrived, if not earlier, but in a bizarre twist he then tried to convince Pemberton to unite with him in striking Grant simultaneously from the front and rear with no intention of actually carrying through with the plan. Johnston's communications with Pemberton therefore misled the Vicksburg commander, placing him in a compromised position. Despite his earlier communication with Richmond, at 9 P.M. on May 13 Johnston sent a message to Pemberton at Bovina via three separate messengers. He urged him to march east and strike Sherman from behind while Johnston kept his attention by operating against Grant's forces from Jackson. Johnston added: "all the strength you can quickly assemble should be brought; time is all important." Pemberton did not receive Johnston's message until dawn on May 14. At 9:10 A.M. Pemberton replied to Johnston, informing him that he was proceeding toward Clinton with more than half his forces. He wrote: "In directing this move, I do not think you fully comprehend the position that Vicksburg will be left in, but I comply at once with your order." On Johnston's word, Pemberton started east with twenty-two thousand of his men, all he felt he could spare for active operations away from the Hill City and its environs. If Johnston did not hold up his end of the bargain to hang onto Jackson and with it Grant's attention, Pemberton would be left extremely vulnerable.[16]

Meanwhile, on the morning of May 14, at least four hours before Pemberton received his orders, Johnston inexplicably decided to abandon Jackson. He instructed Gregg to move his troops out on the road toward Clinton to cover the evacuation of the city, long before Grant had placed any pressure on the capital, and even before Johnston knew the full number of Union troops bearing down on him. Gregg put the orders into motion at 3 A.M. on May 14, which means that Johnston had issued them less than six hours after ordering Pemberton to conduct an operation that would necessitate Johnston's defense of Jackson. As Gregg took command of the troops in the city Johnston and his staff departed for Canton, almost twenty-five miles to the northeast. In light of the pouring rain, Johnston instead initially stopped for the night at Tougaloo, just a half-dozen miles north of the city.[17]

After Johnston's departure, Gregg went about making his dispositions for the defense of Jackson. He placed Colonel Peyton Colquitt in command of his own brigade and ordered it into position three miles east of Jackson on the Clinton Road. He then ordered Walker to bring his command up to support Colquitt. Gregg also placed the Mississippi state troops and several artillery batteries in place to support Colquitt. Lastly, the Texan placed Colonel Albert Thompson's 3rd Kentucky Mounted Infantry southwest of Jackson on the Raymond Road.[18]

At 9 A.M. on May 14 James McPherson's Federal skirmishers made contact with Colquitt's men, and shortly thereafter Sherman's skirmishers engaged Thompson's mounted infantry along the Raymond Road. The Confederates managed to hold off McPherson and Sherman until 2 P.M., when a determined assault routed Colquitt's men and sent them racing back toward Jackson. Fortunately for the Confederates, Gregg received a message at the same time informing him that the last of the supply trains had cleared the city. Gregg then gave the order to retreat toward Canton while the state troops and their artillery temporarily held the Federals at bay. At 4 P.M. on May 14, Grant triumphantly assembled with his commanders in Jackson, altering the entire complexion of the campaign for Vicksburg.[19]

It is almost impossible to overestimate the importance of the fall of Jackson and to overemphasize Joseph Johnston's failure during the events of May 13 and 14. For the Confederates, the loss meant sheer disaster, logistically and strategically. Logistically, it deprived the Confederacy of factories, munitions, and stores they badly needed, as well as an important railroad hub. Strategically, the capture of Jackson doomed Pemberton and more than half of his command, which had started east. Now, with Johnston for all intents and purposes having sidelined himself and his small army, Grant could turn west and concentrate on crushing Pemberton and capturing Vicksburg. In less than a day on the scene, Joseph Johnston, instead of helping save Vicksburg, immediately gave up on saving Jackson, changed his mind, issued confusing orders that left Pemberton extremely vulnerable, and then abandoned Jackson after all, leaving Grant with the strategic upper hand.

After Gregg's retreat from Jackson, Johnston sent orders to Pemberton by courier urging him to continue to take his army toward Clinton to intercept Grant. Johnston informed Pemberton that "no more than half" of the Union army occupied Jackson, and that if Pemberton hurried he could defeat Grant in detail. How Johnston arrived at these conclusions is a mystery, but what is clear is that Johnston never intended to support Pemberton in any kind of move against Grant. After dawn on May 15, Johnston continued marching his troops northeast toward Canton, directly *away* from Pemberton.[20]

Unbeknownst to Johnston, by the time Pemberton had reached Edwards Station on his way toward Clinton he had come to his senses. He realized that the Federals had possession of Clinton, so he altered his march, instead moving southeast toward Dillon's Farm to try to cut Grant's supply line. At 5:30 P.M. on May 14, he sent Johnston word of his planned maneuver, unaware that his commander had already abandoned him to face Grant alone. To make matters worse, one of the couriers to whom Johnston had entrusted his orders to Pemberton on the night of May 13 turned out to be a Union agent, who turned the orders over to Grant. With this information in hand, Grant decided to leave Johnston's small force in his rear and advance with his entire army against Pemberton.[21]

At 8:30 A.M. on May 15 as Johnston marched toward Canton, he received Pemberton's message, sent the previous afternoon, informing him that he was heading toward Dillon's. Johnston had not received Pemberton's message notifying him of his compliance with his original orders, so he assumed that Pemberton had disobeyed him. With this mistaken impression Johnston exploded, sending Pemberton an angry note that instructed him to march immediately toward Clinton to effect a junction of the two forces, even as Johnston himself continued to march northeast in the *opposite* direction. Johnston apparently intended his orders on May 15 to emphasize that Pemberton had disobeyed his earlier orders and therefore should bear the blame for the loss of Vicksburg. By the end of May 15, Johnston and his small force were resting quietly at Calhoun Station, north of Canton.[22]

At 6:30 A.M. on May 16, Pemberton received Johnston's angry dispatch written the previous morning, and he decided to obey by moving his army northeast in hopes of joining Johnston and striking Grant in the flank. However, by 9 A.M. Pemberton's Confederates, moving to meet Johnston, ran into most of the Union army, initiating the Battle of Champion Hill. As the skirmishing began, Pemberton quickly hurried off a note to Johnston, informing him of his position and attempted compliance with his orders. Unfortunately for the Confederates, even as Grant fought Pemberton at Champion Hill, Johnston sat with his command at Calhoun, twenty-five miles away, without even enough urgency to send out scouting patrols. By May 18, Grant had trapped Pemberton in the defenses of Vicksburg, all but guaranteeing the eventual fall of the Gibraltar of the South.[23]

Joseph Johnston's actions during the maneuvering for Vicksburg comprise some of the worst decisions ever made by a Civil War commander in the field. From the beginning of his assignment to the West, Johnston refused to take any sort of proactive approach because he did not like his assignment. Despite their personal differences, Jefferson Davis trusted Johnston to command a vital region of the Confederacy that included Davis's own plantation not far from Vicksburg, but Johnston remained convinced that Davis wanted to ruin his reputation by placing him in an impossible position. Deciding that he could only manage the war in Tennessee, despite the fact that he would not take personal command of the Army of Tennessee, he focused all of his attentions there and flatly refused to do anything about Mississippi. When events began to accelerate, Johnston proceeded to make up a series of elaborate excuses to avoid going west. This behavior apparently stemmed from the fact that Johnston already considered the situation in Mississippi impossible and refused to risk his reputation in trying to salvage a victory.

As negligent as Johnston's actions were before heading to Mississippi, his actions in the six days from May 13 to May 19 border on the criminal. After reaching Jackson, he consulted only John Gregg before giving up, writing to Davis, "I am too late." Critics maintain that Gregg bears most of the blame for misleading Johnston, but it remained Johnston's responsibility to ascertain the true state of affairs for himself rather than relying on the word of a single subordinate. Then Johnston, after learning the true state of affairs, sent off an urgent order to Pemberton to unite their forces. The Virginia general's defenders can point to the fact that Johnston did not receive Pemberton's reply until the afternoon of May 16, but Johnston never gave Pemberton time to reply, ordering the evacuation of Jackson less than six hours after issuing orders that placed Pemberton in a very vulnerable position. After giving up perhaps the second most strategic city in Mississippi without a fight, Johnston then continued to urge Pemberton to unite with him at Clinton, even as Johnston marched in the opposite direction. These renewed orders then placed Pemberton in an even more compromised position, allowing Grant to defeat him at the decisive Battle of Champion Hill while Johnston sat in camp at Calhoun Station twenty-five miles away without even enough urgency to send out patrols. From the very beginning, Joseph Johnston decided that Vicksburg could not be held, and to protect his own reputation he deliberately misled John Pemberton, Jefferson Davis, and others, creating a self-fulfilling prophecy that doomed the Hill City.

Notes

1. U.S. War Department, *The War of the Rebellion: A Compilation of the Official Records of the Union and Confederate Armies*, 128 vols. (Washington, D.C., 1880–1901), series 1, vol. 23, pt. 2:825–26. (Hereinafter cited as *OR*. All references are to Series 1 unless otherwise indicated); Joseph E. Johnston, *Narrative of Military Operations, Directed, during the Late War between the States by Joseph E. Johnston, General, C.S.A.* (New York: D. Appleton and Co., 1874), 173.

2. Johnston's biographer Craig Symonds employs the apt phrase "concentration of force." Craig Symonds, *Joseph E. Johnston: A Civil War Biography* (New York: W. W. Norton, 1992), 140.

3. Steven H. Newton, *Joseph Johnston and the Defense of Richmond* (Lawrence: University Press of Kansas, 1998); Alan Downs "'The Responsibility Is Great': Joseph E. Johnston and the War in Virginia," in Steven E. Woodworth (ed.), *Civil War Generals in Defeat* (Lawrence: University Press of Kansas, 1999), 29–70; Symonds, *Joseph E. Johnston*.

4. For a more full explanation of the feud between Johnston and Davis, see Symonds, *Joseph E. Johnston*, 125–39.

5. Jack D. Welsh, *Medical Histories of Confederate Generals* (Kent, Ohio: Kent State University Press, 1995), 119–20.

6. Special Order No. 275, November 24, 1862, and Joseph Johnston to Samuel Cooper, November 24, 1862, *OR*, vol. 17, pt. 2:757–58; Johnston, *Narrative*, 150.

7. Joseph E. Johnston to Louis Wigfall, December 16, 1862, Louis T. Wigfall Papers, Dolph Briscoe Center for American History, University of Texas at Austin.

8. *OR*, vol. 20, pt. 2:459–60; Johnston, *Narrative*, 154–55.

9. Johnston to Wigfall, March 4 and March 8, 1863, Wigfall Papers; Johnston, *Narrative*, 167–73.

10. *OR*, vol. 23, pt. 2:745, 799; Johnston, *Narrative*, 170–73; correspondence December 4, 1862–February 14, 1863 from Johnston to Wigfall, Wigfall Papers.

11. *OR*, vol. 23, pt. 2: 613–14, 632–33; Johnston, *Narrative*, 170–73; Grady McWhiney, *Braxton Bragg and Confederate Defeat*, vol. 1 (Tuscaloosa: University of Alabama Press, 1969), 379–89.

12. *OR*, vol. 17, pt. 2: 757–58; Johnston, *Narrative*, 173.

13. William L. Shea and Terrence J. Winschel, *Vicksburg Is the Key: The Struggle for the Mississippi River* (Lincoln: University of Nebraska Press, 2003), 109–20.

14. *OR*, vol. 24, pt. 1: 239; Johnston, *Narrative*, 174–75.

15. *OR*, vol. 24 pt. 1: 213, 239. For the view that Gregg should be blamed, see Edwin C. Bearss and Warren Grabau, *The Battle of Jackson, May 14, 1863* (Baltimore: Gateway Press, 1981) 11; Warren E. Grabau *Ninety-Eight Days: A Geographer's View of the Vicksburg Campaign* (Knoxville University of Tennessee Press, 2000), 248.

16. *OR*, vol. 24, pt. 1: 239; pt. 3: 877; Grabau, *Ninety-Eight Days*, 246–47; Gilbert E. Govan and James W. Livingood, *A Different Valor: The Story of General Joseph E. Johnston, C.S.A.* (Indianapolis: Bobbs-Merrill, 1956), 199.

17. *OR*, vol. 24, pt. 1:785–86; Grabau, *Ninety-Eight Days*, 247.

18. *OR*, vol. 24, pt. 1:785–87.

19. Ibid., 785–86; Grabau, *Ninety-Eight Days*, 254–56.

20. *OR*, vol. 24, pt. 1:240; Grabau, *Ninety-Eight Days*, 266–67.

21. *OR*, vol. 24, pt. 1:240; Grabau, *Ninety-Eight Days*, 257. Grant had no supply lines, but Pemberton could not have known this.

22. *OR*, vol. 24, pt. 1:240. Johnston eventually received Pemberton's original note, written at 9:10 A.M. on May 14, on the afternoon of May 16.

23. Grabau, *Ninety-Eight Days*, 282–83.

Major General Ulysses S. Grant ended a winter of
deadlock outside Vicksburg by unleashing a fast-moving
campaign that became the Civil War's most masterful
demonstration of the operational art. Library of Congress

Confederate Lieutenant General John C. Pemberton, a northerner
by birth who seemed to have neither much experience nor aptitude
for command, was charged with defending Vicksburg but proved
no match for Grant and his spring campaign. Library of Congress

Union Rear Admiral David Dixon Porter commanded the Union gunboat
flotilla that provided vital support to Grant's campaign. Library of Congress

Union Colonel Benjamin H. Grierson led a cavalry raid that helped distract Pemberton as Grant's campaign began to unfold. Library of Congress

A contemporary illustrator from *Harper's Weekly* made this print from
J. R. Hamilton's sketch of Grierson's troopers riding triumphantly through
Baton Rouge on May 2, 1863, at the conclusion of their raid. *Harper's Weekly*

Confederate Brigadier General
John S. Bowen used highly
advantageous terrain to
put up a stiff but ultimately
unsuccessful defensive fight
against Grant's advance at
Port Gibson. Library of Congress

Confederate Brigadier General John Gregg thought he would surprise a lone Union brigade near Raymond, Mississippi, but he was the one surprised when the column he struck turned out to be the entire Federal Seventeenth Corps. Library of Congress

Union Major General James B. McPherson commanded the Seventeenth Corps. Library of Congress

Artist Theodore R. Davis sketched the Battle of Raymond for the June 13, 1863, edition of *Harper's Weekly* magazine. *Harper's Weekly*

Musician Alfred E. Mathews, of the 31st Ohio Regiment, was serving on detached duty with Grant's army when he made this sketch depicting the charge of Sandborn's and Boomer's brigades at the Battle of Jackson, Mississippi. Library of Congress

Union Major General William Tecumseh Sherman
was Grant's chief lieutenant and commander of the
Fifteenth Corps throughout the campaign, including
the assault on Jackson. Library of Congress

Confederate General Joseph E. Johnston failed to assist Pemberton in the decisive struggle for control of the interior of Mississippi. Library of Congress

Union Major General John A. McClernand was the most difficult of Grant's subordinates and remains controversial to the present day. Library of Congress

7

GRANT, McCLERNAND, AND VICKSBURG
A CLASH OF PERSONALITIES AND BACKGROUNDS

Michael B. Ballard

Traditional Civil War history has demeaned John McClernand as a bombastic, mediocre soldier who should never have been allowed to serve in the Union army, certainly not as a general. The story usually goes that McClernand used his political status to wedge his way into the war, and that U. S. Grant put up with him, especially during the Vicksburg campaign, because of McClernand's status in Washington. In recent years, a more balanced view of McClernand and his relationship with Grant has emerged in the historiography of the Vicksburg Campaign.[1] The following essay further reevaluates the McClernand-Grant story.

If the Civil War had not brought them together, chances are they would never have met. John Alexander McClernand and Ulysses Simpson Grant came from very different backgrounds and had personalities that made a good relationship between the two implausible and ultimately impossible. Yet their common purpose, to defeat the Confederacy, kept them together for many, often uncomfortable, months.

Born May 30, 1812, in Kentucky, McClernand grew up in southern Illinois. Self-educated, he studied Latin, Greek, and law. By 1832, he had prepared himself enough to pass the Illinois bar exam. His first military experience came in the Black Hawk War, and he earned praise for his bravery. Afterward, he dabbled in river trade on the Ohio and the Mississippi, the newspaper business (editing a Democratic paper) and entered the world of politics, for which he proved to be well suited. Elected to the Illinois state legislature, he worked with Stephen A. Douglas and met Abraham Lincoln, a fellow legislator and a Whig. McClernand and Lincoln agreed on some issues and differed on others. On the question of slavery, both supported the rights of the states over the Federal Government, though Lincoln thought this position did not cover the District of Columbia and McClernand did.

His friendship with Douglas ultimately led to McClernand's accepting the doctrine of popular sovereignty.

McClernand served terms in the state legislature and later in the United States House of Representatives. He developed a reputation as an unequivocal expansionist and fully supported the war with Mexico. In 1846, Lincoln joined McClernand in the House. Their wives maintained a close friendship that did not necessarily characterize the interaction of their husbands, though the men remained on good terms through the fiery 1850s preceding the Civil War.

McClernand opposed the Wilmot Proviso and worked mostly behind the scenes to draft the Compromise of 1850. Despite his personal feelings, he considered the Kansas-Nebraska Act an anathema because he feared it would damage his party. He supported a constitutional right to own slaves, and he detested abolitionist troublemakers. Personally, McClernand found slavery repugnant and looked forward to its elimination. He remained active in Illinois and national politics and continued to hone his political skills. McClernand became a political animal in a most positive sense, and he enjoyed great popularity in his home state. When war came, his decision was easy; he fully supported maintaining the Union. He became a soldier, but he never ceased being a politician. Practicing the two arts simultaneously would not play well with West Pointers, who, as a rule, did not like non-West Pointers in command of anything.[2]

Born Hiram Ulysses Grant in the small southwestern Ohio town of Point Pleasant, Grant became the beneficiary of one of the most significant clerical errors in American history. When nominated to attend the United States Military Academy at West Point, New York, Thomas Hamer, the congressman who appointed Grant, could not remember the youngster's full name. Knowing that Simpson was the maiden name of Grant's mother, Hamer wrote "Ulysses Simpson Grant." Thus Hiram Ulysses became Ulysses Simpson, and Grant never corrected the error. At the academy, he became known as "Sam," due to the initials U. S. being translated into Uncle Sam by fellow cadets.

Grant grew up prowling the Ohio River and exhibited natural skills as a horseman. He also demonstrated a personality trait of tenacity, which served him well in coming years. Grant was not particularly thrilled when his father Jesse arranged for him to attend West Point. Jesse did not necessarily want Ulysses to be a career soldier, but he hoped the academy's engineering curriculum would open career doors for his son.

Ulysses later wrote that though he had doubts, he never expressed objections to going to West Point, but he did believe his educational level would not be suitable for staying there very long. He managed to graduate, however, finishing twenty-first in a class of thirty-nine; excelling in mathematics, and many fellow cadets were awed by his horsemanship. Grant did not have an outgoing personality, which gave him time to observe classmates. His ability to read people would benefit him in his later years. He also met his future wife Julia through his roommate, Frederick Dent, Julia's brother from St. Louis.

Within a relatively short time after graduation, Grant found himself on the front lines of the United States' war with Mexico. Grant, unlike McClernand, was no expansionist. He later criticized his government for warring against a country without just cause. Still, he, and other future Civil War combatants, learned much in Mexico. Grant was drawn to the commanding style of future president Zachary Taylor, whose low-key personality and casual dress appealed to the young Ohioan. Grant admired Winfield Scott's military ability, but he was uninspired by Scott's fancy dress habits, which earned the general the title "old Fuss and Feathers."

Grant performed well in Mexico, earning two brevet (honorary) promotions. He exhibited bravery under fire and emerged from the war with a solid reputation. Yet he welcomed peace, married Julia, and looked to whatever future his military career might offer. It did not offer much that pleased him, for he had to endure many separations from Julia while he served in New York and Michigan and finally on the Pacific coast. He tried several schemes to earn extra income for Julia and the children but failed in every case. Grant grew very despondent about his separation from his young family and occasionally turned to liquor, for which his body had a low tolerance. Soon tales of his drinking circulated in the gossipy army. He had no idea that his infrequent drinking would haunt his reputation for years.

Finally, he resigned from the army and came home to Julia, his children, and St. Louis, where he failed at farming and had to cut and sell wood to bring in a meager income. He moved his family in 1860 to Galena, Illinois, in the far northwestern corner of the state, to work in a family business there. Along the way, he began suffering from malarial symptoms of chills and fever, conditions that continually haunted him.

Grant was aware of the political storms of the 1850s, but, as a Democrat, he hoped war would not come. He voted for James Buchanan in 1856 and Stephen Douglas in 1860. Though opposed to slavery, he, like McClernand, feared that Abraham Lincoln's election would tear the country apart. When war did come, he immediately supported the Union, and he used his military acumen to train local volunteers in Galena.[3]

Grant entered the war as the same quiet, tentative man he had been at West Point and in Mexico, but he had a determination to do the best he could for the Union cause. He never had the bombastic demeanor of a politician like McClernand, but the two men, so different in background and personality, shared a resolve to preserve the Union. Their resolve, however, would be highlighted by personality conflicts.

A clue of the sort of future problems McClernand could cause began on April 10, 1861, in a McClernand letter to Abraham Lincoln. Though the war had not begun, McClernand, mostly a military novice in spite of his Black Hawk service, wrote Lincoln that the United States army and navy should attack Texas to get that state back into the Union. McClernand did not stop there; within a few weeks, he, along with Illinois governor Richard Yates, wrote Lincoln and Winfield Scott, at the time general-in-chief, that New Madrid, Missouri, Memphis, Tennessee, Corinth, Mississippi, and Columbus, Kentucky should be fortified. The plan sounded grand, as one would expect from two politicians, but militarily, at the time, it made no sense. Undeterred, McClernand contacted outgoing president James Buchanan and others in Washington about the vital importance of maintaining control of the Mississippi River. Though west-to-east railroads in the Mid-West made commerce viable, loss of free access down the Mississippi due to secession must not be tolerated. Many others understood the significance of the river, but McClernand's obsession with that waterway led to later actions that would infuriate Grant.[4]

During this period of strategic visions, McClernand met Grant for the first time. Since Galena, Grant had become colonel of the 21st Illinois, and in early May the regiment had responded unenthusiastically to Lincoln's call for enlisted men to stay in the army for three years. McClernand and John Logan, another southern Illinois politician, asked Grant's permission to speak to the regiment. The two orators had a dynamic effect on the men and all agreed to the three-year stint. Since southern Illinois was viewed by many as filled with Southern sympathizers, the actions of McClernand and Logan were welcomed by Lincoln.[5]

On November 7, 1861, Grant and McClernand first shared military action at the Battle of Belmont, Missouri. Both had received the rank of brigadier general in July, but Grant had been ranked 19th on the list approved by Lincoln and McClernand 33rd. So Grant commanded, and he came close to having his forces partially trapped during the fighting against Leonidas Polk's Confederates, stationed across the Mississippi in Kentucky. Polk decided to retreat, from fear of becoming isolated more than the actions of Grant's troops. Grant's first battle as a commander was hardly a tactical masterpiece, but he had survived and avoided losing. Grant wrote his father, Jesse, the day after the battle that McClernand had "acted with great coolness and courage throughout, and proved that he is a soldier as well as statesman."[6]

McClernand could not restrain himself in trumpeting the victory. He wrote George McClellan, detailing the battle, and acknowledged Grant only as being in command. In his official report, he was generous in his praise of Grant and the whole army. McClernand knew that he could not afford to ignore Grant, not in an official document; and then he proceeded, as anyone knowing his background would have suspected, to tell the world of his own heroic conduct. He had unsolicited help from the press, for many editors saw the battle as a defeat, and there were calls for Grant to be dismissed from the army. To make matters worse, from Grant's perspective, McClernand received a letter of congratulations from Lincoln, though the prewar Lincoln-McClernand relationship must be taken into account. Lincoln also knew that politically he should not pass up a chance to cheer on a Democrat. Mc-Clernand also began a practice that ultimately led to his downfall: he issued a congratulatory order to his men. Though innocent enough, McClernand's orders of this sort always seemed to give his troops more credit than others thought they deserved.

Grant shrugged off the negative news stories, and he stood by McClernand, who in some cases had not escaped editorial criticism. Writing to his father three weeks after Belmont, Grant said, "All who were on the battle field know where Gen. McClernand and my self were and it needs no resort to Public press for our vindication."[7]

In 1940, Helen Todd wrote a biography of Grant that is undocumented and mentions few sources, none of which apply to post Belmont. Todd claims that positive press treatment McClernand received, compared to Grant, caused Grant's chief aide, John Rawlins to have a profanity-filled tantrum against McClernand. According to Todd, Grant defused Rawlins by stating that he did not "have time for newspaper fighting." Whatever the story's accuracy, the tone does fit Grant's demeanor.[8]

Grant's and McClernand's next major campaign involved the taking of forts Henry and Donelson on the Tennessee and Cumberland Rivers, respectively. Grant succeeded and became a national hero due to his telling Confederate general Simon Bolivar Buckner that the only terms offered would be unconditional surrender. Once again Grant's first two initials benefited him, and people started calling him "Unconditional Surrender" Grant.

After Donelson fell, Grant wrote in his report, February 16, 1862, that when he gave an order for his left wing to attack, an assault that was key to Union victory, his division commanders, including McClernand, "were with their commands in the midst of danger, and were always ready to execute all orders, no matter what the exposure to themselves." McClernand, near the end of his report to Grant, wrote in the style of political oratory: "I am happy in congratulating you as the respected commander of a victorious army engaged in a just cause, and in believing that no stain will be found, no word of reproach or disparagement coupled with the record which shall bear the history of this great event down the stream of time, but that it will endure as an imperishable example of duty bravely, manfully, and nobly performed."[9]

Despite patting each other on the back, discord arose between Grant and McClernand rooted in language in McClernand's report. McClernand wrote that he had urged Grant to make a "simultaneous assault" all along the line, a claim that Grant denied in his report to Henry Halleck. Grant wrote, "I have no special comments to make on it [McClernand's report], further than that the report is a little highly colored as to the conduct of the First Division, and I failed to hear the suggestions spoken of about the propriety of attacking the enemy all around the lines on Saturday." McClernand's battle reports and hyperbole were synonymous, in effect politicized. He congratulated his troops once more, casting, intentionally or not, glory on himself, and he sent a copy of his remarks to Lincoln. McClernand never showed appreciation for the chain of command, not when it came to corresponding to powerful acquaintances in Washington. Despite the tension, both Grant and McClernand received promotions to major general as a result of the victory at Fort Donelson.[10]

Then came Shiloh, the April 6–7, 1862, battle that temporarily turned Grant's military career upside down and led McClernand to seek his own fortune. Grant's army camped along the Pittsburg Landing plateau on the southern bank of the Tennessee River, some twenty-five miles from Corinth, Mississippi, a small town that surrounded an important railroad junction. The Union forces were surprised by a vicious Confederate attack on April 6. McClernand and William T. Sherman combined to reestablish a wrecked Union line on the right of Grant's army, and the next day reinforcements provided by Don Carlos Buell and his Army of the Ohio joined with Grant's survivors to turn the tide and force the Confederates back to Corinth.

Grant gave Sherman most of the credit, though Sherman's performance had not been spectacular, but he was Grant's friend, and, importantly, a fellow West Pointer. McClernand got good reviews from lower-level commanders but not from Grant. Grant sent a message of congratulations to his army, the same kind of laudatory commentary usually written by McClernand. Eventually, Henry Halleck arrived and took command of the army, leaving Grant in a command limbo, officially second in command, unofficially in a position that meant nothing.[11]

Meanwhile, McClernand took an initiative that came naturally to his impatient nature, when he wrote Grant that it seemed likely Confederate forces would leave Virginia and assemble en masse in the lower South. To counter this likelihood, McClernand advised that Grant's army build strong entrenchments to counter expected Confederate attacks or move at once to Corinth and finish whipping the Confederates there. McClernand's ideas about Virginia revealed his ignorance of the reality of the eastern theater of the war. Ultimately, Halleck chose to march to Corinth, though McClernand's advice to Grant had nothing to do with the decision.[12]

While the Union army regrouped, Governor Yates from Illinois visited twice and talked with McClernand. Richard Kiper, McClernand's biographer, suspects that on the second trip the two political allies may have talked about an independent command for McClernand, especially since McClernand had already broached the subject to Lincoln. McClernand never let an opportunity pass to press the politically powerful for his own benefit.

For the present, McClernand was content to continue promoting himself and his men, but this time he went further and openly criticized Grant in a letter to Lincoln. The McClernand message was sent the same day that Grant ordered all official correspondence be confined to the chain of command. McClernand spread the word to his officers and then proceeded to disobey Grant's directive. It is difficult to believe McClernand did so intentionally; he simply could not stop wearing two hats, the army general and the politician.

McClernand told Lincoln that his division had been at the forefront of the fight at Shiloh as it had been in other battles. Then he said, in a thinly disguised insult to Grant, that the army should have pursued the enemy during its retreat after the second day of the battle. McClernand's judgment was faulty in two aspects. First he had ignored the work of other officers, including Sherman, who had, with varying degrees of success, helped stem the tide of the initial Confederate attack. Secondly, to criticize Grant for not ordering a pursuit was to ignore the condition of the Union army after the two-day battle. Most companies, regiments, divisions, and corps were decimated and scattered, and though Buell's army was in relatively better shape, pursuit would have been ill-advised. McClernand did not let such facts stand in his way.[13]

McClernand kept his troops active while he waited for Halleck to order the advance on Corinth. Yates's two visits no doubt fueled speculation about some sort of behind-the-scenes shenanigans by McClernand. As Halleck organized his forces, he gave McClernand command of the army's reserve. McClernand in turn gave up his division, no doubt realizing he could only lead one force at a time. He reported to Grant who passed messages on to Halleck. The frustration of both Grant and McClernand grew as Halleck marched his men very slowly toward Corinth. Lincoln warned Halleck not to be reckless, for Lincoln had his hands full trying to get George McClellan to do anything. Halleck, a recognized military scholar who had never led an army in the field, took Lincoln's order to heart. So Grant's embarrassment and McClernand's impatience were dragged through muddy roads at a snail's pace to Corinth. Before the town could be captured, Confederate General P. G. T. Beauregard evacuated the place, but not before sending supplies and men safely south.[14]

While Grant kept his fury mostly to himself, his friend Sherman had to talk him out of resigning from the army. McClernand meanwhile had decided Halleck was treating him unfairly, probably because he was not a West Pointer. He wrote to Halleck that as a commander of the reserve, he felt he had been given an inferior position. McClernand hastened to add that justice, not his ego, prompted his protest. That was no doubt half true. Halleck in turn told McClernand that leading the reserve was not an inferior job, and that in fact McClernand had more men under his command than before. McClernand again felt an urge to turn to his only dependable allies—political friends.[15]

Following the taking of Corinth, Halleck sent his troops hither and yon for a while, accomplishing nothing, and he finally decided to break up his large army and send portions to Arkansas and east to northern Alabama to work on repairing railroads. Then Halleck was called to Washington to take command of all Union armies, and Grant reassumed command of his Army of the Tennessee. McClernand reported to Grant once more, but the two clashed occasionally, mainly due to menial issues.

The lack of action during the Corinth Campaign and postcampaign duties furthered McClernand's frustrations. On June 20, McClernand, again ignoring the chain of command, wrote directly to Lincoln to ask for an independent command to cover southern Arkansas, Texas, western Louisiana, and the Indian Territory west of Arkansas. Lincoln ignored the message. McClernand then turned to Grant's political ally and fellow Illinoisan, U.S. Representative Elihu Washburne. He asked Washburne to arrange for him to come east with two divisions to support George McClellan. A nice byproduct would be that McClernand would rise to command of a corps. It was shortly after this message that Halleck left for Washington, and McClernand's request likely, and intentionally, got lost during Halleck's settling into new duties. There is no evidence that Washburne responded to McClernand's message. McClernand later wired Senator Orville Browning of Illinois to ask for help to go east. McClellan's failures in Virginia were not enough for the Lincoln administration to pull troops from the west, especially since such a move might weaken the Union hold on Corinth.[16]

McClernand soon found that his messages to Washington, even to Lincoln, were now being turned over to Halleck. Halleck ostracized McClernand for not "transmitting [his messages] through prescribed channels," for in doing so, "you have violated the Army Regulations." He noted that he had warned McClernand about such practices in the past. Time would prove that McClernand paid no heed to Halleck's warning. In fact this warning came after McClernand had sent a copy of a message that he had sent to Grant, protesting the placement of McClernand's troops. Halleck ruled in McClernand's favor, but the new commanding general in Washington obviously did not like McClernand's methods. This was yet another instance of how McClernand would pull whatever strings necessary to get his way and make enemies in high places in the process.

McClernand continued confronting Grant in a number of areas, and each encounter expanded the scope of their mutual dislike. McClernand especially seethed when Grant accused him on occasion of not carrying out the details of orders as issued. Grant also accused McClernand of exercising authority that undercut Grant's geographic area of command. McClernand angrily replied that he had done no such thing. McClernand also created hard feelings with General James McPherson, a favorite of Grant's and Sherman's. McPherson, superintendent of railroads in the area at the time, lashed back at McClernand for implying that improper goods were being shipped in railroad cars. Aside from Grant, McClernand had made another enemy, one who would be around in the future Vicksburg Campaign.[17]

Flustered by Lincoln and Washburne ignoring his missives and sensing that he could not rely on Halleck as an ally, McClernand contacted Andrew Johnson, military governor of Tennessee at the time and future vice president and president, about an independent command to patrol west Tennessee. McClernand and Johnson had served together in the U.S. House of Representatives. Johnson responded that he could raise a sufficient force, but all military equipment must come from McClernand. McClernand sent Johnson's message to Grant, who without doubt must have been angered that McClernand had struck again behind his back.

Not surprisingly, nothing came of the scheme, and in August McClernand wrote Lincoln to ask for a leave of absence, and he wrote Richard Yates that he felt sure if he could return to Illinois, he could recruit enough troops to replace losses and perhaps add more men to the original Illinois regiments. He told Yates to make the proposal to Secretary of War Edwin Stanton. This time McClernand was fortunate, for the government had called upon Governor Yates to provide over twenty-six thousand more men for the war effort, and if Yates thought McClernand could help him reach that goal, then Lincoln made sure, through Stanton, that McClernand should be given leave. On August 25, Halleck wrote the order, and McClernand left for Illinois three days later. Halleck was not happy, for on August 20, he had written a stern letter to McClernand that current War Department policy dictated no leaves of absence "except in extraordinary circumstances." Up to that point, Halleck wrote, no leaves had been given to any officers in Grant's army. Political manipulation prevailed, and Halleck had to eat his words, yet he was not likely to forget McClernand's actions.[18]

Working together, Yates and McClernand did an admirable job recruiting and training Illinois men. McClernand, however, had more than recruiting on his mind. He had long desired an independent command, and he certainly knew neither Grant nor Halleck would come to his aid. They were, after all, West Pointers, and McClernand had seen how the former cadets took care of each other. Yet in the western theater, action had slowed to a crawl after the victory at Corinth. McClernand still considered clearing the Mississippi a high priority, and he was not the only one. Lincoln felt the same way, and the president knew that people in the Mid-West were growing restless at the lack of progress.

Yates gave McClernand a letter of introduction, ostensibly to ask the Lincoln administration to let the latter assist in organizing new troops in Illinois, something McClernand in fact was already doing. McClernand tried to cover additional political bases. First, he talked with Secretary of the Treasury Salmon Chase about the need to open the Mississippi. Chase in turn arranged a McClernand interview with Lincoln. Meanwhile Secretary of War Stanton asked Lincoln about McClernand, and the president, while admitting his fellow Illinoisan had shown good qualities in battles in the west, expressed his concern about McClernand's obsession with having an independent command. Lincoln understood it would take teamwork to open the river, especially to take the Confederate bastion of Vicksburg. Lincoln no doubt understood the West Point mystique, and he knew placing McClernand in a position ahead of Grant and likely against Halleck's advice could cause trouble.[19]

Unaware of Lincoln's concerns, McClernand lobbied the president personally on every occasion that presented itself about his desire to take an independent command down the Mississippi and attack Vicksburg from the Yazoo River (something Sherman would fail to do in December). McClernand had other grandiose plans, including capturing Mobile, operating west of the Mississippi, and marching toward Atlanta.

Few, if anyone, took McClernand seriously. Halleck would never endorse such nonsense; ironically Halleck thought McClernand undisciplined in that the latter's campsites were disorderly and ill kept, the same criticisms the Illinoisan had made against Grant at Shiloh. McClernand took his case to Stanton who kept Halleck informed about McClernand's lobbying. The general outlined to Stanton his plan to take a force of some twenty-six thousand men down the Mississippi. According to McClernand's biographer, Richard Kiper, there is no evidence that McClernand ever met personally with Halleck, for he likely felt if he could convince Stanton, the secretary of war would order Halleck to cooperate.[20]

Lincoln seemed impressed enough with McClernand's record to give McClernand what he wanted, as much for political as military reasons. David Dixon Porter, a naval commander who would play a key role in several stages of the coming Vicksburg Campaign, claimed that in a private conversation with Lincoln, the president vigorously praised McClernand. Porter, however, habitually stretched the truth and sometimes lied outright, so whether his account of the conversation is true is questionable. Porter hated West Pointers, so perhaps he felt a kinship with McClernand and exaggerated Lincoln's views.[21]

On October 21, McClernand at last got what he wanted, a command to move down the Mississippi to assault Vicksburg. At the same time, Grant had worked up a plan to push his army into north Mississippi and attack Vicksburg by following the Mississippi Central Railroad south and then turning west. Grant did not learn of McClernand's plan until early November.

Had McClernand, the skilled politician, read closely the order issued in Washington, he would have seen that his mission was not the panacea he envisioned. Like other politicians through the ages, McClernand did not carefully read what he embraced. The order directed McClernand "to proceed to the states of Indiana, Illinois, and Iowa, to organize the troops remaining in those States and to be raised," and to assemble them in Memphis or Cairo or wherever else Halleck directed. When McClernand had a sufficient force "not required by the operations of General Grant's command," then McClernand could organize a command to campaign against Vicksburg. Further, "The forces so organized will remain subject to the designation of the general-in-chief, and be employed according to such exigencies as the service in his judgment may require."

The order clearly did not give McClernand carte blanche to command the troops as he wished. When Grant heard about McClernand's gambit, he fired off a November 10 message to Halleck: "Am I to understand that I lay still here while an Expedition is fitted out from Memphis or do you want me to push as far South as possible? Am I to have Sherman move subject to my order or is he & his forces reserved for some special service? Will not more forces be sent here?" Halleck replied promptly the next day. "You have command of all troops sent to your Dept, and have permission to fight the enemy when you please."

So the fine print, which was not fine print to anyone except McClernand, essentially doomed McClernand's efforts to operate independently. Just as Grant had not known what McClernand was up to, now McClernand headed south under an illusion of support from Lincoln to operate independently. Grant understood now that he had Halleck's backing, which meant the implied backing of Stanton and Lincoln, to control McClernand's designs on Vicksburg. When push came to shove, the Lincoln administration backed off from giving McClernand a free hand, further casting doubt on Porter's account of Lincoln's words.[22]

While appeased, Grant had no intention of waiting for McClernand to reach Memphis. Grant suspected that a confrontation would take place, and he wanted to act before there was any need. He sent Sherman from the north Mississippi operation back to Memphis to hurriedly throw together a force to take down the Mississippi to attack Vicksburg. Grant would coordinate the land campaign with Sherman's expedition. If things worked out, Vicksburg would be trapped between Grant and Sherman. Things did not work out. Earl Van Dorn raided Grant's main supply base at Holly Springs, Mississippi, well north of Grant's main force, thus forcing him to retreat from Mississippi. Sherman attacked the hills north of Vicksburg along Chickasaw Bayou and was easily thrown back by Confederates who used the railroad Grant had intended to take advantage of to concentrate troops to meet Sherman. Sherman showed little tactical imagination, and his attacks were grossly uncoordinated.[23]

Meanwhile McClernand experienced many delays before he received permission to go south. On December 16, he complained in messages to Browning, Stanton, and Lincoln that Halleck was doing all in his power to keep McClernand from carrying out his orders. The next day Stanton responded by assuring McClernand that Halleck had done nothing to harm his status, and that he was surprised by his concerns. Then Stanton proceeded to open McClernand's eyes. The secretary of war wrote, "The operations being in General Grant's department, it is designed to organize all the troops of that department in three army corps, the First Army Corps to be commanded by you, and assigned to the operations on the Mississippi under the general supervision of the general commanding the department. General Halleck is to issue the order immediately." There was the rub, and McClernand could not ignore reality this time. He knew he would not be independent, but he would report to Grant. When Halleck's order came out, McClernand learned he would lead the Thirteenth Corps, not the First Corps. Halleck told Grant that McClernand was to be a part of the river expedition, and, in a politically ambiguous phrase that under other circumstances McClernand would have admired, Halleck added that "he [McClernand] shall have the immediate command under your direction." Clearly Lincoln's grasp for middle ground fogged the situation and must have further aggravated and confused McClernand. Whatever conclusions he reached, McClernand had clearly been shafted with such great expertise that he remained confused for a time about what it all meant.[24]

Finally receiving orders to head south, he reached Memphis December 29, while Sherman was in the midst of getting hammered at Chickasaw Bayou. En route McClernand took a brief respite to marry his late wife's sister in Jacksonville, Illinois. When McClernand reached Memphis, he was handed a December 18 order giving him command of the Thirteenth Corps. Grant was not present due to the negative developments in his North Mississippi Campaign, but McClernand did not wait. He wrote Grant a lengthy message that included copies of his orders that stated Lincoln's wish for McClernand to command a river expedition and Halleck's order to do so, and, when he had been informed that Sherman had already taken an army downstream, he grew angry. In his own mind, he believed that Sherman had taken an army intended for him. Obviously, McClernand decided to ignore the Washington instructions that took decision-making out of his hands.

McClernand notified Lincoln, and he made no effort to mask his fury. He noted that the situation forced him to ride downriver in a steamer, without much protection, to take command of the army. Once more McClernand pointedly told Lincoln that the odor of a conspiracy against his Mississippi plan was everywhere. He did not like having to give up his position as commander of the river operation to command a corps, and even worse, his command had been sent on to Vicksburg without his presence. On December 30, McClernand began his trip downriver unaware of Sherman's disaster.[25]

Once he arrived north of Vicksburg, he met with Sherman and David Porter, both of whom left contradictory accounts of the meeting, so it remains anybody's guess as to the facts. One thing for certain came of the meeting—McClernand did nothing to impress Sherman or Porter. McClernand had counted on Porter and his naval force to participate in his campaign against Vicksburg, but he had not bothered to cultivate a personal relationship with Porter. Porter meanwhile, despite his disdain for West Pointers, became friends with Sherman and Grant.

The Sherman, Porter, and McClernand meeting resulted in a plan for a joint army-navy operation up the Arkansas River to attack a river fortress called Arkansas Post. Arguments later arose over whether Sherman or Mc-Clernand first had the idea. Evidence indicates that McClernand had mentioned such a campaign en route to Vicksburg. Sherman later claimed he had to convince McClernand to carry out the plan, and Porter, unreliable Porter, agreed. Whatever the case, McClernand, who outranked Sherman, commanded, and the campaign produced a complete success. No longer could Confederates ship supplies to Vicksburg via the Arkansas, which emptied into the Mississippi north of the town. Grant's order denying McClernand's request to undertake the campaign arrived too late, so Grant termed the whole thing a "wild goose chase," blaming McClernand for wasting time.[26]

Sherman changed Grant's mind. In a January 17 message, Sherman wrote that if Major General Nathaniel Banks, who had been trying to capture Port Hudson, had shown up at Vicksburg during McClernand's campaign, he could understand Grant's anger. But, Sherman argued, capturing Arkansas Post eliminated a threat to Union operations on the Mississippi. Sherman's stamp of approval quieted Grant's criticisms. Yet McClernand was miffed by the criticism and again ignored the chain of command, complaining directly to Lincoln, who replied directly that McClernand's Arkansas triumph was "both brilliant and valuable," and that the disgruntled Illinoisan could do much greater things than engaging "in open war with Gen. Halleck." Whether McClernand had already figured out that all his messages had been referred to Halleck, he knew it now, for Lincoln had made that point clear. Lincoln wrote frankly, "I have too many *family* controversies (so to speak) already on my hands," and he intended to avoid any others.[27]

The Grant-McClernand sniping nevertheless continued in separate messages to Washington. On February 1, Grant wrote, "I have not confidence in his ability as a soldier to conduct an expedition of the magnitude of this one successfully." Given the manner in which Grant later used McClernand in the Vicksburg Campaign, Grant's words are ironic and no doubt written more out of anger than realistic analysis. McClernand continued to harass Lincoln. On March 15, he wrote that he had heard Grant was drunk two days earlier, and he could provide testimonies to that fact. Grant had so often been accused of drunkenness during his army career, McClernand likely was passing along gossip. The Ohioan suffered migraine headaches that some around him mistook for inebriation. As Grant had written in anger, so had McClernand or the latter would not have resorted to such an aged charge. Behind all the bickering lay McClernand's lingering refusal to accept the fact that his only authority was as a corps commander, and that he must accept Grant as his superior. McClernand placed the blame now on Grant's shoulders rather than on Washington, where it belonged. Halleck, Grant,

Sherman, and James McPherson, now commanding a corps under Grant, were all West Pointers, and Lincoln had tired of McClernand's complaints. McClernand knew he had no advocates, which doubtless made him more determined to be obstinate, more so than usual. His moods depended to a large extent on how he was treated, and his situation made him quite sensitive. His pride kept him from yielding gracefully to those he felt were at least complicit in the destruction of his dream, especially Grant.[28]

Grant came down from Memphis, took command, and McClernand had to live with it. After a time, he went about doing his job, for in reality he had no choice other than resigning. He still wanted to see the Mississippi cleared of Confederates, and he could not walk away and not be part of it.

In the early months of 1863, Grant tried myriad strategies to reach Vicksburg, none of which worked. In trying to determine why McClernand ultimately led the army's march down the Louisiana side of the river, his biographer has offered several suggestions, starting with the observation that perhaps some of Grant's operations north of Vicksburg were intended to keep McClernand downriver at Young's Point while Sherman, whose Fifteenth Corps was near and just north of McClernand's, could successfully reach Vicksburg. Perhaps, but Sherman's recent failure at Chickasaw Bayou might have been repeated.

Additionally, McClernand was Grant's senior commander, but that did not mean Grant had to allow McClernand to take the lead. Did other situations such as high water and terrain play roles in Grant's decision? Such analyses are not unreasonable, but they go against Grant's postwar claims that since early in 1863, he had focused on getting his army south of Vicksburg, crossing the river and driving inland to attack Vicksburg from east to west. In fact, he likely had been told by one of his aides, James Wilson, that McClernand had likely had the same idea earlier. Wilson also gave credit to John Rawlins, Grant's chief aide, for coming up with the idea. No doubt, the fact that the plan worked caused many to claim being its author. Grant also wrote that he never really expected his many trials and errors to work, but that he at least he kept his army active and in good physical condition. His view was disingenuous, for he knew that many men in Sherman's and McClernand's sickened and died in large numbers on the swampy Louisiana side of the Mississippi. Grant's other corps, the Seventeenth, commanded by McPherson, enjoyed better conditions north of Vicksburg at Lake Providence.[29]

Once Grant decided to move down the Louisiana side of the river, McClernand was his only corps commander who endorsed the plan, indicating that perhaps he indeed had had the same idea earlier. McPherson did not like it, and Sherman wanted to return to Memphis and strike down through north

Mississippi again. Grant knew going back up the river would appear to be a retreat, no matter the intent, and he had no intention of going back. He did take one last look at the bluffs along the Yazoo River north of Vicksburg to see if there might be a possibility of success. The same bluffs that Sherman could not conquer were still there, and Porter, who had to run boats by the Vicksburg batteries to get them downstream to carry Union soldiers across the Mississippi, grew impatient. He told Grant that a decision must be made, for Porter's gunboats, once downstream, would have trouble chugging back upriver against the current. So Grant made his decision to go.[30]

The deployment of Grant's corps did dictate that McClernand, whose men were farther south, take the lead and that McPherson follow. To the north, Sherman would make a demonstration against the Yazoo bluffs (which failed to fool any of the Confederates). So the argument can be made that the positions of Grant's three corps made McClernand's Thirteenth Corps the logical one to take the lead. Yet how much sense did it make for Grant to trust a man he obviously detested? This movement put Grant's future on the line. If he failed, would Washington continue to support him? With much riding on this operation, why would he put a general he strongly disliked in the lead position? The possible explanations involve several nuances. Yes, McClernand was in place to take the lead. Could Grant have ordered McPherson to move downriver in front of McClernand? There is no reason to doubt that he could have. McPherson was a highly regarded West Pointer, liked by both Grant and Sherman. McPherson had primarily been Grant's chief engineer for most of the war until the north Mississippi invasion, when he commanded two divisions. But that campaign had produced no major battles that would have given McPherson experience he needed and did not have. Grant was well aware that giving McPherson the lead role in the forthcoming campaign might be risky. He likely thought it would be a mistake to put too much pressure on the young general.

Sending Sherman downriver before McClernand arrived would have been a logistical challenge, but surely if Grant had no confidence in McClernand, he would have managed it. Sherman had not shown any brilliance in battle, however. He was a fighter, but he was a poor tactician as he had demonstrated at Chickasaw Bayou. At Shiloh, he had been a better defender than fighter, but circumstances had forced him into that role. Later in the war in Georgia, Sherman would show he was much better at maneuver than combat. Grant surely would never have expressed any lack of concern about Sherman's generalship, for the two men were very close friends. James Wilson, however, wrote afterward that one of the reasons Sherman came up the rear was his strong opposition to the plan.[31] Grant may well have decided he would rather have a general who believed strongly in the upcoming campaign than one who did not. Grant could also make a good case that he wanted someone he could trust to cover the rear of the army and to carry out the attempted diversion along the Yazoo.

Adam Badeau, one of Grant's aides later in the war, wrote a three-volume study of Grant's generalship after the war, offers another possibility. Grant gave McClernand the lead position, Badeau wrote, "to appease the unappeasable ambition and conceit of his subordinate." In effect, Badeau argued that Grant let McClernand go first to keep the latter from sending more letters to Lincoln that would wind up on Halleck's desk. That and to avoid McClernand's protests if he was not allowed to lead. Certainly it is possible that Grant felt exactly as Badeau describes.[32]

Badeau's assertion is interesting if unconvincing, but it does lead to another piece of the puzzle of why McClernand led the way. If Grant felt so strongly, why had he not replaced McClernand already? Certainly he had grounds for doing so, and Halleck, Stanton, and Lincoln, all of whom had been worried by McClernand's barrage of letters, would have found Grant another general, perhaps even a West Pointer. Yet there might have been political ramifications, and Grant did not need more distractions. Grant seemed willing, if not delighted, to overlook the personality conflicts and put his most experienced combat commander out front. Whatever McClernand's personality flaws and political habits, he had proven at Belmont, Donelson, and Shiloh that he would fight and fight well. His biggest problems had been self-inflicted; he clung to his political background and contacts like a lifeline, and in the process turned both military and civilian leadership against him.

Taking all factors into consideration, one can make the assertion, arguable to be sure but based on actions that overshadow the written record, that Grant trusted McClernand to lead the way downstream and counted on him to make the campaign a success. He may have dreaded McClernand's boasting that surely would come with victory, but victory would be worth more than worrying about a subordinate's big mouth. McClernand's corps had done a masterful job of conquering the swampy, bayou-infested Louisiana side of the Mississippi, and though they were not able to do the impossible and cross over to Grand Gulf and hold it as Grant had wanted, they moved at an admirable speed. Grant found out firsthand just how tough the Grand Gulf position was when Confederate general John Bowen's big guns hammered Porter's fleet, forcing the Union columns to move farther south to a safe crossing at a place called Bruinsburg.

McClernand's corps led the march inland toward Port Gibson, a town a few miles southeast of Grand Gulf. There were two roads to Port Gibson,

Grant's first target. One road led directly to the town, while another wrapped around hills south of the direct road. For unknown reasons, McClernand chose the second route. Perhaps he felt that Confederates would be waiting on the main road, and by taking the other, he could flank them. No written explanation of the decision has been found.[33]

Grant did not accompany McClernand and the Thirteenth Corps as it wound its way through the rugged, hilly terrain, but rather remained in Louisiana for the night before riding hard the following day to Port Gibson, arriving at 10 A.M. An argument has been made that McClernand, being in the lead, and Grant being close by, was a case of Grant keeping his eye on the man he did not like. Perhaps, but where else would Grant likely be than with the lead corps? Another factor could well have been that Grant wanted to keep an eye on McPherson, whose corps followed McClernand's. McPherson, as noted, was inexperienced, and Grant doubtless wanted to be sure the young general he was so fond of did not get into trouble. Only one division of McPherson's corps participated in the battle near Port Gibson, and that division did not fight as well as McClernand's men, despite Grant's hints to the contrary in his memoirs.

McClernand twice powered his way over the Rebels in his front, and he could rightly claim that his troops caused the Confederate army to retreat. He again annoyed Grant, for after the initial enemy retreat, McClernand made brief victory remarks, in which he was joined by Illinois governor Yates, who accompanied the Thirteenth Corps, and Grant's political ally, Illinois congressman Elihu Washburne, probably added a few words. Whatever negative feelings Grant had, he had to mute them since he would not be critical of Washburne, which kept him from lashing out at Yates and McClernand. Grant did remind the three that the battle was not over, and McClernand needed little urging to order his troops forward to ultimate victory.

An interesting sidelight occurred afterward when Grant aides John Rawlins and James Wilson approached Grant about a *"rapprochement,"* suggesting that Grant personally congratulate McClernand. They were taken aback when Grant refused. Grant said he was angry with McClernand for asking that Governor Yates be allowed to "review the troops" before they began to cross the Mississippi. If so, McClernand was being true to his political roots, and Grant should not have been surprised. Grant also said that McClernand had violated orders by bringing wagons along behind his column, wagons which were supposed to "have been left at the river during preliminary movements." Surely Grant could have overruled McClernand on the spot and held the wagons in place if he felt that strongly. McClernand had also, according to Grant, ordered his artillery to keep firing after Grant had told the artillery "to harbor its ammunition." Supposedly a messenger from McClernand told Grant that the former had declared that he had fought well and did not want to let up or to be interfered with. McClernand had a point, however bombastic his response, and Grant ordinarily would have understood, especially if McPherson or Sherman had been in McClernand's position. If this account is accurate, Grant's protestations seem petty, and one wonders if none of the irritations had occurred would Grant have personally congratulated McClernand? Given Grant's feelings toward his subordinate, he probably would not.

Once the Confederates evacuated Port Gibson, they also gave up Grand Gulf, so Grant had a supply base and could continue inland. Sherman had still not arrived, but Grant decided to move ahead, his initial target being the Southern Railroad of Mississippi, a supply line that connected Vicksburg to Jackson and points east. Grant knew that the main Confederate force would be on his left flank, scattered along the opposite bank of the Big Black River that ran southwest from east of Vicksburg to the Mississippi. If Grant had little confidence in McClernand, he again did not show it, for he chose to place McClernand and his corps on the army's left during the push north. McClernand, not McPherson, protected Grant's most vulnerable flank. If Grant still fretted about McClernand, he could have waited on Sherman and put Sherman on the left. But Sherman was not a believer, and he had not done well at Chickasaw Bayou. Moreover Grant did not want to pause too long, for he had momentum and did not intend to lose it. So he ordered his army north, which meant he surely trusted McClernand to repel any attempt by Confederate general John Pemberton to strike the Union left.

When Sherman finally arrived, Grant placed his corps in the center between McClernand and McPherson, further shielding McPherson from a potential Pemberton attack. However, McPherson found himself confronting Rebels south of Raymond, a town southwest of Jackson. John Gregg's Confederate brigade had occupied the position to keep track of Grant's right flank. Pemberton had warned Gregg not to be drawn into battle, but Gregg, thinking McPherson's advance consisted only of a small force covering Grant's right, attacked on May 12. Not until the fight was well underway did he realize he faced a larger Union force; whether he ever knew until afterward that he faced a whole corps is unclear. McPherson did not lead well, sending in his divisions piecemeal, and Gregg's men fought fiercely. Numbers soon told, and solid leadership by McPherson's division commanders turned the tide, forcing Gregg to retreat to Jackson.

By that time, Grant had heard that Joseph E. Johnston had arrived in the capital city and was gathering an army to reinforce Pemberton. So

Grant turned his attention to Jackson, leaving McClernand in the Raymond area to keep Pemberton at bay. Once again McClernand deployed in the more dangerous position of potentially facing Pemberton's entire force, much larger than Johnston's. McClernand, still on Grant's left, had to move right toward Raymond while fighting off Confederate details nipping at his heels.

Grant sent McPherson and his corps to attack Jackson from the west, while Sherman advanced from the south to attack the town. Interestingly, Grant ordered McClernand to send one division to cover McPherson's rear, while using the rest of his corps to help Sherman if needed. Thus Grant placed McClernand in the position of not only watching for a possible advance by Pemberton but also protecting Sherman and McPherson from that same advance or any other problems that might arise. Grant personally rode with Sherman. The battle at Jackson on May 14 did not take long to win; Johnston hurriedly withdrew northeast, leaving the town to a token, sacrificial force. The taking of Jackson did not challenge the military abilities of Sherman or McPherson.[34]

Grant meanwhile received a message from a Union spy that told him Pemberton had been ordered to join forces with Johnston. So, leaving Sherman behind to sack Jackson, Grant pushed McPherson's corps west to join with McClernand to block Pemberton.

Pemberton initially ignored Johnston's order and moved toward Raymond to strike at Grant's supply line rather than unite with Johnston as ordered. Pemberton did not want to leave Vicksburg vulnerable. However, when he received word from Johnston that Jackson had been evacuated and that Pemberton must march east to join him, Pemberton tried to turn his army around and go north. Grant's two corps reached Pemberton's army too soon, and the battle of Champion Hill ensued on May 16. Sherman's corps missed the battle because it was still in Jackson. Sherman did not move west until the night of May 15 and arrived too late to join in the battle. So Grant went into the fight with McPherson's corps on the right and McClernand's on the left. Grant saw no need to keep track of McClernand, for he chose to stay with McPherson.

McClernand had already moved his corps forward, and he met briefly with McPherson and asked McPherson to send one division to support the Thirteenth Corps' advance. McClernand, in his too often undiplomatic way of dealing with West Pointers, told McPherson that once the Thirteenth Corps had chased the Rebels back toward Vicksburg, McPherson could bring up the rest of his men to mop up. McPherson ignored the slight and went along with McClernand's idea, for it was sound strategy.

As the battle developed, Grant sent word to McClernand to push forward if conditions allowed. McClernand took Grant's words to mean not to risk an all-out aggressive attack unless he was sure of success. McClernand, knowing how Grant felt about him, decided he must be cautious. Grant later in the day sent word for McClernand to speed up, but McClernand did not receive the message until mid-afternoon. Once he did, he acted and pushed forward forcing Pemberton's rear guard, William Loring's division, to retreat away from the rest of Pemberton's army. Loring did a roundabout march and joined forces with Johnston at Jackson. McClernand's push had cost Pemberton a division.

Grant later strongly criticized McClernand for holding back, but the charge is disingenuous. By riding with McPherson rather than placing himself between the two corps, Grant cut himself off from communicating effectively with McClernand. Thus, while McPherson's division commanders, especially John Logan, smashed Pemberton's left flank, McClernand received word of the successes on the Union right too late to coordinate his own actions with McPherson's. Could McClernand have moved more quickly and made the Union victory even greater than it was? Certainly he could have, but under the circumstances, he cannot be solely blamed for not doing so. McClernand did march his corps aggressively forward to the town of Edwards, and the next day he singlehandedly beat Pemberton's forces at the Big Black River, sending the Confederates retreating to Vicksburg.[35]

After failed attacks on May 19 and May 22 against the well-fortified Confederates at Vicksburg, Grant settled on regular siege operations. McClernand on the left, McPherson in the center, and Sherman on the right comprised Grant's alignment. Grant had another negative encounter with McClernand during the May 22 attack. McClernand's corps made greater headway than the other two, and he begged for help, though his political mindset led him to exaggerate his success. Grant finally sent troops from McPherson's corps, but the detachment arrived too late to be of much aid. Grant did not take McClernand's messages seriously, but his reaction was rather petty. He did give Sherman permission to attack again on the right to turn Rebel attention in that direction, but Sherman, as had been the case all day, did nothing but increase his casualty list. Grant in fact had no idea of how much progress McClernand had made, for he had established his headquarters behind Sherman's corps. Might McClernand have scored a breakthrough if Grant had sent more of McPherson's men sooner? There is of course no way to know what might have happened. Grant made sure of that; this was one time that Grant's dislike of McClernand clouded the commanding general's judgment.[36]

The final act in the McClernand-Grant relationship came later in the siege. A week after the May 22 failure, McClernand sent out his usual congratulatory message to his troops. The corps had fought well during the land campaign, and McClernand's words seemed innocuous enough. However, he did intimate that his corps could have done more on the twenty-second if it had received more support. This, of course, was a not so thinly veiled criticism of Grant's inaction. The order might have gone unnoticed had it not appeared in print in a Memphis newspaper, a copy of which reached Sherman's hands. Sherman, who hated McClernand more than Grant did, exploded, pointing out to Grant that McClernand had violated the 1862 order that no official reports of any kind were to be sent to newspapers. Grant first coldly asked McClernand for an explanation. McClernand admitted that he had written the message as published, and he apologized for Grant's not having received a copy, an oversight he blamed on his adjutant.

Grant did not care for any explanation. McClernand's action gave him an opening that he felt free to use, now that the siege was in progress and reinforcements were pouring in every day. The bottom line was Grant no longer needed McClernand, for he had had other grounds for dismissal if he had adhered to strict military parameters. Edwin Stanton had already told Grant that if McClernand or anyone else in the army caused trouble, Grant had permission to remove said perpetrator from his army. McClernand had certainly made waves on more than one occasion, and Grant had ignored them. Now ready to act, Grant knew that Stanton's words gave assurances that he would have the full support of the government. McClernand had no doubt overplayed his hand with his many messages to Lincoln and his disrespect for Halleck. Halleck in turn had no doubt influenced Stanton. On June 18, Grant formally dismissed McClernand from command. McClernand wrote many long letters denouncing the injustice of Grant's act, but no one in Washington listened. They had stopped listening when McClernand kept arguing there was a conspiracy against him. His claims were not totally an illusion, but he had fed his problems with his personality. McClernand stayed in the army, but his future assignments were in the backwater of the war.[37]

The story of Grant and McClernand demonstrated that men of diverse backgrounds and personalities could not avoid confrontations. The confrontations did not keep them from doing the jobs they had to do to make the campaign a success. Though they understood victory to be the goal, that did not mean they ever found personal common ground. Tension between the two persisted as an undercurrent of their relationship and overshadowed the campaign without derailing its success. McClernand's overt political demeanor collided with Grant's reserve and military training, which gave him little patience with a non–West Pointer. Yet Grant's actions after he decided on his final Vicksburg strategy indicate that no matter how much he disliked McClernand, he respected him as a field commander. Grant never would admit as much, but McClernand led the inland march, covered Grant's potentially vulnerable left flank, and was placed in position to bail out McPherson and Sherman during the campaign against Jackson. Whatever McClernand's failings at Champion Hill, Grant had to bear some responsibility, and the victory at Big Black River belonged to McClernand. During the May 22 attack at Vicksburg, McClernand's corps had accomplished more than McPherson's or Sherman's. That fact is clear: how much McClernand actually did, or how much more he might have done with reinforcements, is debatable.

The traditional, oversimplified view of McClernand does not hold up under close scrutiny. He can rightly be called loud-mouthed, annoying, overbearing, arrogant, and possessed of a consistent ability to create friction with other commanders. Yet in campaigns and battles, he often performed admirably. Grant understood that, and he tolerated McClernand and used him accordingly. Whatever Grant's feelings, he put victory first, something he had in common with the political general he detested. Both deserve credit for the ultimate success of the Vicksburg Campaign. Grant justly received recognition for his great victory; McClernand deserves to receive more credit than history has given him.

Notes

1. Examples are Richard L. Kiper, *Major General John Alexander McClernand: Politician in Uniform* (Kent, Ohio: Kent State University Press, 1999); Michael B. Ballard, *Vicksburg: The Campaign That Opened the Mississippi* (Chapel Hill: University of North Carolina Press, 2004); William L. Shea and Terrence J. Winschel, *Vicksburg Is the Key: The Struggle for the Mississippi River* (Lincoln: University of Nebraska Press, 2003). Examples of traditional negative views are in T. Harry Williams, *Lincoln and His Generals* (New York: Vintage Books, 1952); Robert Leckie, *None Died in Vain* (New York: HarperCollins, 1990); Geoffrey Perret, *Ulysses S. Grant: Soldier and President* (New York: Random House, 1997).

2. The discussion of McClernand's prewar years is from Kiper, *McClernand*, 1–21.

3. The discussion of Grant's prewar years is from Michael B. Ballard, *U. S. Grant: The Making of a General, 1861–1863* (Lanham, Md.: Rowman and Littlefield, 2005), 1–9.

4. Kiper, *McClernand*, 20, 64.

5. Ibid., 22; Ballard, *Grant*, 11.

6. Roy P. Basler, ed., *The Collected Works of Abraham Lincoln*, 8 vols. plus index (New Brunswick, N.J.: Rutgers University Press, 1953–55), 8:593–94; John Y. Simon, ed., *The Papers of Ulysses S. Grant*, 31 vols. to date (Carbondale: Southern Illinois University Press, 1967–), 3:138; Kiper, *McClernand*, 24.

7. Kiper, *McClernand*, 47–48; *The War of the Rebellion: A Compilation of the Official Records of the Union and Confederate Armies*, 128 vols. (Washington, D. C.: Government Printing Office, 1894–1927), series 1, vol. 3, pt. 1:277–83 (hereinafter cited as *OR*. Unless otherwise indicated. all citations are from series 1); Simon, *Grant*, 3:239.

8. Helen Todd, *A Man Named Grant* (Boston: Houghton Mifflin, 1940), 30.

9. *OR*, vol. 7, pt. 1:160–61, 182.

10. Ibid., 170, 179; Kiper, *McClernand*, 88–89; Ballard, *Grant*, 39–40.

11. Ballard, *Grant*, 51, 53, 58–59; Kiper, *McClernand*, 109–10; *OR*, vol. 10, pt. 1:111–12.

12. Kiper, *McClernand*, 114.

13. Ibid., 119; *OR*, vol. 10, pt. 1:110; Simon, *Grant*, 5:49.

14. Kiper, *McClernand*, 119; *OR*, vol. 10, pt. 2:99, 189.

15. *OR*, vol. 10, pt. 2:240–41, 256–57.

16. Ballard, *Grant*, 66; Kiper, *McClernand*, 122, 124–25; Simon, *Grant*, 5:331.

17. Kiper, *McClernand*, 124–31; Simon, *Grant*, 5:403–4, 412–14.

18. Kiper, *McClernand*, 127; Simon, *Grant*, 5:331.

19. Kiper, *McClernand*, 133–36.

20. Ibid., 136–37.

21. David Dixon Porter, *Incidents and Anecdotes of the Civil War* (New York: D. Appleton and Co., 1885), 122–23.

22. Quoted statements regarding McClernand are by Edwin M. Stanton, Secretary of War, October 21, 1862, in *OR*, vol. 17, pt. 2:282; Ballard, *Vicksburg*, 80–81, 83–84; Simon, *Grant*, 6:288–89; Kiper, *McClernand*, 139.

23. Ballard, *Grant*, 89–90.

24. Kiper, *McClernand*, 148–53; *OR*, vol. 17, pt. 2:420, 432–33.

25. Simon, *Grant*, 7:61–62, 135–37; Kiper, *McClernand*, 155.

26. Ballard, *Vicksburg*, 147–50, 154; Kiper, *McClernand*, 144.

27. *OR*, vol. 17, pt. 2:570–71; Basler, *Lincoln*, 6:70.

28. Simon, *Grant*, 7:274–75; Kiper, *McClernand*, 207.

29. Kiper, *McClernand*, 211; Ballard, *Vicksburg*, 172, 191–98; Ulysses S. Grant, *Personal Memoirs of U. S. Grant*, 2 vols. (New York: Charles L. Webster and Co., 1885–86), 1:449; James Harrison Wilson, *Under the Old Flag*, 2 vols. (New York: D. Appleton and Co., 1912), 1:159; James Harrison Wilson, *The Life of John A. Rawlins* (New York: Neale Publishing Co., 1916), 114–15.

30. Ballard, *Vicksburg*, 195.

31. Wilson, *Under the Old Flag*, 1:197.

32. Adam Badeau, *Military History of U. S. Grant*, 3 vols. (New York: D. Appleton and Company, 1885), 1:194.

33. On Port Gibson, see Ballard, *Vicksburg*, 221–50.

34. Wilson, *Under the Old Flag*, 174–75. On Raymond and Jackson, see Ballard, *Vicksburg*, 251–81.

35. On Champion Hill and Big Black, see Ballard, *Vicksburg*, 282–318, especially 295–96; see also Ballard, *Grant*, 129–30.

36. On the May 22 assault, see Ballard, *Vicksburg*, 338–51, especially 343–44.

37. Simon, *Grant*, 8:384–87, 428–31; Kiper, *McClernand*, 268–78.

8

"DEVELOPED BY CIRCUMSTANCES"
GRANT, INTELLIGENCE, AND THE
VICKSBURG CAMPAIGN

William B. Feis

On July 4, 1863, Major General Ulysses S. Grant telegraphed the War Department with news he had been longing to send for months: "The Enemy surrendered this morning."[1] These five words marked the end of the Vicksburg Campaign, one of the more remarkable and significant military victories in the Civil War and, for that matter, in American military history. On that day, Lieutenant General John Pemberton's Confederate forces gave up Vicksburg, Mississippi, one of the last major Confederate bastions guarding a strategically significant stretch of the Mississippi River. Pemberton's surrender resulted, in part, from Grant's relentless siege operations that began on May 22 and by Independence Day had starved the Vicksburg garrison into submission. However, the siege was but the capstone of an earlier, rapidly unfolding maneuver campaign conducted by Grant's Army of the Tennessee between April 30 and May 19. This "Mississippi Blitzkrieg" phase began when Grant crossed the Mississippi at Bruinsburg on April 30 and ended with two failed assaults on Vicksburg's fortifications on May 19 and 22. During this period, the Army of the Tennessee marched 180 miles through hostile territory, fought and won five battles against isolated Confederate forces, captured the state capital at Jackson, drove Pemberton's troops into the city's fortifications, and cut them off from outside aid, essentially dooming the garrison. Coupled with the simultaneous Confederate defeat at Gettysburg in the East, the war seemed to turn decisively in favor of the Union. But what Major General William T. Sherman told Grant after they reached the outskirts of Vicksburg in May speaks to the importance of the maneuver campaign in its own right. "Until this moment I never thought your expedition a success," he remarked. "But this is a campaign. This is a success even if we never take the town."[2]

Reflecting upon the campaign in his memoirs, Grant that it seemed "as though Providence had directed the course of the campaign while the Army of the Tennessee executed the decree."[3] Divine intervention notwithstanding, he also declared that the course he pursued was, from beginning to end, "suggested and developed by circumstances." He started with a large strategic objective and the broad outlines of a plan to achieve it, but the campaign on the ground was essentially an ad hoc affair, dependent upon local conditions, enemy reactions, and the blind crossroads where paper plans and reality collide to give it shape, texture, and direction. The only clarity Grant could hope to scratch out of this swirling chaos would come from the information he received in the midst of it, either from intentional intelligence collection efforts or by sheer happenstance. This essay will examine how Grant procured and used intelligence during the opening weeks of the Vicksburg campaign (roughly mid-March through mid-May) and will argue that the Union general not only outmaneuvered his opponent but also outgeneraled him in the "intelligence war." As Grant would attest, however, merely possessing the right intelligence did not by itself bring success. The difference between triumph and failure came down to what he *did* with that information. It was in those lonely moments of truth that he came face to face with one of war's many object lessons: intelligence does not make decisions, commanders do. By the time Grant penned those five words on July 4, he had not only embraced that lesson but transcended it.

Before the Vicksburg Campaign unfolded in the spring of 1863, Grant had perhaps more experience than any other Union officer in confronting fortified Confederate positions along or near major waterways. In late 1861, he led an unsuccessful attempt to outflank Columbus, Kentucky, a fortress on the Mississippi River, by attacking a Confederate outpost at Belmont, Missouri, directly across the river. This action failed to turn Columbus, but in early 1862, after a short but sharp campaign, Union forces captured Fort Henry on the Tennessee River and Fort Donelson on the Cumberland, breaking the Confederates' major defensive line in the West and forcing the evacuation of *both* Columbus and Nashville. Later that spring, Grant positioned his forces along the Tennessee River for an assault on the fortifications ringing Corinth, Mississippi. Though the Confederates' surprise attack at Shiloh delayed that campaign, Corinth soon fell, followed shortly by New Orleans, Baton Rouge, and Memphis. By late 1862, one of the last significant Confederate strongholds on the Mississippi River was at Vicksburg, a heavily fortified city known as the "Gibraltar on the Mississippi." The imposing fortifications both along the river and east of the city defended a stretch of the Mississippi containing the last remaining logistical connection with the

Confederate Trans-Mississippi. When Grant zeroed in on Vicksburg in late 1862, his past success against similar positions augured well for his future campaign, especially since they were valuable learning experiences in using intelligence against enemy forces tethered to fortified positions. But it had also been, at times, a hard-earned education.[4]

The months before Grant turned his gaze upon Vicksburg, however, proved frustrating. Still smarting from the surprise attack at Shiloh that nearly shattered his army and his reputation along with it, he was forced to play second fiddle to Major General Henry W. Halleck during his successful bid to capture Corinth in May 1862. Grant eagerly resumed command after Halleck's departure that summer but instead of moving toward the next objective, his troops were dispersed in garrisons along a 115-mile defensive front arcing across northern Mississippi and southwestern Tennessee. By summer's end, Grant had spent many frustrating weeks protecting over 360 miles of railroad tracks, rebuilding bridges and torn up rail lines, managing a hostile population, chasing ubiquitous guerrillas, and watching Confederate activity in northern Mississippi. "With all the vigilance I can bring to bear," he complained at the time, "I cannot determine the objects of the enemy."[5] The Confederate invasion of Kentucky caused substantial commotion in the fall of 1862 and, with all eyes on General Braxton Bragg's attempt to reach the Ohio River, Grant remained sidelined. This state of affairs frustrated him deeply because, as staff officer Horace Porter later observed, he possessed "an inborn dislike to be thrown upon the defensive" because it not only handed the initiative to the enemy but threw the burden of uncertainty on the Federals. The impact on the overall strategic picture also troubled Grant. He later assessed the situation this way: "The problem for us was to move forward to a decisive victory, or our cause was lost. No progress was being made in any other field, and we had to go on."[6] On the operational level, sitting still multiplied his difficulties by allowing Confederates to interdict supply lines and to pounce on isolated garrisons seemingly at will while Union troops fumbled around trying to stop them. Moreover, without Grant keeping them at home, Confederate troops in Mississippi could reinforce Bragg's invasion without much fear of detection, let alone disruption. To turn the tables required going on the offensive, but until that happened, Grant had to rely on his ability to find accurate and timely intelligence to counteract Confederate operations. But this was easier said than done. No wonder Grant called this idle stretch his "most anxious period of the war."[7]

Throughout the summer of 1862, a number of obstacles prevented Grant from getting quality information, including Confederate guerrillas and cavalry preying on his communications and, as was becoming clear, the lack of a centralized intelligence service within his army.[8] The actions on Union-held Iuka and Corinth that fall—aggressive moves that Grant had great difficulty uncovering, let alone tracking with any accuracy—only underlined the great difficulty of getting a fix on an enemy operating on his own turf. Posing an even greater challenge was detecting Confederate reinforcements either coming from Tennessee or heading there from Mississippi. His anxiety lessened considerably when, in early November, he received the go-ahead for an attempt on Vicksburg. His plan called for driving south along the Mississippi Central Railroad to Jackson, then turning west toward the fortified city. As he got underway, however, rumors surfaced that a portion of Bragg's army—now in Middle Tennessee after the failed invasion of Kentucky—was headed toward Mississippi. Alarmed, Grant discovered how little he truly knew about the potential threats lurking behind him in Tennessee. If left unaddressed, this intelligence gap might well prove disastrous for his upcoming campaign if Confederates decided to squeeze the Army of the Tennessee from both front and rear. Not only might Vicksburg get farther out of reach, but such an event could seriously threaten the Union's hard-fought gains since Forts Henry and Donelson. Grant therefore had to find out what was going on beyond his lines in Tennessee. But how to get that information remained a difficult proposition.[9]

On November 12, 1862, nearly two weeks into Grant's first Vicksburg campaign, three Union spies arrived in Corinth with news that Bragg was en route to Mississippi. The commander of the post, Brigadier General Grenville M. Dodge, quickly relayed the report to Grant in the field. Concerned, Grant replied: "Can you get information from the East, say as far as Florence [Alabama]? I want to hear from along the Tennessee [River] from Tuscumbia eastward to know if any rebel troops are crossing there." In another dispatch, Grant's chief of staff John Rawlins told Dodge to "send out spies and scouts [to the] east and obtain all information possible." Believing he had "carte blanche to take care of that front," Dodge began constructing an intelligence network, and before long his scouts were watching Tennessee River crossings for signs of Confederate activity.[10] As Dodge's network shifted into gear, Grant stressed the importance of its unique mission. Dodge's Corinth operations would be, he wrote, "a much more important command than that of a division in the field."[11]

As Grant's campaign continued into late November, Dodge consistently reported that Bragg remained in Middle Tennessee and posed no threat to Union operations in Mississippi. Focused as they were on the Union rear, however, Dodge's men were not in a position to get information on Pemberton's forces confronting Grant in northern Mississippi. And without a way to consistently locate and track Confederate forces, especially fast-moving enemy cavalry units, disaster was never far away. When Union scouts missed Major General Earl Van Dorn's December raid on Holly Springs, which destroyed Grant's main supply depot, the dangers of this liability became clear, especially since the raid wrecked the campaign and forced a retreat.[12]

After the Holly Springs debacle and the nearly simultaneous defeat of Sherman's expedition at Chickasaw Bayou north of Vicksburg, Grant buried the overland approach for good, opting instead to use the Mississippi River as the new axis of advance. But where his main blow would fall remained an open question. Respect for the city's imposing river defenses in the center negated that option, and Sherman's failed assault on the Confederate right flank (the Walnut Hills) northeast of the city in December boded ill for another attempt there. Grant searched for ways to circumvent the most impressive of these defenses by digging canals and using natural waterways like Lake Providence, Yazoo Pass, and Steele's Bayou to bypass the big river guns. All these attempts failed, though they did confuse Pemberton as to Grant's true intentions. In a last ditch effort, on April 2, Grant personally surveyed the Walnut Hills fortifications for an opportunity to exploit but came away firmly against another attempt there, a decision that ended "the last hope of turning the enemy by the right."[13]

With dwindling options, Grant settled on a bold gamble that promised significant dividends if successful. His army would march down the river's west bank to a point below Vicksburg and cross over to Warrenton or Grand Gulf where good roads led inland. But for this scheme to work, Vicksburg had to be isolated from outside assistance while Grant went after Pemberton, placing a premium on intelligence about Confederate reinforcements coming from Tennessee or elsewhere. To meet that need Dodge's network grew in both size and operational reach. In November 1862, Dodge had only eleven men in his fledgling "secret service." Between February and April 1863, however, an average of twenty-five operatives per month received pay, and in May, the most important month of Grant's second Vicksburg Campaign, Dodge sent out thirty-two scouts on sixty separate missions, most of them looking for Confederate reinforcements coming from Tennessee but a few also ranging beyond Grant's front in Mississippi. For example, on February 23, Dodge submitted a lengthy report summarizing news from scouts "posted at Mobile, Meridian, and Jackson." These men reported that Pemberton had not received any reinforcements since December and that train loads of sick soldiers departed daily from Vicksburg, all of which were corroborated by Confederate deserters "flocking" to Union lines.[14]

Two months later, Grant grew concerned that news of "a large accumulation of engines and cars at Meridian" meant the Confederates might be preparing to transport a large force to Vicksburg and instructed Dodge to look into it. Before long, Dodge's scout returned declaring that the rail cars in question had been "run off on wooden rails for storage purposes as the confederacy [sic] had no use for them."[15] Dodge eventually penetrated deeper into the Confederacy using spies (often Mississippi and Alabama Unionists) planted in Meridian, Selma, Mobile, Chattanooga, and even Atlanta. By the time Vicksburg fell, Dodge had employed nearly 130 operatives, authorized over 200 covert missions, and expended over $21,000 on "secret service" activities in the cause of toppling the "Confederate Gibraltar."[16]

Before the second campaign got underway, however, Dodge's network had not penetrated Vicksburg and, with Federal armies too far from the city, information gleaned from prisoners, deserters, "contrabands" (escaped slaves), and local civilians remained scarce. Unfortunately for Grant, what did come in was often contradictory and confusing. By late February, a number of reports claimed that Pemberton was determined to hold Vicksburg at all costs while others depicted a distraught enemy prepared to give up the city without a fight. More confusing, some sources suggested that a landing below Vicksburg would be welcomed by the Confederates because it would open West Tennessee to invasion.[17] These conflicting reports only darkened the mood at headquarters. "It is impossible to get information from [Vicksburg]," Grant complained. "Even deserters who come can tell nothing except of their own regiments or Brigade at furthest." A month later, he still grumbled that he possessed "no means of learning anything from below except what is occationally [sic] learned through Southern papers." In late March, the situation remained discouraging, prompting Charles A. Dana, a War Department official traveling with the army, to report that Grant's headquarters was "not so well informed a place as I hoped to find it."[18]

Despite this near-blindness, Grant forged ahead with the campaign and on March 31 Major General John McClernand's corps headed downriver toward Richmond and New Carthage, Louisiana, with Major General James McPherson's corps not far behind. Once underway, however, Grant realized Pemberton would likely detect the activity on the west bank, especially after learning that some northern war correspondents with the army had reported the move in graphic detail to their papers. Furious about the leak, Grant fumed that these reports had given the Confederates "important news, and probably in time to defeat the consummation of our plans," and the next day ordered all Memphis newspapers shut down "for giving aid and comfort to the enemy by publishing in their columns every move made here by troops."[19] Several days later, however, Charles Dana revealed that the security breach might have worked in Grant's favor. "The probability," he observed, "is that the rebels regard the publication as a blind to cover other designs" because Pemberton seemed to "believe Snyder's or Drumgould's Bluff [the Confederate right along Walnut Hills] is to be assaulted, and there and at Chickasaw Bayou they are making considerable preparations."[20]

Grant was also doing all he could to foster this false impression. Understanding Frederick the Great's dictum that "He who tries to defend everything defends nothing," Grant knew Pemberton had little margin for error in deploying his troops to meet potential threats while holding on to points vital to the defense of Vicksburg.[21] Like a guard dog tethered to a post, Pemberton could growl and snap ferociously along his perimeter, but he could neither lunge beyond the length of his leash nor be everywhere at once, making the slightest miscalculation in his deployment scheme potentially disastrous. To help Pemberton make such a mistake, in early April Grant dispatched troops under Major General Frederick Steele to establish a base upriver at Greenville to strengthen the impression that the Federals were focused on the Confederate right. In the end, Steele's expedition, combined with the Federal withdrawal from Yazoo Pass, a reported decline in Union forces outside Port Hudson, and reports of transports loaded with Union troops moving upriver, misled his opponent more than Grant could have hoped. All this activity convinced Pemberton that Grant's army had been ordered to Tennessee, and Steele's force was covering the retreat. Union movements had meshed so perfectly with Pemberton's own wishful thinking that, despite numerous warnings from subordinates monitoring the east bank, he not only ignored McClernand but detached two brigades (about eight thousand men) to help Bragg confront a newly reinforced Union army in Tennessee.[22] Clearly, distinguishing the real from the ruse required better Confederate intelligence and an intrepid and intuitive commander, both of which were lacking in Vicksburg.

About this same time, a spy named W. I. Morris arrived in Corinth with information showing that the ploy was working. Though one of Dodge's men, Morris at times worked directly for Grant, who had sent him into Vicksburg around March 21. Prior to this time, information about the city trickled in from Dodge's operatives, southern refugees, Confederate deserters, and smuggled copies of Vicksburg newspapers, though much of it was dated or untrustworthy. Morris's report was the first significant peek inside the city by an experienced scout. His April 13 report stated accurately that Pemberton had ordered eight thousand of his troops to Tennessee and that the Vicksburg garrison faced serious supply shortages. Morris also observed that Pemberton's forces—estimated to be between twenty-five thousand and thirty-two thousand men (also accurate)—were thinly stretched from Grand

Gulf on the Mississippi north to Greenwood, and that most of the large-bore guns were deployed in the river defenses. More important, however, was his description of the fortifications ringing the city. Pemberton had constructed continuous works three miles east of the city, some several lines deep. "Every Hill and ridge," warned Morris "has a work upon it." Despite the seemingly formidable nature of these fortifications, however, Morris was confident that the Confederates did "not fear an attack from that direction," an indication that Pemberton still expected the main Union attack to strike the Walnut Hills.[23] This news was evidence that Union diversions had indeed, as Grant wrote, "tended to confuse and mislead" the enemy. More important, Morris's intelligence revealed that Pemberton's army was dispersed and that advancing from below the city might hit him where he was least expecting it.[24] A day later, in fact, Dana reported that the consensus at headquarters was that the Confederates "still, apparently, have no idea of [McClernand's] movement, but look constantly for an assault on Haynes' Bluff or Vicksburg direct" from the north.[25] Based on his past experience confronting fortified positions and bolstered by Morris's intelligence, Grant pushed to get across the river below the city before this critical opportunity vanished.[26]

On the night of April 16, Union gunboats and transports passed the Vicksburg batteries without suffering serious damage. Six days later, another flotilla survived the gauntlet and moved into position to ferry Grant's infantry across the river. Flooding on the Louisiana side, however, delayed the arrival of his columns. If running the batteries failed to tip his hand, Grant feared this last delay might give Pemberton time to figure it out.[27] In fact, by this time Pemberton had already woken up to the fact that Grant's army was not Tennessee-bound and cancelled the transfer of his two brigades headed for Bragg's army. But he still remained uncertain as to the true intent of Union operations. To keep the Confederate commander in the dark, on April 17 Grant sent Colonel Benjamin H. Grierson's cavalry on a sweep through central Mississippi to sever Pemberton's communications and divert attention from Grant's operations. At the same time, two other raids led by Dodge and Colonel Abel D. Streight knifed into Alabama to further distract the Vicksburg commander and hopefully lure Confederate cavalry out of Mississippi and away from Grierson.[28] Until his army crossed the Mississippi, however, Grant would not know for sure whether Pemberton had taken any of the bait.

By April 18, Grant had decided upon Grand Gulf as the main landing point. But soon some disturbing information made him rethink his choice. A "local preacher" had told Admiral David Porter, in command of the naval component supporting the campaign, that Pemberton had "known all about this move" on Grand Gulf and had "been preparing this place six weeks." This report, along with testimony from naval scouts sent to view the works, gave Porter cold feet. To settle the matter, Grant personally surveyed Grand Gulf from across the river but saw nothing to support the clergyman's story or the admiral's fears. In fact, he told Sherman that if Grand Gulf were attacked soon, "the place will fall easily."[29] The next step was to find a good road running from Grand Gulf across the Big Black River toward Warrenton. For this mission, he sent Lieutenant Colonel James H. Wilson, a topographical engineer on his staff, to scout the area north of Grand Gulf near Cox's Ferry on the Big Black for a possible landing place connected to a "practicable road to the highlands." The area was inundated with water, but Wilson found a suitable landing place above Thompson's Ferry with the only passable road between Grand Gulf and Warrenton that led to higher ground. Moreover, from his own observations and interrogations of slaves "who had been working on the fortifications only that morning," Wilson determined that the Confederate defenses overlooking the Big Black were not all that imposing. Upon hearing this news, Grant requested that the navy steam up the Big Black and seize the ferry crossing. Fearing the narrowness of the river would endanger his boats, Porter declined. In his report dated May 30, Wilson complained, "Subsequent events have clearly demonstrated the weakness of the rebel defenses at the ferry and along the Big Black, as well as the practicability of the route" he proposed. [30]

Without Porter's gunboats, Grant scuttled the Big Black River operation and instead instructed McClernand to cross and seize Grand Gulf. Around the same time, Sherman's corps steamed upriver on transports to demonstrate against Haynes Bluff and make Pemberton think twice about weakening his right to meet the emerging threat downriver.[31] Though one historian argues that Sherman's demonstration "had little impact" and another called it "a wasted effort," Grant wrote afterwards that information from Confederate prisoners indicated that "this ruse succeeded most admirably."[32] On April 29, Grant watched as Porter's gunboats pounded the Grand Gulf fortifications in preparation for a landing, but it soon became evident that the defenses were far stronger than first believed. Adapting quickly, he postponed a crossing until the following day, ran the gunboats and transports past the Grand Gulf batteries with slight loss, and looked downriver at Rodney, Mississippi, as the new landing site.[33] Area maps, which were very poor, showed a steamboat landing there connected by a road to Port Gibson, a small hamlet southeast of Grand Gulf where several inland roads converged. Seizing Port Gibson would secure the beachhead and put the Federals in a position to force the evacuation of Grand Gulf and a long stretch of the Big Black's south bank.[34]

Likely impatient and worried that Pemberton had by now comprehended what was going on, Grant searched for a landing spot closer than Rodney. Late on April 29, he sent a reconnaissance force across the river to find a local resident familiar with the roads and terrain south of Grand Gulf and bring him back for questioning. A small detachment from the 3rd Illinois Cavalry crossed in a rowboat, found an "intelligent contraband" and delivered him to Grant early the next morning. The informant stated that "a good landing would be found at Bruinsburg," a spot upriver from Rodney free of Confederates and connected to Port Gibson by a serviceable road.[35] Adapting once again to new information, the Union commander ordered McClernand to cross at Bruinsburg and head toward high ground in the direction of Port Gibson.

With regard to the "intelligent contraband" who gave Grant the crucial information about Bruinsburg, geographer/historian Warren Grabau has argued that it was unlikely the Federal commander would have made such a momentous decision based *solely* on the word of an unknown slave picked up in the middle of the night. To explain this, Grabau claims that Grant's man was but one of many "contrabands" on the east bank of the Mississippi who were "both intelligent and intelligence agents" and "part of an elaborate and highly efficient service operated by the Union command."[36] He clearly believes Grant directed his patrol not to find just *any* individual on the other side, but to locate a specific slave who was part of an organized covert intelligence network in Mississippi run from Army of the Tennessee headquarters. Grabau's conclusion, however, is purely speculative since no evidence points to the existence of such an "intelligence network" in that area. Moreover, he apparently assumes that quality intelligence of this nature could *only* come from a "secret service" organization overseen by Union officials. But throughout the war, Union commanders in all theaters learned quickly that local slaves could provide a wealth of information on terrain, road networks, and the location and movement of Confederate forces. Just living and working in the area made them experts on those things, but they were also willing informants who sought out Union camps and readily shared what they knew to help the "Soldiers of Jubilee." Union officers pumping contrabands for information happened all the time, as a perusal of the *Official Records*, the *Grant Papers*, and a myriad of other sources quickly reveals. Even General Robert E. Lee knew all about this information hemorrhage. "The chief source of information to the enemy" he complained in 1863, "is through our Negroes."[37] Thus, it is *not* a stretch to conclude that the contraband Grant questioned that night provided actionable intelligence without, as Grabau contends, being part of a Union intelligence system along the Mississippi. [38]

Once McClernand's corps rushed ashore unopposed at Bruinsburg on April 30, the intelligence environment for Grant changed. No longer focused on where and when to land, his operational and tactical decisions would now be driven by rapidly changing circumstances on the ground and by what he knew at any given moment about his opponent's situation. The first instance where intelligence impacted his decisions across the river occurred even as McClernand's men disembarked from transports. According to Grant, his plan had been to cross the river and establish a foothold, build up his forces and collect supplies, and then send McClernand's corps south to assist Major General Nathaniel Banks in operations against Port Hudson, Louisiana. President Abraham Lincoln preferred that the two armies unite and operate together against both Vicksburg and Port Hudson, and Grant had agreed to this in principle back in March. He later claimed, however, that once McClernand made it across the river, intelligence indicating that "troops were expected at Jackson from the Southern Cities with [P. G. T.] Beaurigard [*sic*] to command" forced him to scuttle that plan and surge inland before Pemberton was reinforced, leaving Banks on his own.[39]

In fact, Beauregard had sent around five thousand troops to Mississippi from his army in South Carolina, but word of this did not reach Grant until eight days *after* he decided to abandon Banks, making this cause and effect relationship rather dubious. The intelligence on Beauregard merely provided Grant with a way to justify—after the fact—what he had likely intended to do all along. And as he watched his army come ashore in Mississippi, his blood was up. "I was on dry ground on the same side of the river as the enemy," he later recalled. "All the campaigns, labors, hardships and exposures . . . were for the accomplishment of this one object."[40] Unwilling to throw all that away to aid the slow-moving Banks, Grant saw an incredible but fleeting opportunity, and he snatched it. And the stunning success of the campaign made the discrepancy irrelevant, except perhaps to Nathaniel Banks.[41] This episode notwithstanding, allowing fluid circumstances and new intelligence to guide his actions remained central in Grant's decision-making for the remainder of the campaign. "Information received from day to day on the movements of the enemy," he later observed, "impelled me to the course pursued."[42]

On May 1, McClernand marched toward Port Gibson based on information supplied by "a fugitive negro" and clashed with Confederate forces under Brigadier General John Bowen on terrain described by Grant as the "most broken and difficult to operate in I ever saw."[43] Before the battle, McClernand—like Grant—had little idea where the enemy might appear, stating that he hoped to "surprise the enemy *if* he should be found in the neighborhood of Port Gibson" (emphasis added). Clearly, his corps operated as a reconnaissance-in-force, feeling for the enemy as it went. At Port Gibson, Bowen's Confederates mounted a stubborn defense but, outnumbered three-to-one, eventually withdrew. Bowen's defeat soon led to the evacuation of Grand Gulf, showing once again the value of Grant's method of turning forti-fied positions rather than tangling with them. But the situation confronting Bowen revealed a reality unfavorable to Pemberton as he attempted to com-prehend and meet the Union threat on his left. In order to protect so many points, the Confederate commander had to deploy his forces across a broad front at different locales, which allowed fast-moving Federal columns to gain local superiority and gobble them up. As Pemberton scrambled to defend everywhere, he risked losing everything. His hope that the main blow would fall on the fortified bluffs northeast of the city combined with his difficulty in grasping the situation on his front after April 30 only added to his troubles.[44]

After Port Gibson, Grant decided upon an indirect approach to Vicks-burg instead of moving immediately toward the city from the south. Sowing uncertainty in Pemberton's mind and geographical considerations all influ-enced this choice, as did his desire to cut the Southern Railroad of Missis-sippi running between Vicksburg and Jackson. Moreover, he also desired to "destroy the rail-road, telegraph [and] public stores" in Jackson and scatter any reinforcements lurking in the area.[45] As he had done in his movements against first Fort Henry and then Fort Donelson, he would swiftly neutral-ize one position (in this case Jackson) and then move rapidly against the stronger one (Vicksburg), having effectively isolated it. This meant, however, first isolating his *own* army deep in hostile territory. But if he could stay on the move and prevent the Confederates from regaining their balance, he could make Pemberton pay for trying to prove Frederick the Great wrong. But success would depend heavily on Grant's ability to make sense of and manage the rapidly changing circumstances on his front.[46]

Finding information on Pemberton's scattered forces, however, posed se-rious challenges. With Grierson's cavalry absent, the Army of the Tennessee in the field had but one full cavalry regiment and a mix of companies from other units. This small contingent quickly discovered that the unforgiving Mississippi terrain made reconnaissance missions nearly impossible, forc-ing some commanders to turn their cavalrymen into couriers.[47] In addition, Grant had few, if any, scouts at his headquarters, probably because he realized they could never keep pace with the swiftly changing environment and be where he needed them at the right time. To confront this reality, he essen-tially decentralized intelligence procurement and left his corps commanders to keep him supplied with information as they felt their way across central Mississippi. McClernand, McPherson, and Sherman all actively employed scouts during the campaign and funneled their reports directly to Army of the Tennessee headquarters. And to ensure enough personnel were available for scouting duty, the Signal Corps stepped into the breach. Limited by terrain that made visual communication difficult, the chief signal officer divided his signalmen into scouting detachments and sent one to each corps commander, boasting later that, as a result, "each corps commander was kept well informed as to his own command and General Grant as to the whole army."[48]

The Union commander also sought other sources of intelligence. For example, newspapers from Vicksburg and other Southern cities provided insight into troop movements, morale, and the general state of affairs behind enemy lines. And if southern war correspondents were as irresponsible as their northern counterparts when it came to keeping secrets, the dailies could be a treasure trove of useful information. To get southern newspapers, Dodge instructed one of his scouts, a Southern Unionist from Chickasaw County, Mississippi, to "make arrangements so that he could receive . . . papers every week" from places like Mobile, Jackson, Augusta, and Atlanta. Being a native Mississippian made this somewhat easier since he could subscribe to several newspapers and then pick them up at his local post office without raising suspicions. A courier system running between the post office and Corinth delivered the papers and other information to Dodge, who then forwarded to Grant a synopsis of the contents.[49] To ensure other human sources were fully exploited, standing orders instructed that Confederate deserters and anyone coming into Union lines undergo a "thorough examination" by the nearest Union officer.[50] In addition, corps commanders obtained newspapers, intercepted correspondence, and interrogated civilians, prisoners, deserters, and "contrabands" as they sliced through the countryside.[51] According to the intelligence log of one of Grant's staff, these efforts generated a steady stream of information throughout the mobile phase of the campaign.[52]

On May 12, Grant won his second engagement of the campaign when McPherson defeated Brigadier General John Gregg's Confederates at Raymond. After putting up a stout fight, an outnumbered Gregg withdrew toward Jackson.[53] Without a doubt, Grant's decision to have the three corps operate separately and advance by different routes worked well, leaving Pemberton confused as to the main axis of advance as Union forces seemingly spread like an ink stain across central Mississippi. This operational approach also allowed Federal troops to gain local superiority over Confederate defenders at both Port Gibson and Raymond. All this activity bred uncertainty in Confederate headquarters and, combined with their mission to hold Vicksburg at all costs, encouraged Pemberton to adopt a passive and reactionary posture, which also fit quite well with his own cautious nature.[54]

Later that night, Grant made a crucial, campaign-changing decision influenced both by Gregg's decision to retreat to Jackson and new intelligence. Before the Raymond fight, Grant learned that Pemberton was digging in at Edwards Station on the Southern Railroad of Mississippi between Jackson and Vicksburg. According to one source, Edwards was where "the rebels intend to make their big stand."[55] These and other reports led him to contemplate a major push northward to cut the railroad—and Pemberton's key supply line—at that point. But some earlier intelligence still remained troubling. Three days before the Raymond fight, McPherson reported that local citizens in Utica disclosed that "Beauregard is at or near Jackson" with reinforcements from the East. On May 11, a southern newspaper forwarded to Grant's headquarters corroborated this news, announcing that "the reinforcements from Charleston [where Beauregard was in command] are arriving—and will continue to come as fast as the roads will bring them." A local Mississippian added that Confederate President Jefferson Davis had ordered Pemberton "to hold the [Mississippi] river at all hazards and that re-enforcements would be sent from the East" while an intercepted letter from Edwards Station noted that the troops from South Carolina had already arrived.[56]

Though Pemberton was indeed receiving additional troops, Grant reasoned that his opponent would wait for the Federals to come to him, which had been the case in much of his experience with Confederate commanders defending fixed points. He gave little weight to the possibility that Pemberton might venture out from behind his works to attack because it would leave Vicksburg exposed. In order to confront Pemberton at Edwards Station, however, Grant had to turn his back on Jackson. But John Gregg's brigade, which had fought hard at Raymond despite being outnumbered, was now there, and reports of Confederate reinforcements headed to the capital made Grant nervous. Uneasy about leaving Gregg and a growing enemy presence behind him when he turned west, Grant decided to "make sure of that place [Jackson] and leave no enemy in my rear" and sent Sherman and McPherson to storm the capital city. But intelligence on the Confederate force assembling in Jackson remained scarce, though McPherson reported that nearly twenty thousand troops manned the defenses.[57]

The night before the assault on Jackson, however, a spy named Charles S. Bell arrived at Grant's headquarters with welcome news. Fresh from the capital, Bell reported that General Joseph E. Johnston had arrived to command Jackson's defense and that two brigades had already reached the city with more expected soon. But at that moment, Bell stated confidently, only six thousand men and fourteen artillery pieces guarded the town. Jackson, he told Grant, was ripe for the picking.[58] And he was right. The following day,

Union troops captured Jackson without much of a fight because Johnston, fearful of getting trapped, had already evacuated the six-thousand-man garrison and retreated thirty miles northeast to Canton. But in an odd twist, the night before the evacuation Johnston had ordered Pemberton to march east to Clinton and hit Sherman's corps in the rear, hoping this might drive Sherman away from Jackson and allow the two Confederate forces to unite. To ensure Pemberton got the message, Johnston dispatched three different couriers, one of whom happened to be a Union covert operative who took it straight to McPherson outside Jackson.[59] By the time Grant saw the note, however, Jackson had fallen and Johnston was in headlong retreat toward Canton. He knew, therefore, that Johnston was out of the picture for now, leaving the Vicksburg army on its own. But if Pemberton received the same order the spy brought in, which Grant had to assume, then a junction of the two forces might still occur, especially if Johnston turned southwest toward Clinton. The two Confederate armies could still unite to defend Vicksburg or squeeze Grant's army between them.[60] Either way, the Union commander was not about to play their game. "The enemy [Johnston] retreated north, evidently with the design of joining the Vicksburg forces," he wrote Halleck. "I am concentrating my forces at Bolton to cut them off."[61]

Pemberton had indeed received Johnston's order on May 14, shortly after moving a large part of his army to Edwards Station. Unaware that Jackson had already fallen, he prepared to march his twenty-four thousand men east toward Clinton as directed. But the Vicksburg commander soon vacillated, calling a war council to decide what to do. When it adjourned, Pemberton and his generals had decided to abandon the march on Clinton and instead attempt a repeat of Holly Springs by heading south to cut Grant's main supply line and force him to retreat. Why Pemberton thought his opponent, who had thus far been bold, relentless, and swift would suddenly grow timid, restrained, and sluggish and allow this scheme to work remains baffling.[62] As Pemberton embarked upon this fool's errand, timely intelligence once again moved Grant to change his plans.

Early on May 16, two employees of the Southern Railroad of Mississippi arrived at Grant's headquarters having just passed through Pemberton's army. Both men insisted that the Vicksburg army was heading Grant's way.[63] Fred Grant, accompanying his father on the campaign, observed that the general "seemed surprised at the news he received," probably because it ran counter to his firm expectation that Pemberton would not likely expose Vicksburg by venturing east of the Big Black. To Grant, however, this information was solid enough to justify abandoning Jackson and pushing the main Union advance westward toward Edwards Station to meet Pemberton.[64]

With the Jackson army still on the loose, however, Grant recognized that Johnston and Pemberton might coordinate an assault on his army from opposite directions, making the decision to abandon Jackson, turn west toward Vicksburg, and leave his rear exposed even more perilous. However, another bit of timely intelligence arrived and neutralized this concern. The same morning the railroad workers appeared with news on Pemberton, one of Dodge's spies—a man known only as "Sanburn"—showed up at Grant's headquarters fresh from Johnston's army. Based on the operative's report, Grant concluded that Johnston was in no position to aid Pemberton any time soon, freeing Union forces to continue westward without fear of an attack from the rear.[65] In fact, Johnston was not only too far away, but was "almost frozen in place in the Canton area" with no intention of coming to save Pemberton or Vicksburg.[66]

As a confident Grant pressed westward, Pemberton was involved in a comic-opera scenario that turned disastrous. On May 16, his army had intended moving southeastward to strike Grant's supply lines. Before they started their march, he received another message from Johnston repeating his order to move on Clinton. This time obeying his commander's directive, the defender of Vicksburg reversed course back toward the railroad. He never reached Clinton but instead collided with Federal forces at Champion Hill and, after getting the worst of a fierce engagement, retreated across the Big Black toward Vicksburg. Thrashed again the following morning at Big Black River Bridge, Pemberton's demoralized garrison filed into the Vicksburg defenses with Grant not far behind.[67]

"The enemy have been so terribly beaten," Grant beamed on May 17 "that I cannot believe that a stand will be made unless the troops are relying on Johnstone [sic] arriving with large reinforcements."[68] Grant decided to test his theory and ordered assaults against Vicksburg's fortifications on May 19 and 22. Before these attacks, Grant knew little about the fortifications he faced but believed the enemy too demoralized to fight effectively from behind them. He also sensed that his troops "believed they could carry the works" and would not have stood the subsequent siege as well "if they had not been allowed to try."[69] Also driving his decision was concern for Johnston's army in Canton, only fifty miles away. If Vicksburg did not fall quickly, he reasoned, the so-called Army of Relief would gain strength and "attack me in the rear and possibly raise the siege."[70] These considerations, to Grant's mind, made it imperative to attack. Both attacks failed miserably in part because Grant misjudged Pemberton's men, neglecting to consider that even a defeated enemy could fight tenaciously when cornered, especially if protected by earthworks. In the end, however, Grant emerged victorious after "outcamping" the Confederates in a siege lasting forty-two days.[71] When he wrote on July 4 that Vicksburg had fallen, he knew that, though it was not as clean or quick a victory as was foreshadowed by the maneuver campaign in the first part of May, in the end, the triumph was no less complete.

In the final analysis, the "Mississippi Blitzkrieg" was heavily dependent upon the shifting sands of intelligence for success. Intelligence helped Grant land "on dry ground on the same side of the river as the enemy" and then guided his decisions on numerous occasions, from the landing at Bruinsburg to the fall of Jackson. The May 16 intelligence bonanza stands out as a critical moment in the campaign, providing Grant an opportunity to thrash Pemberton twice before arriving on the outskirts of Vicksburg. Information came from many different quarters and although it was sometimes imperfect, Grant was adept at discerning what was useful and discarding what was not. And he was not afraid to make critical decisions based upon a single report. It must be remembered, however, that intelligence alone did not lead to the final crowning success. Grant's ability to think clearly in a fluid and chaotic environment, plus a remarkable flexibility that allowed him to adjust seamlessly to developing circumstances and to interpret intelligence quickly and correctly, were critical factors behind the victory. In the final analysis, Grant's ultimate victory on July 4, 1863, stemmed from his uncompromising faith in the power of the initiative and from a mental dexterity that allowed rapidly changing circumstances and intelligence to "suggest and develop" his course of action. In other words, his talent for making it up as he went along, guided by instinct and information, not fear and uncertainty, transformed the campaign into a stunning success, even though at times his operations were rather unconventional. On this point, perhaps Henry Ward Beecher's 1885 "Eulogy on Grant" summed it up best. "If he neglected the rules of war, as at Vicksburg," he observed, "it was to make better rules."[72]

Notes

1. Ulysses S. Grant, *The Papers of Ulysses S. Grant,* edited by John Y. Simon, 32 vols. to date (Carbondale: Southern Illinois University Press, 1969–), 6:31. Hereinafter cited as *GP.*

2. Quoted in James M. McPherson, *Battle Cry of Freedom: The Civil War Era* (New York: Oxford University Press, 1988), 631.

3. Ulysses S. Grant, *Personal Memoirs of U.S. Grant* (reprint, New York: Da Capo, 1982), 301.

4. For a detailed analysis of these earlier experiences using intelligence, see William B. Feis, *Grant's Secret Service: The Intelligence War from Belmont to Appomattox* (Lincoln: University of Nebraska Press, 2002).

5. Feis, *Grant's Secret Service,* 109–18; *GP,* 6:31.

6. Quoted in McPherson, *Battle Cry of Freedom,* 627.

7. Horace Porter, *Campaigning with Grant*, ed. Wayne C. Temple (reprint, New York: Bonanza Books, 1961), 5; Grant, *Memoirs*, 205–6.

8. Grant, *Memoirs*, 205–6.

9. For the lack of a systematized, armywide intelligence service in the Army of the Tennessee at this time, see Feis, *Grant's Secret Service*, 3–6, 109–38.

10. Feis, *Grant's Secret Service*, 313; *GP*, 6:310–12, 373–74; Grenville M. Dodge, "The Secret Service in the Civil War," 1–47, Manuscript in Grenville M. Dodge Papers, State Historical Society of Iowa, Des Moines. (Hereinafter cited as Dodge Papers.)

11. U.S. War Department, *The War of the Rebellion: The Official Records of the Union and Confederate Armies*, 128 vols. (Washington, DC: Government Printing Office, 1880–1901), series 1, vol. 17, pt. 2:399. (Hereinafter cited as *OR*. All references are to Series 1 unless otherwise indicated.)

12. Feis, *Grant's Secret Service*, 130–38.

13. *GP*, 8:4.

14. *OR*, vol. 24, pt. 3:64–65.

15. Dodge, "Secret Service," 8.

16. Records of the Provost Marshal General, RG 110, entry 31, box 2, National Archives and Records Administration, Washington, D.C.; inventory of Dodge's Scouts and Secret Service Vouchers, box 148, Dodge Papers. See also Feis, *Grant's Secret Service*, 126–30.

17. *GP*, 7:240; *OR*, vol. 24, pt. 3:17; *GP*, 7:292–93, 362.

18. *GP*, 7: 361, 428; *OR*, vol. 24, pt. 1:64.

19. *GP*, 8:37–38.

20. *OR*, vol. 24, pt. 1:72–73; Charles A. Dana, *Recollections of the Civil War* (New York: D. Appleton, 1898), 20–22.

21. Owen Connelly, *On War and Leadership: The Words of Combat Commanders from Frederick the Great to Norman Schwarzkopf* (Princeton, N.J.: Princeton University Press, 2002), 17.

22. Michael B. Ballard, *Vicksburg: The Campaign That Opened the Mississippi* (Chapel Hill: University of North Carolina Press, 2004), 203–6; Edwin C. Bearss, *The Vicksburg Campaign*, 3 vols. (Dayton, Ohio: Morningside, 1986), 2:107–26; *OR*, vol. 24, pt. 1:251–52; pt. 3:729–30, 738, 733, 745.

23. For Morris's report, see Dodge's Secret Service Diary, box 149, and Secret Service Vouchers, box 148, Dodge Papers; *OR*, vol. 24, pt. 3:191. See also "Final Report of Receipts and Expenditures of Col. Wm. S. Hillyer, Provost Marshal General, Department of the Tennessee, February–May, 1863," box 1, William S. Hillyer Papers, University of Virginia, Charlottesville.

24. *GP*, 8:485; Bearss, *Vicksburg Campaign*, 2:19–21.

25. *OR*, vol. 24, pt. 1:75.

26. *GP*, 8:109.

27. Bearss, *Vicksburg Campaign*, 2:53–82; *GP*, 8:109.

28. Ballard, *Vicksburg*, 205; Bearss, *Vicksburg Campaign*, 2:129–236; Stephen V. Starr, *The Union Cavalry in the Civil War*, 3 vols. (Baton Rouge: Louisiana State University Press, 1985), 3:185–97; *GP*, 8:46–47, 506–7.

29. *OR*, vol. 24, pt. 3:211; *GP*, 8:114–15, 117; Ballard, *Vicksburg*, 214–15.

30. *OR*, vol. 24, pt. 1:127–28.

31. *GP*, 8:126–27, 130–31, 114–15; Ballard, *Vicksburg*, 213.

32. Ballard, *Vicksburg*, 213; Bearss, *Vicksburg Campaign*, 2:267; *GP*, 8:494.

33. *GP*, 8:133, 494; Bearss, *Vicksburg Campaign*, 2:317.

34. Walter Grabau, *Ninety-Eight Days: A Geographer's View of the Vicksburg Campaign* (Knoxville: University of Tennessee Press, 2000), 143.

35. *GP* 8:512; *National Tribune*, July 1, 1886, 3; Grant, *Memoirs*, 251.

36. Grabau, *Ninety-Eight Days*, 507–8.

37. Quoted in Edwin C. Fishel, *The Secret War for the Union: The Untold Story of Military Intelligence in the Civil War* (New York: Houghton-Mifflin, 1996), 419.

38. Two examples of blacks providing information during this phase of the campaign can be found in *GP*, 8:227, 397. For a discussion of the use of "contrabands" in the eastern theater, see Fishel, *Secret War for the Union*, 5, 120–21, 139, 152, 424, 437–38.

39. *GP*, 8:494.

40. Grant, *Memoirs*, 252.

41. *GP*, 8:183; Ballard, *Vicksburg*, 247–48; Bearss, *Vicksburg Campaign*, 2:432–35.

42. *GP*, 8:494.

43. Bearss, *Vicksburg Campaign*, 2:317–46; *GP*, 8:143.

44. *OR*, vol. 24, pt. 1:143; *GP*, 8:147; Bearss, *Vicksburg Campaign*, 2:351–52, 417; *OR*, vol. 24, pt. 3:792–93, 807.

45. *GP*, 8:495.

46. *GP*, 8:494–95; Grant *Memoirs*, 259–61; Bearss, *Vicksburg Campaign*, 2:431–57, 480.

47. Starr, *Union Cavalry*, 3:182–83.

48. *OR*, vol. 24, pt. 1:130.

49. Levi H. Naron, *A Mississippi Scout for the Union: The Civil War Memoir of Levi H. Naron*, ed. Thomas D. Cockrell and Michael B. Ballard (Baton Rouge: Louisiana State University Press, 2005), 101, 105.

50. *GP*, 5:247. For a discussion of the overall value of deserters as information sources, see Feis, *Grant's Secret Service*, 198–200.

51. For examples of these different sources being tapped by McClernand, McPherson, and Sherman, see *OR*, vol. 24, pt. 3:208, 293, 296, 347, 365.

52. James H. Wilson, "A Staff-Officer's Journal of the Vicksburg Campaign, April 30 to July 4, 1863," *Journal of the Military Service Institution of the United States* 43 (July 1908): 93–109, 261–75.

53. Ballard, *Vicksburg*, 251–69.

54. Michael B. Ballard, *The Civil War in Mississippi: Major Campaigns and Battles* (Jackson: University Press of Mississippi, 2011), 153.

55. *GP*, 8:208, 173, 177; Wilson, "Staff-Officer's Journal," 95, 97–99.

56. Wilson, "Staff-Officer's Journal," 100; *OR*, vol. 24, pt. 3:842; *GP*, 8:183. Beauregard sent two brigades (five thousand men) from South Carolina, but did not accompany them to Mississippi. Bearss, *Vicksburg Campaign*, 2:525; Wilson, "Staff-Officer's Journal," 99.

57. *GP*, 8:208, 494–96; *OR*, vol. 24, pt. 3:309.

58. For Bell, see *New York Ledger*, March 27, 1869; and William B. Feis, "Charles S. Bell, Union Scout," *North and South* 4 (Sept. 2001): 26–37; Wilson, "Staff-Officer's Journal," 105.

59. *OR*, vol. 24, pt. 3:870; Wilson, "Staff-Officer's Journal," 105–6.

60. *GP*, 8:213–14, 220, 215; Wilson, "Staff-Officer's Journal," 106; Ballard, *Vicksburg*, 278–79.

61. *GP*, 8:220.

62. Ballard, *Vicksburg*, 283–84.

63. Wilson, "Staff-Officer's Journal," 106–7; Grant, *Memoirs*, 268; *GP*, 8:497; Bearss, *Vicksburg Campaign*, 2:579.

64. Frederick D. Grant, "A Boy's Experience at Vicksburg," in *Personal Recollections of the War of the Rebellion*, ed. A. Noel Blakeman (New York: G. P. Putnam's Sons, 1907), 93; *GP*, 8:226; Ballard, *Vicksburg*, 289; *GP*, 8:497–98.

65. Dodge, "Secret Service," 14, Dodge Papers. See also "Address by Gen. Frederick D. Grant," in *Report of the Proceedings of the Society of the Army of the Tennessee, 1909–1911* (Cincinnati: Charles O. Ebel, 1913), 200. Fred Grant's rendition of this incident differs from Dodge's version, but he notes that "The plan of battle . . . was made on information conveyed from General Dodge." Apparently, Sanburn never returned to Corinth nor was he heard from again. See Dodge's unpublished "Personal Biography," 1:106, Dodge Papers.

66. Ballard, *Vicksburg*, 279–80.

67. Ibid., 282–318.

68. *GP*, 8:233.

69. Grant, *Memoirs*, 277.

70. *GP*, 8:502.

71. Grant, *Memoirs*, 278.

72. Henry Ward Beecher, "Eulogy on Grant," in *Patriotic Addresses in America and England*, ed. John Howard (New York: Fords, Howard, & Hulbert, 1887), 851.

9

"A VICTORY COULD HARDLY HAVE BEEN MORE COMPLETE"
THE BATTLE OF BIG BLACK RIVER BRIDGE

Timothy B. Smith

L ieutenant General John C. Pemberton was in a no-win situation, literally.
He had just been soundly defeated earlier that day, May 16, 1863, at the
Battle of Champion Hill, where Major General Ulysses S. Grant's Army of
the Tennessee had shattered the mobile Confederate army defending Vicksburg. Now, Pemberton's traumatized army was hurriedly retreating westward
through Edwards Station toward Vicksburg on the mighty Mississippi River.
One lieutenant in command of a train of wagons described the miserable
retreat from the Champion Hill battlefield: "It was slow progress from then
until we arrived at Big Black—as it was covered with Artillery, the trains of
the Army—straggling and wounded men—every conceivable conveyance
with women and children fleeing their homes and abandoning them to the
Yankees." And if that was not bad enough, as Pemberton and his devastated
army sullenly moved onward, the general no doubt also rehearsed in his
mind the fact that he was disobeying his departmental commander, General
Joseph E. Johnston, by falling back into Vicksburg. Johnston had ordered him
to get away from the trap that was Vicksburg and join him near Jackson, but
Pemberton chose to follow his commander in chief's opposite direction to
hold Vicksburg at all costs. Pemberton was truly in a no-win situation; he
had to disobey someone.[1]

But the larger strategic context was not the most difficult decision Pemberton had to make that night. His army had been devastated and literally
broken apart. The best-case scenario was to concentrate the divisions and
march to Vicksburg as a cohesive army. Unfortunately, that was not possible. The divisions were terribly confused and scattered, with the crossing
of Bakers Creek on the western edge of the Champion Hill battlefield causing
most of the confusion. And one of those divisions itself had broken apart,

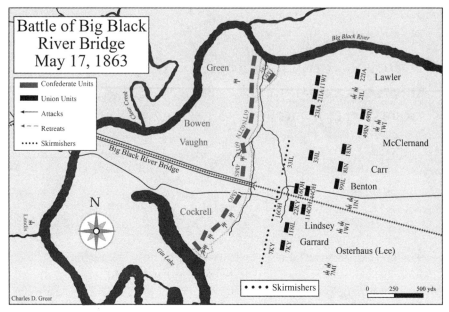

Battle of Big Black
River Bridge
May 17, 1863

Confederate Units
Union Units
Attacks
Retreats
Skirmishers

After taking Jackson and defeating Pemberton at the Battle of
Champion Hill, Grant pursued the retreating Confederates westward
toward Vicksburg. At the Big Black River, eleven miles east of
Vicksburg, Pemberton attempted to hold a bridgehead.

the brigades having crossed the creek at two different points. Moreover, the
divisions did not all cross together, but rather left the battlefield piecemeal.
The army was not concentrated, Pemberton had no idea where much of it
was, and Grant was not giving him much of a chance to catch his breath;
Pemberton was in dire straits.[2]

Such a disastrous situation only became worse as the night hours unfolded. Pemberton knew Major General Carter Stevenson's division was
moving safely toward Vicksburg; in fact, having crossed the Big Black River,
a formidable watershed that ran southwestward from the central portion of
the state to its confluence with the Mississippi River south of Vicksburg, the
division had moved on toward Bovina during the night. Brigadier General
John Bowen's division was next to arrive at the river, having held the ford
and bridge at Bakers Creek long enough to meet the lead elements of Major
General William Loring's retreating division. But when the hard-charging
Federals who had crossed Bakers Creek to the north suddenly took Bowen's
men in the flank, the Missourian ordered his division westward, telling Loring to get out as best he could. Thus, when Bowen arrived at the Big Black
River, Pemberton ordered him to man the defenses at the bridge and await

Loring, who all thought would be only a short distance behind Bowen. But as the night hours drug on and Loring never showed, Pemberton began to fret about what to do. For all he knew, Loring was still marching westward to join the rest of the army, perhaps fighting a rearguard effort on his way out. "It was necessary to hold the position to enable him [Loring] to cross the river, should the enemy, which was probable, follow him closely up," Pemberton wrote. Then again, Loring could conceivably have been delayed by the darkness and would arrive after daylight. And even if Loring did not cross at the railroad bridge, he could still cross somewhere else, which even more necessitated holding the line at the Big Black. Obviously, Pemberton needed all his troops to defend Vicksburg. If Bowen could hold the river crossing for Loring, Pemberton would then have his entire army concentrated once again west of the Big Black River—stunned, but concentrated and ready to defend Vicksburg. It was a gamble Pemberton had to take.[3]

The agony of the night can be felt in Pemberton's correspondence and reports. "I awaited in vain intelligence of the approach of General Loring," Pemberton later wrote. But Loring never arrived. He had determined that he was cut off by the flanking Federals who had driven Bowen away from the Bakers Creek crossing. He thus set out on a roundabout route through swamps and forests in an attempt to escape. He would, but lost all his artillery, much of his arms and ammunition, and many of his men in the process. He eventually emerged at Crystal Springs several days later and ultimately joined Joseph E. Johnston's army in Jackson, the state capital.[4]

All that was in the future, however, and on the night of May 16, Pemberton had no way of knowing what Loring was up to. Thus, he determined to hold at the river. The result was disastrous. As to waiting all night for Loring to show, Pemberton sadly confessed, "For this purpose alone I continued the troops in position until it was too late to withdraw them under cover of night." He later related that he had "determined not to abandon so strong a front while there was yet hope of his arrival." Instead of Loring, the next morning, Sunday, May 17, Grant's blue columns arrived. Obviously, Loring was not coming, at least not on the direct route. But Loring's whereabouts, although he was the reason Pemberton had determined to hold at the Big Black, was now of secondary importance to the Confederate commander. He now confronted Grant's victorious army east of the river, and he could not retreat quickly. His men would have to fight another battle.[5]

By the evening of May 16, U. S. Grant sat in an ideal position. He had defeated the enemy at Champion Hill and could pursue with vigor. He had wounded the Confederate army; now he hoped for the kill. He thus made plans to move his Army of the Tennessee westward toward Vicksburg. Even better, more units steadily arrived during the waning hours of May 16, including the majority of Major General William T. Sherman's corps that had recently been destroying Jackson. Now with his entire army, Grant could take several routes toward Vicksburg, hoping to mop up the shattered Confederate commands, turn any defensive positions Pemberton might take, and perhaps bag the whole lot. Leaving the hardest fighting units to rest on the Champion Hill battlefield itself, Grant shoved Brigadier Generals Eugene Carr's and Peter Osterhaus's divisions farther toward Edwards on the Jackson road that night. Brigadier General A. J. Smith moved his division across Bakers Creek and also turned toward Edwards. Grant sent Sherman's corps northward to Bridgeport, the place the Confederate wagon train had crossed the night before. In addition to the swelled numbers, spirits were high in the Federal ranks; they had just won a magnificent victory and even reveled in rumors that Pemberton himself had been killed.[6]

With Edwards in Federal hands, Grant resumed the pursuit when the sun rose the next morning, units of Carr's and Osterhaus's divisions leading the way. The only impediment was the Big Black River. Grant knew that if the Confederates made a stand, it would be there. Thus Grant and his high-spirited Federals moved onward to locate the enemy. Union soldiers described the dawn of May 17 as bright and beautiful, much like the day before. Unfortunately, this day would also see bloodshed and destruction as the armies continued to grapple with one another.[7]

On the surface, Pemberton's new line at the Big Black River was a strong one. The river made a huge curve exactly where the main Jackson-to-Vicksburg road as well as the railroad crossed over, an area Pemberton described as "somewhat in the shape of a horseshoe." The road and railroad entered the open end of the horseshoe on the eastern side and crossed the river on the extreme western edge. The sixty-foot bluffs on the western side of the river were substantially higher than the flood plain on the east bank, thus offering the Confederates an opportunity to cover the crossing points with artillery and infantry. In addition, a line of breastworks had been erected earlier in April across the opening of the horseshoe, east of the river, about midway between the opening and the river crossings. These had gone up in the first two weeks of May as part of a larger Big Black River line of defense intended to protect the Vicksburg approaches from Grant's inland advance east of the river. Made of cotton bales covered with dirt, these works provided ample cover for infantrymen and also contained embrasures for artillery along the southern end, where everyone seemed to think an attack would develop. Only one artillery unit took position on the northern end of the line. Confederates manning these defenses on a line running north to south had an extremely favorable position in that their flanks were secured by the bending river on the northern end and a small lake that once was part of the river to the south. Moreover, the field of battle for an attack on this line was constricted, offering a smaller zone to cover and crowding Federal units into a somewhat manageable area of combat. Perhaps most important, there were natural factors that aided the Confederate defense as well, such as wide open fields along most of the line to the south and center, and a large slough some ten to twenty feet wide and two to three feet deep that meandered along the northern and middle part of the line and ran into the river on the north side of the horseshoe. This small bayou would not be an absolute deterrent to the enemy, but hopefully it would slow any attacking column long enough to allow the defenders to rake them with artillery and musketry. Pemberton himself noted that it "opposed a serious obstacle to an assault upon the pits." In addition, the sharpened branches of felled trees formed an abatis at points along the line, mainly in the bayou itself, and there was a detached section of works east of the bayou on the extreme northern end of the line, from which southern soldiers could enfilade any attack moving toward the bayou and the main Confederate line. Only on the northern sector along the river would an attacking army have any cover in the form of what one soldier described as "a copse of wood." A stand of cypress trees stood along the southern portion of the Confederate line, but it was far too small to provide any aid to the Federals in approaching from that direction. Thus, most any Federals attacking this Confederate line of earthworks would have immediate difficulty in even getting to the enemy line.[8]

As his tired troops reached this new position, Pemberton had a decision to make. Obviously, he would keep his forces at the river crossing to allow Loring a chance to rejoin the army, but how he would deploy his men and who he would deploy would be critical. Instead of forming his entire line west of the river on the higher ground, which in retrospect would have been the better option, Pemberton decided he needed to man the line of entrench-ments east of the river to allow Loring a chance at an uninterrupted crossing, especially if followed closely by the enemy. Loring would have a hard time crossing the river if the Confederate line was on the western side, taking the pursuing enemy under fire. Loring would likewise have to cross his men while fighting a rear guard action. Pemberton deemed it best to hold the line of entrenchments east of the river and allow all the divisions to hopefully cross without molestation, maybe during the night. Unfortunately, not all agreed with the commanding general, and their viewpoint would be proved correct in time. One Missourian, for instance, later wrote: "The position would have been a strong one, if the fortifications had been on the other side of the stream, and it would certainly have been better to take position there with no fortifications, than to be in them where we were, with a river at our back to cross in case of accident or disaster."[9]

Still, by the early hours of May 17, Pemberton's hopes rested on crossing all of his army, including Loring, without fighting another battle. The Confederate commander was obviously gun-shy after the whipping he had taken at Champion Hill the day before, and his main goal was to reach the Vicksburg defenses, where additional troops awaited his mobile army and where major fortifications could help the tired foot soldiers fend off a Union attack. In fact, Pemberton had already begun to move in that direction himself, riding to Bovina and leaving Bowen in charge at the river. In order to make the crossing as easy as possible, the Confederates planned to use the railroad bridge as well as a steamboat, the *Dot*, which had had its machinery removed and had been converted into a bridge by turning it crossways in the river and building approaches on and off the vessel. Engineers also planked the railroad bridge to allow wheeled vehicles to move across, and Confederate teamsters soon had the wagons that still accompanied the individual brigades across safely, which was a high priority for Pemberton. In order to place a major obstacle between them and Grant as soon as Loring arrived, engineers also prepared to douse the bridge and boat with turpentine and set them afire.[10]

With the decision to hold east of the river made, Pemberton also had a decision to make about who was to man the trenches. Most of Stevenson's division, which was just now concentrating after the debacle at Champion Hill the day before, had already marched on through the area and was moving toward Bovina. With Loring still missing and Pemberton's other two divisions under Major Generals M. L. Smith and John H. Forney back at Vicksburg, that left only Bowen's depleted division to man the works. But that division was not in ideal shape. It had been mauled at Port Gibson sixteen days earlier and then made the dramatic counterattack at Champion Hill the day before, losing nearly a thousand men in the process. When the attack lost its steam, the division had recoiled under the pressure of a Federal counterattack and had retreated during the night to the river and crossed it. Tired as they were, the Missourians were nevertheless all Pemberton had to man the trenches and hold out for Loring's arrival. They crossed back over to the east side of the river and moved toward the trenches.[11]

Bowen's exhausted division thus had to defend the works, which one southerner affectionately termed "our ditches." Bowen placed his best men, Colonel Francis M. Cockrell's brigade, on the right of the line where there was no covering bayou and the line was accordingly more exposed. Bowen put Brigadier General Martin Green's men on the left, with Colonel Elijah

Gates's 1st Missouri Cavalry (dismounted) eventually occupying the detached works east of the bayou, near the river. In between, along the railroad where Pemberton felt sure no attack would come, was the only fresh unit Pemberton had at his disposal: a small brigade of Tennesseans commanded by Brigadier General John C. Vaughn of M. L. Smith's division. The 60th, 61st, and 62nd Tennessee had manned these works for several days and, as a result, had seen no fighting as yet, but they were somewhat circumspect in their loyalty. Most of the men had been conscripted from east Tennessee, a region blatant in its Unionism. Fortunately, the 4th Mississippi of Brigadier General William Baldwin's brigade took position amid the Tennesseans to add to their strength and morale. Among the infantry, artillery crews placed some twenty guns at advantageous spots, mostly south of the railroad where all expected any attack would come.[12]

Despite the issues, Pemberton was confident that Bowen could hold the line. He stated matter of factly, "I knew that the Missouri troops, under their gallant leaders, could be depended upon." He also noted that the four thousand or so men manning the trenches were "as many as could be advantageously employed in defending the line." In fact, Pemberton's only major worry was Grant turning his position. "So strong was the position," Pemberton later wrote, "that my greatest, almost only, apprehension was a flank movement by Bridgeport or Baldwin's Ferry, which would have endangered my communications with Vicksburg."[13]

Not every one was so convinced, however. Some questioned the length of the line with only four to five thousand troops to defend it; one historian has even surmised there was only about one man to every foot of earthworks. Likewise, Pemberton's chief engineer, Major Samuel H. Lockett, later wrote that he began preparing to destroy the bridges in the event of a break because even early that morning he was "seeing signs of unsteadiness among our troops." No doubt the situation made them unsteady. If the men in the fortifications did not hold, there was little hope for the troops. Pemberton himself noted that "between the works and the bridge, about three-quarters of a mile, the country was open, being either old or cultivated fields, offering no cover should the troops be driven from the trenches." Hemmed in by the curve in the river, which one Federal described as "muddy and turgid at this time of the year," the men would be stranded. Moreover, a bottleneck would undoubtedly occur at the river. The only means of escape were the railroad bridge and the steamer *Dot*. Even in possession of those two means of escape, Bowen's entire division with Vaughn's brigade could not evacuate before the Federals surrounded them. Accordingly, Bowen had to hold—at least until Loring arrived.[14]

Major General John A. McClernand, commander of the Federal Thirteenth Corps, had his men up and marching early on May 17, even before daylight. One member of Carr's division remembered that "the unwelcome sound of the bugle greeted our ears" at 2:00 A.M. Rations were quickly issued, and the soldiers sleepily downed what one Federal described as a "pint of corn meal and a slice of bacon." Another reported, "we made much of the meal and broiled our meat on forked sticks." By this time, some soldiers had had enough. One grumbled, "There is no fun in soldiering neither is there any fun on the battlefield when bullets are whistling around our heads[.] Shells bursting and cannon balls and grape shot tareing up the ground all around us[.] my curiosity is satisfied." Nevertheless, Brigadier General William Benton's men of Carr's division led the way westward at 3:30 A.M. After skirmishing with Confederates in the early hours after sunup, during which locals told them they would have to fight to get across the river to the west, McClernand's Thirteenth Corps arrived near the Big Black, where the troops found the Confederate positions across their path complete with artillery and battle flags flying.[15]

With Grant looking on, Carr's division led the advance and ultimately deployed in line along the northern section of the Confederate fortifications. Brigadier General Michael Lawler's brigade, after supporting Benton's initial brigade in a second line, formed with its right on the river in response to the Confederate occupation of the extended works east of the bayou, which was deemed an advance and thus a threat to the right flank. Peter Osterhaus, next in line, formed his division along the middle and southern portions of the line, although two of his regiments of Brigadier General Theophilus Garrard's brigade went northward to support Carr's men. Colonel Daniel Lindsey's brigade formed the right, and the remainder of Garrard's men, although initially in a second line behind Lindsey, took position on the left rear to watch the flank when unidentified Confederate movements in that area also falsely signaled an enemy attack. A space still existed south of Garrard's line, but Brigadier General Stephen Burbridge's brigade of A. J. Smith's division soon arrived and filled that expanse. Finally, McClernand's artillery took position near the line, mainly Captain Jacob T. Foster's six guns of the 1st Wisconsin Battery. Eventually, the guns of the 1st Indiana, 7th Michigan, Chicago Mercantile, and Battery A, 2nd Illinois Artillery also deployed and raked the Confederate line as well.[16]

Soon after the lines formed, a spirited artillery duel ensued. The exhausted soldiers of Bowen's division huddled quietly behind their breastworks during the bombardment, keeping an open eye for Loring and the end of such misery. With the arrival of Federals across the way, however, it looked increasingly less likely that Loring would show up. Thoughts thus turned to getting out of what was becoming a trap, but the officers nevertheless tried to calm the unsteady soldiers' nerves. Such bravery almost cost General Vaughn his life; a Union cannonball came close enough to cut the reins of his horse. An aide tied the reins together, noting "he seemed unconscious of fear." As bad as the barrage was for the Confederates behind the breastworks, however, even worse conditions existed for the Federal soldiers. They had absolutely no cover and could only lay flat in the dusty fields and hope the Confederate gunners missed their mark. Many did. One Federal infantryman described how "the rebels replied with very heavy artillery[.] the shells flew thick and over our heads bursting in the tops of the trees[.] the rebels over shot us and not a man was touched." That may have been the case at points, but there were some casualties elsewhere. A 22nd Iowa soldier on the northern portion of the line, Samuel D. Pryce, reported, "broadside after broadside came hurtling through the woods. Havoc was terrific among the big trees. Earth and sky seemed tumbling together. . . . Missiles crashed through the giant elms and tore them to pieces. Great lordly trees were peeled and stripped and looked like splintered bones." Aquilla Standifird of the 23rd Iowa wrote in his diary how the enemy shot and shell was "making it [a] very unsafe place to stop." Illustrating the exposed nature of the Federal line, a Confederate shell hit a Union limber, causing a tremendous explosion. The blast sent shrapnel flying, some of which hit General Osterhaus in the leg as he conversed with Captain Foster about where to locate his artillery pieces. The wound was severe enough to force Osterhaus from the field. Brigadier General Albert Lee took command of the division.[17]

Amid the barrage, one Federal commander saw his men's plight and determined to remedy the situation. Three-hundred-pound Michael Lawler, the hard-fighting Irishman described by one of the soldiers that day as "rushing around in his shirt sleeves," reported that his men faced large open areas, a deep bayou with felled trees in it, and formidable earthworks to the front. Lawler admitted the Confederate position was "really formidable and difficult of approach." He nevertheless formed his brigade with the 11th Wisconsin on the left of a line and the 21st Iowa on the right. The 23rd Iowa took position in a second line a hundred yards behind the Wisconsin regiment, and the last regiment of the brigade, the 22nd Iowa, remained in the rear as a reserve and support for the section of the Illinois artillery battery engaging the enemy even then. As Lawler's men moved through the woods and into the open fields fronting the enemy line only about four hundred yards away, they could see their work would be difficult if called to attack. And because of the wooded area through which they had moved, only two guns of Battery

A, 2nd Illinois Artillery, were able to deploy. One of the soldiers wrote his brother that they "engaged them with their muskets but the rebels were so well protected that our firing did but little execution and it seemed as nothing but a bayonet charge would drive them from behind their strong position."[18]

But then came good news. Lawler received word from McClernand's chief of cavalry, Colonel John J. Mudd, that a covered opening had been found near the bank of the river toward a small grove of trees. It was a meander scar, an old bed of the river that was now dry, that ran parallel with the river on the south bank. With the Confederates' attention diverted because of the artillery exchange as well as other arriving units such as A. J. Smith's division, Lawler led the three front line regiments of his brigade into cover on the extreme right of the Union line where a small copse of woods and the scar offered protection. One Iowan described the move: "We was soon ordered to the right through some timber to the river. We was ordered to move down the river and to get as near the enemy's intrenchments as possible which we did." Ultimately, Lawler reached the river bank and deployed the men in a line behind the bluff, the 11th Wisconsin, 21st Iowa, and 23rd Iowa, left to right. A soldier described the place as "a growth of small timber between the bank and water which gave us good protection." The 22nd Iowa was not as fortunate and remained farther to the left in the field for a time before moving to the bank as well and deploying near the 11th Wisconsin.[19]

By the time his men had gained cover, despite the continuous blistering fire from Confederate artillery and small arms, Lawler saw that he was surprisingly close enough to assault the Confederate works. In fact, Colonel William H. Kinsman of the 23rd Iowa, closest to the enemy line, came to Lawler and told him of the situation and asked permission to assault. Knowing better than to send only one regiment, Lawler ordered his entire brigade to fix bayonets. One officer in the 21st Iowa remembered, "The command was quietly passed along the line to fix bayonets, and as quietly obeyed."[20]

In what Grant described as a "brilliant and daring movement," Lawler's brigade then burst from the lowland in columns of fours with a yell that took the Confederates by surprise. An Iowan described the brigade "yelling like the furies." One Confederate also described the Union yell: "It is much more regular than ours and is clearly distinguishable from it." The screaming 23rd Iowa, closest to the Confederates, "sprang forward to the works," Lawler remembered, followed closely by the 21st Iowa on their left. The 23rd's colonel, William Kinsman, had worked out a plan by which his left wing would start first by moving into the open field, whereupon the right wing would follow when the left moved as far as the colors. One member of the regiment remembered in his diary that all planning went awry once the attack began: "when we leaped up over the bank a perfect storm of lead was hurled at us but did not check those that was not hit." A member of the 21st Iowa agreed, later writing that the regiment "began to toil up the steep bank, but as the head of the column appeared above the bank it was met by a storm of shot. The movement in that order would have been impossible, and Colonel [Samuel] Merrill, seeing the difficulty, immediately shouted the order: 'By the left flank, CHARGE!'" He added, "And the silent river overflowed its banks and poured a flood of living men upon the plain—living, yelling, screaming madmen." The 11th Wisconsin followed closely behind the 23rd Iowa as the two frontline Iowa units angled southwesterly toward the Confederate line. "We went on the run[,] the boys falling all the way across," an Iowan remembered. Meanwhile, the 22nd Iowa moved out into the field behind the 21st Iowa and toward the Confederate line as well, while Lawler also got Garrard's two regiments, the 49th and 69th Indiana, going forward farther to the left. But in the main attack, the Iowans and Wisconsin troops swept forward across Green's front toward Vaughan's Tennesseans near the railroad. Lieutenant Colonel Cornelius W. Dunlap of the 21st Iowa reported that his men moved forward some eight hundred yards: "the bullets came in showers from the flanks, and, combined with those coming from the horde of rebels in the rifle-pits in front, made an awful hail storm, through which it seemed a miracle that a single man passed uninjured." Many did not. One Iowan told of passing a fellow soldier lying wounded, yelling, "Go in boys, . . . they have fixed me." Another member of the regiment described how "regimental and company organizations immediately broke . . . , the fastest runners ahead."[21]

Unfortunately, several high-ranking Federals went down as the charge moved onward. Colonel Kinsman, closest to the Confederate line, was hit as his Iowans raced toward the Confederate line. He went down, but somehow managed to get to his feet and push his men onward. "He staggered a few paces to the front," Lawler reported, ". . . and fell again, this time to rise no more, pierced through by a second ball." Colonel Merrill of the 21st Iowa also went down in the assault, shot through both thighs. Even the 23rd Iowa's sutler fell; Lawler described him as "a brave old man, who took a gun at the commencement of the battle, went into the ranks, fought nobly, and fell, mortally wounded." Scores more Iowa and Wisconsin troops fell as well. But other officers soon raced forward to take the positions of wounded leaders. Lieutenant Colonel Samuel L. Glasgow took command of the 23rd Iowa; and because Lieutenant Colonel Dunlap of the 21st Iowa was still recovering from having been wounded at Port Gibson earlier in the month, Major Salue G. Van Anda took over the 21st Iowa while Dunlap watched from the rear with pride.[22]

As the Union regiments neared the bayou, they stopped only to deliver a volley into the Confederate line. One Federal remembered, "the rebels poured in a dreadful volley of musketry into the ranks of our brave boys but on they went yelling like demonds[.] the rebs stood firm until our boys got within a few yards of their breastworks." Lawler reported the men then "dashed forward through the bayou, filled with water, fallen timber, and brush, on to the rebel works with the shout of victors, driving the enemy in with confusion from their breastworks and rifle-pits, and entering in triumph the rebel stronghold." Another Iowan reported, "Leaping from tree to tree, from branch to branch, through mud and water, none knew how, but the bayou was passed."²³

Despite the wounding of several important officers, the Federal attack accomplished its goal of shattering the Confederate line where the unnerved 61st Tennessee stood. Colonel Elijah Gates, commanding one of the Confederate Missouri regiments of Green's brigade, later admitted that the Federals had massed "on the river in the timber where we could not see them." Moving southward along and somewhat parallel to the Confederate defenses and the bayou, the Federals were on top of the Confederate line in no time, literally before they could react. One Confederate remembered, "our troops were completely surprised and were really surrounded before they knew it." The stunned Missourians and Arkansans let out a wild volley as the Union regiments passed, but watched them, no doubt in relief, move on to their right. There, Lawler's men, after stopping and delivering a massive volley, hit Vaughn's brigade. The Tennesseans, although some of the freshest men in the entire Confederate army, simply could not hold their positions. As Lawler's men poured over the "deep, miry slough," as McClernand described it, and scaled the accompanying earthworks, Vaughn's Tennesseans melted away. They were headed for Vicksburg. A Federal reported to his brother that "some of them ran but the majority of them threw down their arms." The veteran 4th Mississippi could not stem the tide either, with so many around them giving way. The Mississippians' honor was tinged in the debacle, one Missourian calling them the "flying Mississippians."²⁴

Panic ran like an electric shock through the remainder of the Confederate army. Although the southerners continued firing, Bowen's men could not hold on. Green's brigade, not hearing much fighting from the right, soon saw the Federals pouring through the line and took to the rear. Colonel Gates alarmingly noted, "I discovered that they had crossed the ditches and were between me and the bridge." He ordered his men to swim the river. Likewise, those of Cockrell's Missourians on the right who braved to climb the railroad embankment saw the Federals making their way down the north side of the railroad toward the river crossings. The disgust can be heard in Cockrell's voice as he later wrote, "I saw the line between the railroad and the first skirt of timber north of the railroad beginning to give way, and then running in disorder." Soon, it dawned on Cockrell that their retreat would have a marked effect on his men. "I watched this disorderly falling back a few minutes, when I saw that the enemy had possession of the trenches . . . and were rapidly advancing toward the bridge," Cockrell reported in disbelief. "The enemy [were] now . . . nearer this crossing than my line," he added. Accordingly, Cockrell ordered his men to the rear to escape, and one Missourian admitted that the brigade "soon showed that they were as fleet-footed and expert in running as they were obstinate, stubborn and courageous in the fight." Another described the "long, hard run of a mile from our position." Due to increasing artillery covering fire from the west bank, many of the Missourians got across, as did Cockrell and Green, but some had to take to the river to get away. Nevertheless, in only three minutes, Lawler had shattered the Confederate line and driven an entire division and another brigade away.[25]

The other Union regiments followed Lawler's example and launched attacks on their own fronts. Lawler managed to ride over toward the 49th and 69th Indiana of Garrard's brigade, which were supporting him, and ordered the Indianans to charge at the same time his Iowans did. They did so, on Lawler's left. Colonel James Keigwin remembered that his men charged over "a heavy abatis" toward the Confederate line. As the Indianans reached the bayou and entered it, they began to see the Confederates "putting cotton on their ramrods and showing a willingness to surrender." Keigwin later noted that despite being in reserve, his unit was the "second in the works, although they had farther to charge and deeper water to wade through than three others that started in advance of us." Despite being in the forefront of the charge, the 49th Indiana only suffered one man wounded. "It was the poorest fight I ever saw the rebels make," Keigwin admitted. Lawler also sent his reserve regiment, the 22nd Iowa, far to the right to dislodge a pocket of Confederates near the river. They did so, and one of the other regiments quickly took them prisoner.[26]

The farther south along the Confederate line, the easier the Union assault was. Several commanders in the lower sectors reported taking the enemy works "without opposition." One of Osterhaus's brigade commanders, Daniel W. Lindsey, went so far as to report that "we had no trouble in possessing the works in our immediate front." Brigade commander Stephen Burbridge, on the far left flank, noted that as his men approached the Confederate line "a white handkerchief was displayed on their intrenchments." Evidently, for all the Confederates cared, Loring could fend for himself.[27]

Colonel Theodore E. Buehler of the 67th Indiana of Burbridge's brigade of Smith's division left a vivid account of the advance on this southern sector of the Confederate lines. Although his men were tired and had not had anything to eat since the previous night, he remembered that "all fatigue was forgotten." "We advanced by the right oblique through brush and bayous," he recalled, "over fences and hedges, at a rapid rate." He continued, "With a shout unequalled, forward we went on the double-quick, over plowed fields and across bayous, to receive the surrender of the Sixtieth Tennessee [Rebel] Regiment." As a testament to just how shocked the Confederates fronting him were by Lawler's advance, the 67th Indiana, as well as the vast majority of the rest of the army, suffered few casualties.[28]

Relatively few Confederate casualties occurred in the charge itself. Pemberton reported a loss of a mere twenty killed and wounded, although the number was surely higher. The loss in artillery was quite severe, however, due to that fact that someone, and none of the Confederate officers would ever admit to such a thing, had ordered all the artillery horses away. Eighteen guns, along with limbers and caissons, were thus stranded, with no way to move them. The Federals took advantage and turned at least one of the guns on the retreating Confederates, one Iowan declaring that Federal general John Logan was on the scene and barking orders to turn the guns around. Conversely, the main Southern loss in men occurred when the retreat began; the Confederates here suffered more than seventeen hundred men taken prisoner, prompting one Iowan to remark that the "rebels were hemmed in like rats in a trap." With only two small avenues over which to cross the river, the feared bottleneck quickly developed. One lowly Confederate termed the region between the river and defenses as the "Jeff Davis Slaughter pen." Pemberton himself wrote that "it very soon became a matter of *save qui peut*," or every man for himself. Indeed, as Bowen's division and Vaughn's brigade tried to cross the river, hundreds fell captive to the pursuing Federals, Lawler marveling that "more men were captured by my brigade than I had men in the charge." Many Confederates tried to swim the river, and some made their way to safety. Others sadly drowned or were shot trying to escape. Most simply threw down their weapons rather than try to run the gauntlet of Union fire. One elated member of the 23rd Wisconsin of Burbridge's brigade wrote home, "our Brigade captured the 60th Tenn. Reg. every single one, the Colonel and all."[29]

But it was not without cost to the Federals. One Union soldier described the fields in front of the breastworks: "the dead and wounded lay thick on the field we were compelled to charge over." Another wrote how he saw "wounded and dead laying in all directions dead horses broken guns and gun carriages." An Iowan even described one soldier who had been hit thirteen times; he was taken to a hospital and left until last because no one thought he would live. Miraculously, he survived, recovered, and later rejoined his unit. That was all in the future, however, and now details were made to gather the wounded and bury the dead. Lawler reported he lost 14 killed and 185 wounded in three minutes. Total Union casualties in the attack amounted to 39 killed, 237 wounded[,] and 3 missing. Obviously, the southerners were even more devastated. One Federal wrote of the results of the chaotic retreat at the river: "Bodies could be seen floating in the brush and deadwood for two or three hundred yards. . . . The banks were covered with guns, hats, and clothing of almost every conceivable description. It is impossible to imagine a wilder scramble." Confederate totals were not fully reported, but killed and wounded were slight; the main loss came in captured, which totaled some seventeen hundred. Even among the carnage, however, most realized that Big Black River was nothing like the battle of the day before. One Federal, in fact, wrote "the engagement was not so severe. They were anxious to get across the river and burn the bridge."[30]

General Lawler himself was in a historic mood after the battle. Perusing the field, he stopped Aquilla Standifird of the 23rd Iowa and asked him to show him exactly where the regiment had begun their attack from behind the river bank. Standifird said the general wanted to know how far the brigade had charged. When Standifird showed him the place, Lawler was amazed, remarking that it was nearly a quarter of a mile to the Confederate works. Later, Grant himself came around and offered Lawler's entire brigade his personal thanks.[31]

Despite the losses, Federals of all ranks were ecstatic. John McClernand later wrote that "a victory could hardly have been more complete." A lower level Federal wrote that "a more gallant charge was never made." William F. Jones of the 42nd Ohio wrote his cousin that "in half a day we whipped them and took 3000 prisoners." Of course, rumors had by that time begun to swell the numbers, one Federal even reporting that they "captured 25000 more prisoners . . . have seen about that many myself." The Federals mopping up the field felt the same surge of enthusiasm, one captain remarking that they had routed "the flower of the rebel army." As the victorious Federals confronted the beaten Confederates behind the surging lines, several struck up conversations. One northerner asked a Confederate what he thought of the Federals. The disheartened Confederate responded, "he thought they could go where they pleased." The same Federal marveled at the sight of the southern soldiers. "None of them have uniforms," he said in disbelief. "They have all kinds of clothing[.] they are hard looking critters."[32]

The commander of those hard luck Confederate soldiers was feeling no better. John Pemberton later wrote in his report, "a strong position, with an ample force of infantry and artillery to hold it, was shamefully abandoned almost without resistance." But with the loss of the Big Black River defenses and nearly two thousand prisoners, Pemberton knew his effort to connect with Loring had gone awry. For all he knew, the Federals had captured or destroyed Loring's division. As a result, Loring now had to fend for himself; Pemberton had to extricate the remaining parts of his army. He sadly admitted, "under these circumstances nothing remained but to retire the army within the defenses of Vicksburg." But the army was falling apart, one officer describing it as "shockingly demoralized." Pemberton noted his first duty was to "endeavor as speedily as possible to reorganize the depressed and discomfited troops."[33]

Indeed, many soldiers had already begun their retreat into the city. One artilleryman reported to his diary, "the retreat of our army may be properly denominated a rout." A wagon master described "the indiscriminate flight . . . wagons at the gallop—men rushing madly along with citizens half crazy and women frantic, asking for assistance, all rendered it as confused a scene as you well could imagine." With so many straggling, Pemberton officially ordered Bowen's whipped command to retreat. The army marched westward, led by Pemberton, who made his way to the city to prepare its defense. He knew the hard-hitting Grant would soon arrive.[34]

As Pemberton made his way toward Vicksburg, he had to realize the terrible situation he was in. He had lost two battles and nearly half his mobile army in two days. Furthermore, he now faced the prospects of becoming trapped in Vicksburg, with no way to escape. Perhaps he best summed up the situation when he calmly confided to an accompanying officer, "Just thirty years ago I began my military career by receiving my appointment to a cadetship at the U.S. Military Academy, and to-day—the same date—that career is ended in disaster and disgrace."[35]

While Pemberton was slipping toward depression, however, portions of his army at the bridge were still holding on. As soon as all who could passed over, Major Lockett ordered the soldiers to destroy the bridge and the *Dot*, thereby halting Grant long enough for Pemberton to make sense of his disorganized situation. Lockett had earlier placed rails and cotton "at intervals," he said, and had a barrel of turpentine ready to ignite the *Dot*. As Lockett watched the retreat in disgust, he gave the signal to torch the bridges when satisfied that all who could had made it out. Fortunately for the Confederates, when lit the bridges burned beyond further use and soon collapsed. "In a few moments," Lockett remembered, "both bridges were in flames, and were quickly and thoroughly burned." Two Confederate brigades, Brigadier Generals Stephen D. Lee's and William Baldwin's, remained to annoy the Federals and delay any bridge building activity, as did artillery, which shelled the Federals across the river. Federal artillery responded while the infantrymen made, according to one Iowan, "Herculean efforts" to extinguish the fires, but they were unsuccessful. Union sharpshooters of Lindsey's Federal brigade of Osterhaus's division also peppered the Confederates, but few casualties resulted.[36]

Confederate sharpshooters on the high bluffs west of the river also helped blunt the Federal advance, which inexplicably included U. S. Grant's son, Fred, who accompanied the commanding general on the campaign. The young boy very much enjoyed himself as he pursued the retreating Confederates to the river and even watched some swim to the west bank. Fred's enthusiasm was quickly dampened when a Confederate sharpshooter hit him in the leg. Thinking he was dead, the younger Grant called to a nearby staff officer, "I am killed." The officer, probably chagrined at his babysitting role in the first place, told the boy to "move your toes," whereupon both learned the wound "was slight but very painful." On realizing the boy would live, the officer "recommended our hasty retreat," Fred remembered years later. "This we accomplished in good order," he added.[37]

Slowly but surely, the defeated Confederate army stumbled into Vicksburg, the residents of which had heard the heavy firing on the morning of May 17 and wondered about its outcome. Soon, they found out. Solemn looks and dejected countenances marked the army's entrance. Stories of defeat and rumors of treachery abounded as many began to lay blame for the debacle. One member of Pemberton's staff described to his diary how "our troops shamefully abandoned the trenches." A member of Cockrell's brigade wrote in his diary, "the troops in line there [on the left] in gloriously gave way, on which account the troops on the right were necessitated to fall back." Several soldiers retold rumors of Pemberton selling Vicksburg, one said for $100,000. As a result, many offered mournful recollections in diaries and letters. One Confederate remembered the army being "all dejected." Another prophesied, "if an attack is made tomorrow, we are lost." He continued to moan, "I have never been low spirited, but things look too dark for even me to be hopeful."[38]

Pemberton's arrival with the army clearly horrified the citizens. The two unengaged divisions, Smith's and Forney's, still presented an effective appearance, but then came the veterans of Champion Hill and Big Black River Bridge. Emma Balfour remembered her anguish as the troops passed: "I hope never to witness again such a scene as the return of our routed army.

From twelve o'clock until late in the night the streets and roads were jammed with wagons, cannons, horses, men, mules, stock, sheep, everything you can imagine that appertains to an army—being brought hurriedly within the intrenchment. Nothing like order prevailed, of course, as divisions, brigades, and regiments were broken and separated." Despite their shock, the people of Vicksburg turned out in full force to aid the troops. Many opened their pantries, and others carried water to the street corners for the exhausted men. Emma Balfour could only look on with desperation, however. "Poor fellows," she wailed, "it made my heart ache to see them." No doubt many soldiers agreed with the desperation. One termed May 17 as "one long day."[39]

Obviously, the exact opposite feeling prevailed in the Union ranks. Grant had reaped huge benefits from his pursuit and attack at the Big Black River, so much so that he could in good faith disregard an order from Washington telling him to support Major General Nathaniel P. Banks's efforts at Port Hudson, Louisiana. Grant had routed the enemy army, captured more than seventeen hundred prisoners, and driven Pemberton headlong into Vicksburg for total casualties of only 279 in a battle that really did not have to take place anyway. And Grant had no mind to stop now. He had Vicksburg within his grasp and would not let go. He thus ordered his three corps across the Big Black River toward his ultimate objective—Vicksburg.[40]

Notes

1. William Drennan to wife, May 30, 1863, William A. Drennan Papers, Mississippi Department of Archives and History, Jackson; Thomas O. Hall, "The Key to Vicksburg," *Southern Bivouac* 2, no. 9 (May 1884): 395. For the Vicksburg Campaign, see Michael B. Ballard, *Vicksburg: The Campaign That Opened the Mississippi* (Chapel Hill: University of North Carolina Press, 2004); Warren E. Grabau, *Ninety-Eight Days: A Geographer's View of the Vicksburg Campaign* (Knoxville: University of Tennessee Press, 2000); William L. Shea and Terrence J. Winschel, *Vicksburg Is the Key: The Struggle for the Mississippi River* (Lincoln: University of Nebraska Press, 2003); and Edwin C. Bearss, *The Vicksburg Campaign*, 3 vols. (Dayton: Morningside House, 1985).

2. For Champion Hill itself and the retreat, see Timothy B. Smith, *Champion Hill: Decisive Battle for Vicksburg* (New York: Savas Beatie, 2004).

3. U.S. War Department, *The War of the Rebellion: A Compilation of the Official Records of the Union and Confederate Armies*, 128 vols. (Washington, DC: Government Printing Office, 1880–1901), series 1, vol. 24, pt. 1: 266. Hereinafter cited as *OR*. All references are to Series 1 unless otherwise indicated; Bearss, *The Vicksburg Campaign*, 2: 654; Grabau, *Ninety-Eight Days*, 332.

4. Timothy B. Smith, "Mississippi Nightmare," *Civil War Times* 48, no. 4 (August 2009): 54–58.

5. *OR*, vol. 24, pt. 1: 266.

6. James H. Wilson Journal, May 16, 1863, James H. Wilson Papers, Library of Congress, Washington, DC; *OR*, vol. 24, pt. 1: 53.

7. William Clemans Memoirs, Rare Book and Manuscript Library, University of Illinois, Urbana-Champaign, 9; William L. B. Jenney, "Personal Recollections of Vicksburg," *MOLLUS-Illinois* (Chicago: Dial Press, 1899), 3: 260.

8. *OR*, vol. 24, pt. 1: 54, 86, 266–67; George Crooke, *The Twenty-first Regiment of Iowa Volunteer Infantry: A Narrative of Its Experience in Active Service, Including a Military Record of Each Officer, Non-Commissioned Officer, and Private Soldier of the Organization* (Milwaukee: King, Fowle, and Co., 1891), 69; Bearss, *The Vicksburg Campaign*, 2: 454, 655–57.

9. Ephraim McD. Anderson, *Memoirs: Historical and Personal, Including the Campaigns of the First Missouri Confederate Brigade* (St. Louis: Times Printing Co., 1868), 317.

10. *OR*, vol. 24, pt. 1: 266; John B. Bannon Diary, May 17, 1863, South Caroliniana Library, University of South Carolina, Columbia; William Drennan to wife, May 30, 1863, Drennan Papers. The larger army reserve wagon train crossed at Bridgeport that night.

11. *OR*, vol. 24, pt. 2: 119. For Bowen, see Phillip Thomas Tucker, *The Forgotten "Stonewall of the West": Major General John Stevens Bowen* (Macon: Mercer University Press, 1997), 286–90.

12. Edmond W. Pettus, "Colonel Franklin K. Beck—A Sketch," Edmond W. Pettus Papers, Alabama Department of Archives and History, Montgomery; Francis V. Greene, *The Mississippi* (New York: Charles Scribner's Sons, 1882), 162; George R. Elliott Diaries, May 17, 1863, Tennessee State Library and Archives, Nashville; *OR*, vol. 24, pt. 1: 266–67; Bearss, *The Vicksburg Campaign*, 2: 665; Phillip Thomas Tucker, *Westerners in Gray: The Men and Missions of the Elite Fifth Missouri Infantry Regiment* (Jefferson, NC: McFarland and Co., 1995), 206. For Vaughn and his brigade, see Larry Gordon, *The Last Confederate General: John C. Vaughn and His East Tennessee Cavalry* (Minneapolis: Zenith Press, 2009), 57–62.

13. *OR*, vol. 24, pt. 1: 267.

14. Ibid., pt. 1:266–67; pt. 2: 73; Samuel D. Pryce, *Vanishing Footprints: The Twenty-second Iowa Volunteer Infantry in the Civil War*, ed. Jeffry C. Burden (Iowa City: Camp Pope Bookshop, 2008), 106; Grabau, *Ninety-Eight Days*, 331.

15. Robert S. Shuey to brother, May 18, 1863, John C. Pemberton Papers, National Archives and Records Administration, Washington, DC; William Drennan to wife, May 30, 1863, Drennan Papers; Bearss, *The Vicksburg Campaign*, 2: 665, 667, 671; Aquilla Standifird Diary, May 17, 1863, Western Historical Manuscript Collection, University of Missouri–Rolla; *OR*, vol. 24, pt. 1: 53–54, 152, 616; pt. 2: 16, 132, 135–36.

16. Bearss, *The Vicksburg Campaign*, 2: 665, 667, 671; *OR*, vol. 24, pt. 1: 53–54, 152, 616; pt. 2: 16, 132, 135–136.

17. Aquilla Standifird Diary, May 17, 1863; Robert S. Shuey to brother, May 18, 1863, Pemberton Papers; Pryce, *Vanishing Footprints*, 105–6; Gordon, *The Last Confederate General*, 60; *OR*, vol. 24, pt. 2: 16, 132, 136; pt. 1: 152; Bearss, *The Vicksburg Campaign*, 2: 666.

18. Jack D. Welsh, *Medical Histories of Union Generals* (Kent: Kent State University Press, 1996), 200; *OR*, vol. 24, pt. 2: 136; Robert S. Shuey to brother, May 18, 1863, Pemberton Papers; Bearss, *The Vicksburg Campaign*, 2: 671; Wilbur F. Crummer,

With Grant at Fort Donelson, Shiloh and Vicksburg: And an Appreciation of General U.S. Grant (Oak Park: E. C. Crummer and Co., 1915), 107.

19. *OR*, vol. 24, pt. 2: 135–37; pt. 1: 152; Charles Boarman Cleveland, "With the Third Missouri Regiment," *Confederate Veteran* 31, no. 1 (January 1923): 19; Aquilla Standifird Diary, May 17, 1863; Steven E. Woodworth, *Nothing but Victory: The Army of the Tennessee, 1861–1865* (New York: Knopf, 2005), 393; Edwin C. Bearss, *Fields of Honor: Pivotal Battles of the Civil War* (Washington, DC: National Geographic, 2006), 231.

20. *OR*, vol. 24, pt. 2: 136–37; Crooke, *The Twenty-first Regiment of Iowa Volunteer Infantry*, 73.

21. Aquilla Standifird Diary, May 17, 1863; Pryce, *Vanishing Footprints*, 106; Robert S. Shuey to brother, May 18, 1863, Pemberton Papers; Crooke, *The Twenty-first Regiment of Iowa Volunteer Infantry*, 73; *OR*, vol. 24, pt. 2: 137, 142; William Drennan to wife, May 30, 1863, Drennan Papers; Bearss, *The Vicksburg Campaign*, 2: 673; S. C. Jones, *Reminiscences of the Twenty-second Iowa Volunteer Infantry: Giving Its Organization, Marches, Skirmishes, Battles, and Sieges, as taken from the Diary of Lieutenant S. C. Jones of Company A* (Iowa City: n.p., 1907), 35.

22. Crooke, *The Twenty-first Regiment of Iowa Volunteer Infantry*, 70; *OR*, vol. 24, pt. 2: 137, 139.

23. Crooke, *The Twenty-first Regiment of Iowa Volunteer Infantry*, 73; *OR*, vol. 24, pt. 2: 137, 142; Aquilla Standifird Diary, May 17, 1863; Pryce, *Vanishing Footprints*, 106; Robert S. Shuey to brother, May 18, 1863, Pemberton Papers.

24. W. L. Foster to his wife, June 20, 1863, Civil War Papers, Mississippi Department of Archives and History, Jackson; *OR*, vol. 24, pt. 2: 119, 128–43; Gordon, *The Last Confederate General*, 60; *OR*, vol. 24, pt. 1: 54, 152, 267; Robert S. Shuey to brother, May 18, 1863, Pemberton Papers; R. S. Bevier, *History of the First and Second Missouri Confederate Brigades 1861–1865, and From Wakaruse to Appomattox, A Military Anagraph* (St. Louis: Bryan, Brand and Co., 1879), 194.

25. George W. Gordon Diary, May 24, 1863, George W. Gordon Papers, U.S. Army Military History Institute, Carlisle; Anderson, *Memoirs*, 319; *OR*, vol. 24, pt. 1: 267–68; Bearss, *The Vicksburg Campaign*, 2: 675; *OR*, vol. 24, pt. 2: 113–14, 119–20; Tucker, *The Confederacy's Forgotten "Stonewall of the West,"* 286; Bevier, *History of the First and Second Missouri Confederate Brigades 1861–1865*, 195.

26. *OR*, vol. 24, pt. 2: 23, 137.

27. Ibid., 24, 26, 32.

28. *OR*, vol. 24, pt. 1: 596.

29. John Griffin Jones to his parents, May 29, 1863, John Griffin Jones Papers, Library of Congress, Washington, D.C.; Pryce, *Vanishing Footprints*, 108; *OR*, vol. 24, pt. 1: 267–68; pt. 2: 113, 131, 138; Anderson, *Memoirs*, 319; Carlos W. Colby, "Bulletts, Hardtack and Mud: A Soldier's View of the Vicksburg Campaign," ed. John S. Painter, *Journal of the West* 4, no. 2 (April 1965): 151; Terrence J. Winschel, "The Guns at Champion Hill (Part II)," *Journal of Confederate History* 6 (1990): 105.

30. Robert S. Shuey to brother, May 18, 1863, Pemberton Papers; Thomas S. Hawley to parents, May 18, 1863, Thomas S. Hawley Papers, Minnesota Historical Society, St. Paul; Pryce, *Vanishing Footprints*, 106; Aquilla Standifird Diary, May 17, 1863; Jones, *Reminiscences of the Twenty-second Iowa Volunteer Infantry*, 35; *OR*, vol. 24, pt. 2: 138; Clemans Memoirs, 9; Crooke, *The Twenty-first Regiment of Iowa Volunteer Infantry*, 73; Ballard, *Vicksburg*, 318.

31. Aquilla Standifird Diary, May 17, 1863; Pryce, *Vanishing Footprints*, 106.

32. Robert S. Shuey to his brother, May 18, 1863, Pemberton Papers; *OR*, vol. 24, pt. 1: 152, 267; pt. 2: 244; Thomas S. Hawley to parents, May 18, 1863, Hawley Papers; William F. Jones to cousin, June 13, 1863, William F. Jones Papers, Western Historical Manuscripts Collection, University of Missouri–Columbia.

33. John C. Taylor Diary, May 17, 1863, Taylor Family Papers, Albert and Shirley Small Special Collections Library, University of Virginia, Charlottesville; *OR*, vol. 24, pt. 1: 152, 267–69; pt. 2: 244.

34. John Power Logan Diary, May 17, 1863, Mississippi Department of Archives and History, Jackson; *OR*, vol. 24, pt. 1: 268–69; William Drennan to wife, May 30, 1863, Drennan Papers.

35. S. H. Lockett, "The Defense of Vicksburg," in *Battles and Leaders of the Civil War*, 4 vols. (New York: Century Co., 1884–87) 3: 488; J. T. Hogane, "Reminiscences of the Siege of Vicksburg," *Southern Historical Society Papers* 2, nos. 4–5 (April–May 1883): 223.

36. *OR*, vol. 24, pt. 2: 73, 124, 132, 229, 350, 352; pt. 1: 268; Jasper N. Whiphers Diary, May 17, 1863, Alexander Roberts Papers, Illinois State Historical Library, Springfield; Clemans Memoirs, 9; John Fiske, *The Mississippi Valley in the Civil War* (New York: Houghton, Mifflin and Co., 1900), 240; Pryce, *Vanishing Footprints*, 108.

37. Frederick D. Grant, "A Boy's Experience at Vicksburg," *MOLLUS–New York*. (New York: G. P. Putnam's Sons, 1907), 3:94–95.

38. Emma Balfour Diary, May 17, 1863, Mississippi Department of Archives and History, Jackson; J. M. Love Diary, May 16, 1863, J. D. Williams Library, University of Mississippi, Oxford; Joseph Dill Alison Diary, May 17, 1863, Southern Historical Collection, Wilson Library, University of North Carolina at Chapel Hill; Theodore D. Fisher Diary, May 17, 1863, Civil War Collection, Missouri Historical Society, St. Louis; John C. Taylor Diary, May 17, 1863, Taylor Family Papers; James E. Payne, "General Pemberton and Vicksburg," *Confederate Veteran* 36, no. 7 (July 1928): 247.

39. Emma Balfour Diary, May 17, 1863; Thomas C. Skinner to "Hannah," May 20, 1863, U. S. Grant Papers, Library of Congress, Washington, DC.

40. Charles A. Dana to Edwin M. Stanton, May 23, 1863, Charles A. Dana Papers, Library of Congress, Washington, DC.

10

THE "STEALING TOUR"
SOLDIERS AND CIVILIANS IN GRANT'S
MARCH TO VICKSBURG

Steven Nathaniel Dossman

On April 30, 1863, Major General Ulysses S. Grant landed twenty-four thousand men at Bruinsburg, Mississippi. With the arrival of Major General William T. Sherman's Fifteenth Corps a few days later, Grant's force exceeded forty thousand hard fighting veterans. Until they reached the outskirts of Vicksburg and established a reliable supply connection furnished by the United States Navy, the entire army would be foraging for provisions in an area that had never before felt the tramp of Yankee boots.[1] In the march to Vicksburg, Grant's men would embark upon their first experiment with a brutal style of economic warfare that historian Mark Grimsley terms *hard war*. Grimsley defines hard war as "actions against southern civilians and property made expressly in order to demoralize southern civilians and ruin the Confederate economy, particularly its industries and transportation infrastructure," which "involved the allocation of substantial military resources to accomplish the job."[2] After fighting and winning the small but savage battle of Port Gibson, the invading Federals immediately came into contact with astounded southern civilians. Catching his Confederate opponent unprepared, Grant secured his beachhead and swiftly dispatched requisitioning parties into the surrounding area.[3]

Lacking a sufficient number of wagons to transport the supplies, Grant ordered "immediately upon landing that all the vehicles and draft animals, whether horses, mules, or oxen, in the vicinity should be collected and loaded to their capacity with ammunition."[4] One Indiana soldier, Thomas Durham, later remembered that "it was equal to a circus parade in a country town to see this ammunition caravan." As Durham recalled, the wagon train contained "fine family carriages loaded with boxes of ammunition and drawn by an ox team, or an old mule and horse hitched together, rigged with plow

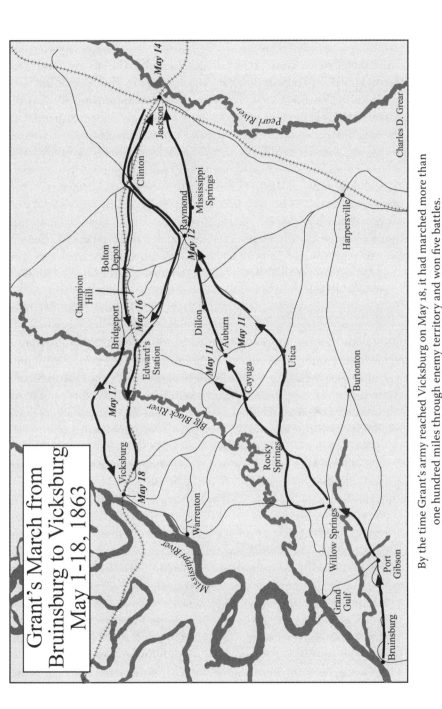

Grant's March from Bruinsburg to Vicksburg May 1-18, 1863

Bruinsburg

Port Gibson

Grand Gulf

Willow Springs

Rocky Springs

Utica

Burtonton

Harpersville

Cayuga

May 11

Auburn

May 11

Dillon

May 11

Mississippi Springs

Raymond

May 12

Jackson

May 14

Clinton

Bolton Depot

Champion Hill

Bridgeport

May 16

Edward's Station

May 17

Vicksburg

May 18

Warrenton

Mississippi River

Big Black River

Pearl River

Charles D. Grear

By the time Grant's army reached Vicksburg on May 18, it had marched more than one hundred miles through enemy territory and won five battles.

harness, shuck collars and rope lines to drive with." He noted that "cotton wagons, ox carts and even dog carts—everything that could be found in the country that had wheels, and every kind of animal and harness with which to pull them, were pressed into service. No such sight has ever been seen since old Noah entered the Ark."[5]

When the Federals entered Port Gibson with the improvised wagon train stretching along behind them, townspeople could only stare in disbelief. One Illinois soldier later remarked that when he "passed through the main street of the city, men, women and children filled the walks or gazed anxiously from the upper story windows, as though a monster show had come to town."[6] Osborn Oldroyd, a member of the Seventeenth Corps from Ohio, stated that after entering the town, "The boys found a lot of blank bank currency of different denominations, upon the Port Gibson bank. They signed some of them, and it is quite common to see a private of yesterday a bank president to-day." Oldroyd observed that the notes "may not become a circulating medium to a very great extent, but it is not at all likely that it will be refused by the inhabitants along our route when tendered in payment for corn-bread, sweet potatoes, etc."[7]

After continuing the march, one member of the 20th Ohio Regiment discovered a coffeepot filled with silver dollars buried under a corner of a house while chasing "a poor lonely confederate chicken" and distributed the money throughout his company. Oldroyd asserted the opinions of most Federal soldiers when he exclaimed in his account, "How foolish it is for southern people to flee and leave their beautiful property to the foe. We only want something to eat." The Ohioan recognized that some soldiers in the Union army had more appetite for the destruction of southern property than others, writing that "there are some who would apply the torch to a deserted home, that would not do so if the owners remained in it. It is quite common here to build the chimneys outside of the houses, and I have noticed them still standing where the house had been burned."[8]

Another Iowa Federal recorded that "during the march this afternoon, we found a lot of bacon the fleeing rebels had left in the woods. Port Gibson is a pleasant business-looking place of about two thousand inhabitants. The inhabitants deserted the town on our approach—only a few families remaining."[9] Port Gibson lost more than bacon during the Federal occupation, as the advancing blue host provided episodes of pillage and plunder as well. One Illinois soldier wrote that "the boys looted the town going through the stores and taking whatever suited them best."[10] Another soldier, bugler Florison D. Pitts of the Chicago Mercantile Battery, noted in his diary on May 2, "occupied Port Gibson at 9 o'clock. . . . Boys jerked every thing they wanted from the stores."[11]

Some violent resistance from the civilians did occur, although it was far less than many Confederate officials had hoped. Oldroyd encountered first-hand the danger from guerrillas when he wandered away from camp along a riverbank on May 5 and recorded that "a bullet flew through the trees not far from my head. I looked across the river from whence it came, but could not see anybody. Did not stay there long, but got back to camp, where I felt safer." While only a few actual attacks took place, enough violence occurred to keep Union soldiers alert to the ever-present threat. When confronted by Federal soldiers, most Mississippians displayed affirmation of loyalty. Old-royd noted, "To our faces these citizens seem good Union men, but behind our backs, no doubt their sentiments undergo a change. Probably they were among those who fired at us, and will do it again as soon as they dare." Old-royd complained that he had "not seen a regular acknowledged rebel since we crossed the river, except those we have seen in their army."[12]

After capturing Port Gibson and the landing at Grand Gulf, which he intended to use as a supply base for the campaign, Grant learned that Major General Nathaniel Banks and his Army of the Gulf would not be in posi-tion to reinforce for weeks. This development persuaded Grant to alter his strategy, as he later explained in his memoirs: "I therefore determined to move independently of Banks, cut loose from my base, destroy the rebel force in rear of Vicksburg and invest or capture the city." The bold resolution to march into the heart of Confederate territory with only minimal logisti-cal support demanded immediate execution and forced Grant to act on his own authority without the approval of his superiors in Washington. Grant's close friend Sherman believed the audacious maneuver doomed to failure and urged Grant to stop until engineers constructed additional roads that securely connected the Grand Gulf supply base to the army. Grant replied that he did not "calculate upon the possibility of supplying the army with full rations from Grand Gulf. I know it will be impossible without constructing additional roads. What I do expect is to get up what rations of hard bread, coffee and salt we can, and make the country furnish the balance." This declaration, while pragmatic in nature, ranks as one of the most influential decisions made by any Federal commander during the war. In one decisive moment, Grant had issued the orders that ultimately transformed his army into an instrument of economic and psychological warfare that would affect southern civilians and their ability to continue the war.[13]

Grant's troops embarked on an epic march that historians often describe as a "Blitzkrieg through Mississippi," and the farms of Central Mississippi provided all rations beyond the basic staples of hard tack and coffee.[14] For-tunately for the Union, the area had suffered little during two years of war, and a rich bounty awaited the conquering Army of the Tennessee. As Grant later stated, "Beef, mutton, poultry and forage were found in abundance. Quite a quantity of bacon and molasses were also secured from the country, but bread and coffee could not be obtained in quantity sufficient for all the men." To remedy the shortfall of bread, Grant ordered soldiers to man occupied plantation grindstones and "these were kept running while we were stopping, day and night, and when we were marching, during the night, at all plantations covered by the troops."[15]

Grant's decision to forage almost entirely off the Mississippi countryside forced Union soldiers and southern civilians into greater and more extensive contact than ever before and substantially increased the amount of damage the Union army inflicted upon civilian property. Foraging and confiscation had occurred before in other areas, but Grant's Vicksburg Campaign vastly surpassed any previous campaign, raid, or expedition in its scale of foodstuffs consumed and material ruin, and it supplied an army of veterans with the knowledge of how effective hard war could be in suppressing Confederate morale. In the entire course of the war, few other decisions would have a greater impact on the war-making methods employed and the eventual outcome of the conflict.

This new policy of reliance on the countryside excited some apprehension from the soldiers. Oldroyd wrote, "My fear is that they may cut our supply train, and then we should be in a bad fix. Should that happen and they get us real hungry, I am afraid short work would be made of taking Vicksburg."[16] To keep the army supplied with rations beyond the hard tack coming up from the Grand Gulf supply base, Grant kept his army advancing at a rapid pace, continuing to forage and gain ground before his men exhausted the local supplies or Confederate adversaries united superior forces against him.[17]

On May 6, General Sherman wrote his wife about conditions he discovered at the Bowie plantation in northeast Louisiana, stating, "We have found some magnificent plantations most horribly plundered. . . . All Rosewood furniture, pier glasses, splendid bedsteads were all smashed, books of the most valuable kind strewn on the floor & about the yard, and every possible indignity offered the palace." Sherman, who had lived in Louisiana before the war, blamed the outrages on "the cursed stragglers who wont fight, but hang behind and disgrace our Cause & Country." The Union general admitted that "devastation marked the whole path of the army, and I know all the principal officers detest the infamous practice as much as I do." Sherman, perhaps remembering his friends in the South, declared to his wife, "Of course I expect & do take corn, bacon, horses, mules and everything to support an army, and don't object much to the using fences for firewood, but this universal burning and wanton destruction of private property is not justifiable in war."[18]

Most common foot soldiers would only have limited interaction with residents while marching through the unforgiving Mississippi heat, but those assigned to foraging expeditions would have extensive contact with civilians. Ohioan soldier Owen Hopkins described a typical expedition in his journal on May 9, 1863, as "a foraging Expedition, alias Stealing tour. I filled my Haversack full of the dainties of the country. We succeeded in Finding a wagon-load of molasses and Bacon which we shipped immediately for the especial Benefit of the Forty-second Regiment Ohio Infantry Volunteers, U.S.A. Returned to camp tired But not hungry."[19]

Hopkins later recorded further information about the incident, writing that "we came to a plantation where no Yankees had ever trod, and after putting to flight a pack of blood hounds and frightening half out of their wits a motly group of alternatively black and white darkies, I discovered the *garden*," while one of his comrades "had the honor of discovering a well-filled smokehouse," another "accidentally fell over a barrel of dried peaches," one companion "in the meantime capturing three or four fat hens," and yet another "encountered a porker with such violence that Porker was killed and his hams amputated with great skill." Hopkins admitted that the pursuit "extended to the mansion and bureau drawers, where I succeeded in finding a dozen pairs of cotton socks, a welcome discovery as my only pair needed the tender care of a mother who could darn. I'll be darned if they didn't!"[20] The foraging party returned to camp, "receiving as a reward from our ravenous comrades a round of hearty cheers, and before morning chickens, turkeys, calves, pigs, and everything had become food for soldiers." Similar expeditions stripped the countryside of food, leaving little substance behind for either the Confederate army or civilian population.[21]

Worse than a foraging expedition would be to have units of the army camp on one's property for any significant time, as Logan's Division of the Seventeenth Corps did on the Bagnell plantation on the Big Black River from May 3 to 7. In a postwar account written for the Southern Claims Commission listing "Stock & Property Consumed & taken off by Gen. U. S. Grant's Army," the estate detailed a total loss of 95 cotton bales either burned or seized, and the confiscation of 15 mules, 2 horses, 40 head of sheep, 15 milk cows, 10 work oxen, 25 calves, 100 hogs, 1 mule wagon, 4 sets of wagon gears, 3,800 bushels of corn, 4,000 pounds of bacon and hams, 5 tons of fodder, 30,000 feet of lumber used in the construction of tent shelters, and 8,000 fence rails burned for fuel. Altogether, the unfortunate plantation owners estimated their loss at $29,855, an amount that calculated the damage using the 1863 price of cotton, raised exponentially by the wartime shortage.[22]

This account does not include the amount of human property lost, which would have raised the total cost by tens of thousands of dollars. A plantation that produced over a hundred bales of cotton would need a sizable slave labor force, who were either relocated by their owners or gained freedom from Grant's army. Interestingly, also missing from this list is any buildings burned or personal property taken, which indicates that the owners most likely stayed during the Union occupation. The damage inflicted by Logan's division in only a few days would prevent this plantation from producing any agricultural supplies for the Confederate army until the war ended. With no slave or animal labor to plant with, and no fences to protect the crops, no large scale production would be possible. Unoccupied plantations suffered even greater devastation.[23]

On May 9, Sherman wrote to his wife Ellen from Hankinson's Ferry, "We are short of wagons and provisions, but in this starving country we find an abundance of corn, hogs, cattle sheep and Poultry. Men who came in advance have drawn but 2 days rations in 10, and are fat."[24] On the same day in Rocky Springs, Grant informed his wife Julia, "People all seem to stay at home and show less signs of fear than one would suppose. These people talk a greatdeel [sic] about the barbarities of the Yankees but I hear no complaints where the Army has been even of insults having been offered." Grant apparently did not know about the outbreak of looting in Port Gibson, or he did not consider the property loss endured by the town's shopkeepers as comparable to the endless rumors of unspeakable northern atrocities against civilians.[25]

The continued foraging not only stripped the material possessions of Mississippi, but also resulted in a substantial amount of interaction with former slave owners, which astounded many of the midwestern Federals who had never before witnessed the nature of slavery in the Deep South. One Union foraging expedition stumbled upon a "young mistress who had just been deserted by her Negroes, all alone, crying with but a scant allowance of provisions left her. She had never learned to cook, and in fact was a complete stranger to housework of any kind." The liberation of slaves forced many owners, especially upper-class women, to rely on their own labor for the first time in their lives, which only increased their hatred of the Yankees as inhuman savages. The exaggerations of northern brutality, created by the secessionist elite, spread throughout all classes of society. Oldroyd discovered that the majority of southerners "have been led, apparently, to expect to find the Lincoln soldier more of a beast than human. At least such is the belief among the lower sort."[26]

As Grant's forces marched deeper into Mississippi, Lieutenant General John C. Pemberton began maneuvering his Army of Vicksburg to repel the

Federal incursion. Undaunted, Grant's systematic foraging continued unabated. As war correspondent Sylvanus Cadwallader of the *Chicago Times* reported, "Army wagons by scores and hundreds were sent out daily from ten to fifteen miles, escorted by infantry details sufficient to protect them from any sudden foray by Confederate Cavalry." After scouring the countryside, Cadwallader added, the wagons "returned at nightfall groaning under the weight of impressed supplies, and increased by the addition to the train of every vehicle, no matter what its description, that could bear the weight of a sack of grain, pieces of salt meat, or pails full of butter, eggs, honey or vegetables."[27]

The region, like much of the Old South, relied largely on livestock for food, which proved a particularly lucrative target for Union foraging parties. Cadwallader affirmed that "horses, mules and cattle were brought in by droves of hundreds. I frequently saw horses, cattle and mules of all ages and condition; milch cows and calves; sheep, goats and lambs; turkeys, geese, ducks and chickens, driven together in one drove." Unionists and neutrals suffered from the requisitions as well as secessionists, as only those who could unquestionably prove their fidelity to the Union received compensation. As Cadwallader declared, "The country was much richer in food products than we had expected to find it. If owners could establish their loyalty they were given regular vouchers for everything taken—if not, not."[28]

One observer, War Department official Charles A. Dana, recognized the substantial impact that voluntary military service and conscription had upon the southern population. Writing after the war, Dana recalled, "A fact which impressed me was the total absence of men capable of bearing arms. Only old men and children remained. The young men were all in the army or had perished in it. The South was drained of its youth." Dana also noticed the dramatic effect that Grant's policies had upon the first southerners to endure the innovative measures. Dana described encountering citizens who "had at first sympathized with the rebellion, and even joined in it, now of their own accord rendering Grant the most valuable assistance, in order that the rebellion might be ended as speedily as possible, and something saved by the southern people out of their otherwise total and hopeless ruin." These former secessionists acted more out of self-preservation than from any patriotic turn of heart. Dana quoted them as declaring, "'Slavery is gone, other property is mainly gone . . . but, for God's sake, let us save some relic of our former means of living.'"[29]

Grant's march introduced the realities of war to the Mississippi home front with an intensity that no one could have imagined two years before. Each animal slaughtered and each bushel of corn consumed meant one less that the Confederates could use to sustain the war. Even if a tactical disaster occurred and Grant's invasion were eventually repelled, those areas of Mississippi through which he had marched would have little value to the Confederacy if recaptured. As Grant pressed on, each step brought his army closer to its ultimate objective of Vicksburg, and each residence visited by the foraging parties brought the Union one step closer on the long road to total victory.

Women, left at home to manage farms and plantations without male assistance, particularly suffered from the deprivation of support from husbands and other male relations. British observer Lieutenant Colonel Arthur Fremantle, one of the most fascinating figures then present in the state, asserted after spending the night in a Mississippi residence that "it is impossible to exaggerate the unfortunate condition of the women left behind in these farmhouses. They have scarcely any clothes, and nothing but the coarsest bacon to eat, and are in miserable uncertainty as to the fate of their relations, whom they hardly ever communicate with." Visiting an area of Mississippi still secure under Confederate control, Fremantle noted, "Their slaves, however, generally remain true to them." Fremantle, quite naively, failed to grasp that the behavior of the enslaved changed dramatically when northern forces and freedom approached.[30]

On May 12, Union major general James B. Mcpherson's Seventeenth Corps collided with Confederate brigadier general John Gregg's brigade outside the small village of Raymond. While the fighting raged, local residents prepared an extensive meal for Gregg's brigade in honor of an anticipated triumph. After repulsing a vicious attack, the superior numbers of the Seventeenth Corps drove Gregg's Confederates back in retreat, hastily leaving the elaborate banquet behind. The Battle of Raymond ended with Union conquest, and the citizens of Raymond found their victory celebration devoured by Federal soldiers.[31] Ohioan Oldroyd remembered wryly that "The citizens had prepared a good dinner for the rebels on their return from victory, but, as they actually returned from defeat they were in too much of a hurry to enjoy it."[32]

The triumphant and well-fed Federals camped in Raymond, helping themselves to more than their enemy's dinner. One Ohioan, Corporal Owen Hopkins, chronicled, "By broad daylight, however, the Brigade was astir, and a regular pillaging of the town commenced; the rain poured in torrents, and the streets were a quagmire, rendered so by the tramping of men and mules." While northern soldiers partook of the shops of Raymond, their wounded comrades filled the largest buildings in town. On May 15, the looting continued, as Hopkins recorded on that date, "A general Plundering prevails. Stores and ware-rooms, Kitchen and dining-room, Parlor and Pantry, undergo alike the ordeal of being Searched by the prying 'Lincolnites.'" Hopkins's diary relates a vivid scene of wreckage: "Furniture and Crockery, Glass-ware and tinware are scattered and Broken promiscuously, and the Forty-second [Ohio] Boys are wreaking their vengeance on the China ware in a Whole Sale establishment just across the Street. . . . Go ahead, boys! It all belongs to Rebels; go in on your 'mus' [muscle]."[33]

Another Federal, Brevet Major Charles Miller, stated that "we passed through Raymond on our march and saw the marks of conflict near that place. It was here that the boys discovered a stock of fine liquors in a druggist's cellar, and the canteens of almost the entire Brigade were filled with choice old wine, brandy and whiskey."[34] The alcohol uncovered in Raymond likely increased the severity of looting. One citizen later wrote that Grant's soldiers "burned all the fences for their cooking pots and emptied the hen houses and the smokehouses. I saw them drive off a cow and calf while my mother begged in vain to spare them."[35]

After securing victory at Raymond, Grant determined to change the direction of his advance. Rather than striking northward to sever the Southern Railroad of Mississippi, Grant oriented his columns to the northeast, against the state capital and industrial center of Jackson. As the Army of the Tennessee proceeded toward its new objective, vast numbers of runaway slaves continued to join the advance. Sylvanus Cadwallader noticed that "afternoon and night refugee 'contrabands' came swarming into our lines by hundreds. They were of all ages, sexes and conditions, and came on foot, on horses and mules, and in all manner of vehicles, from the typical southern cart, to elegant state carriages and barouches." Cadwallader witnessed that "straw collars and rope harness alternated with silver plate equipments, till the moving living panorama became ludicrous beyond description."[36]

The influx of former slaves further drained Mississippi's labor potential, already severely diminished by the manpower demands of Confederate military service. As each slave became free, the power of the Confederacy to feed itself and produce the necessary articles of war diminished; while conversely, the Federal army gained the labor of the freedmen, who served as teamsters, cooks, laborers, and eventually, Union soldiers. Furthermore, in many instances former slaves appropriated valuable wagons and property from their masters before departing, a further material loss upon slave owners. As Cadwallader detailed, "The runaway darkies who had made sudden and forcible requisition upon their old masters for these varied means of transportation, generally loaded their wagons and carriages with the finest furniture left in the mansions when their owners had abandoned them at our approach."[37]

By May 13, Grant had maneuvered his army into a central position, completely outgeneraling his opponent and feasting upon the rich surplus of the Mississippi heartland. As Grant's army approached Jackson, his maneuver divided Confederate forces on either side of his own and presented the Union with a decided operational advantage. That same day, Confederate general Joseph E. Johnston arrived to defend Jackson and assess the strategic situation. Johnston quickly concluded his position was hopeless and decided to evacuate Jackson after a brief rear-guard action rather than defend the city. The battle and occupation of Jackson would result in a new degree of destruction and present the first major urban demolition of the campaign.[38]

Inside the Mississippi state capital, Junius Henri Browne, a captured northern war correspondent from the *New York Tribune*, surveyed the panicked evacuation with elation. Browne noted that at "the street corners were knots of excited men, discussing the prospects of the future with more feeling than logic. To us, who had long been careful observers, it was evident they were at a loss what to do; and you can imagine we rather enjoyed the trepidation of the Rebels." As the Yankees approached, many Jacksonians fled to the surrounding countryside. Browne commented that he "saw a number of vehicles of various kinds loaded with household furniture, and men, women, children, and black servants, all greatly excited, moving rapidly out of town."[39]

In stark contrast to the secessionists, the town's enslaved population welcomed the invaders. Browne documented that "a panic of the most decided kind existed among all classes of society; but we had no difficulty in perceiving that the negroes of both sexes, young and old, enjoyed the quandary of their masters and mistresses." Despite pleas from the city's mayor for violent resistance from the civilian population, few Jacksonians undertook any organized defiance against Union forces. Browne sarcastically observed that, "If the citizens were flying to arms, they must have concealed them somewhere in the country, and have been making haste in that direction to recover them. They were certainly leaving town by all possible routes, and by every obtainable means of conveyance."[40]

After driving back Confederate delaying forces in a brief action on May 14, the Army of the Tennessee entered Jackson in triumph. Rather than detach valuable units to remain as an occupying garrison, Grant determined to eliminate Jackson's capacity as a war production center and railroad junction. In a foreshadowing of events that would occur the following year in Atlanta, Grant selected Sherman's Fifteenth Corps to destroy the manufacturing facilities. Grant later explained concisely that "Sherman was to remain in Jackson until he destroyed that place as a railroad centre, and manufacturing city of military supplies. He did the work most effectually."

The destruction of Jackson marked a turning point in the career of Sherman. Although Sherman had ordered small southern towns burned in response to guerilla attacks on the Mississippi River, no large scale urban destruction had taken place previously in the occupation of major southern cities in the western theater such as Nashville and New Orleans. Before the Vicksburg Campaign, Sherman had lamented the material damage associated with the conquest of the South and had felt that Grant's audacious attempt to supply his army off the civilian population would be unlikely to succeed. With the capture of Jackson, Sherman learned just how effective the use of the torch could be in modern warfare, and it was a lesson he would later apply with brutally effective results in Georgia and the Carolinas.[41]

At one particular textile factory, Grant and Sherman watched as workers, mostly young women, labored at looms producing cloth labeled "C.S.A." The two Union commanders stood by silently observing the scene until, as Grant later recalled, "I told Sherman I thought they had done work enough. The operatives were told they could leave and take with them what cloth they could carry. In a few minutes cotton and factory were in a blaze." Later, when Grant served as president of the United States, the owner of the razed factory traveled to Washington in an attempt to gain restitution for the property on the grounds that it had been private, not government property. President Grant swiftly denied the request.[42]

Grant, preparing to turn his march to the west, gave little time or consideration to the concerns of residents for the protection of private property. As war reporter Cadwallader remembered, "Many calls were made upon him by citizens asking for guards to protect their private property, some of which perhaps were granted, but by far the greater number were left to the tender mercies of Confederate friends."[43] Those "Confederate friends" had started Grant's work of ruin before he had even arrived. As Johnston's army retreated, they set fire to commissary stores that could not be removed, which were still blazing when Federals entered the city. In an appalling case of poor judgment, prison officials released the incarcerated inmates of the state penitentiary at the approach of Grant's forces. The freed convicts took full advantage of the lapse in law and order to pillage freely from Jackson merchants and residents. As the Army of the Tennessee began its mission of wreckage, flames were already spreading throughout the city.[44]

When Union soldiers embarked upon reducing Jackson's war-making potential, they transformed much of the city into ashes. Cadwallader asserted that "foundries, machine-shops, warehouses, factories, arsenals and public stores were fired as fast as flames could be kindled. Many citizens fled at our approach, abandoning houses, stores, and all their personal property, without so much as locking their doors."[45] In addition to the military supplies, the conflagration consumed an immense amount of cotton stored in the capital. Charles Dana recorded that "I remained with Sherman to see the work of destruction. I remember now nothing that I saw except the burning of vast quantities of cotton packed in bales, and that I was greatly astonished to see how slowly it burned."[46]

As the destruction and fires raged, total anarchy was unleashed before Grant could restore order. Cadwallader watched helplessly as "the negroes, poor whites—and it must be admitted—some stragglers and bummers from the ranks of the Union army—carried off thousands of dollars worth of property from houses, homes, shops and stores, until some excuse was given for the charge of 'northern vandalism,' which was afterwards made by the South." The newspaperman further testified, "The streets were filled with people, white and black, who were carrying away all the stolen goods they could stagger under, without the slightest attempt at concealment, and without let or hindrance from citizens or soldiers." Certainly, Union soldiers were not solely responsible for the acts of plunder that occurred in Jackson, as Confederate deserters, lower-class whites, released prisoners, and freed slaves took full advantage of the lapse of civil authority to sack storefronts, shops, and private homes at will. The looting of Jackson lasted throughout the night of the fourteenth, and it was not until the following day that Sherman established order under martial law.[47]

During the ransacking, a group of soldiers entered the Jackson Masonic Lodge during the mayhem. Private J. W. Greenman wrote that they "soon were decorated with aprons and sashes and collars, and then started to go out on the street for a parade but Col. [Joseph] Mower heard of the business and met the Boys just as they came down the stairs from the Lodge room." Mower apparently felt a great deal of regard for the fraternal organization, as Greenman recorded, Mower "ordered the Boys to take everything back and then get out, which was quickly done."[48]

Another Federal present, Charles A. Wilson, wrote of the Jackson inferno that "what grieved me most I think was to see the sugar warehouses with their tiers upon tiers of sugar hogsheads, going up in fire and smoke. I loved sugar—it had always been a luxury with me." Despite the reigning confusion, Wilson managed to leave with "eight or nine canteens of it, hung to my shoulders, as we marched out of the city. But my endurance proved not equal to my zeal for sugar. One by one the canteens had to go as the straps cut into my shoulder."[49]

The Federals also discovered a large supply of tobacco in Jackson, as Wilson affirmed: "An immense amount of plug tobacco was brought out by the soldiers, their hankering for the weed evidently on the same scale as mine for sugar. I think enough was left strewed over the ground at our first camp to thatch a good-sized village." Johnston's retreating forces burned the Pearl River railroad bridge, and Grant's army tore up the remaining railroad tracks that entered the city for at least three miles. Sherman's men placed the rails upon burning ties to twist the track beyond repair into a worthless pile of metal termed "Sherman's neckties."[50]

Not even the state library escaped unscathed during the orgy of destruction. Charles Dana Miller remembered that on May 16 he "visited the Mississippi State Library where the soldiers were helping themselves to books apparently without objections being made by General Sherman. I secured a few small volumes such as I could carry conveniently, but saw a good many expensive works I would have liked, could I have obtained transportation."[51] Books were common items always desired by soldiers who had little reading material to help pass the long hours of drudgery in camp. On the march to Jackson, Osborn Oldroyd wrote that "the boys frequently bring in reading matter with their forage. Almost anything in print is better than nothing. A novel was brought in to-day, and as soon as it was caught sight of a score or more had engaged in turn the reading of it."[52]

The fires that raged within Jackson did extensive damage and smoldered for days afterward. On the evening of the fourteenth, Private J. W. Greenman of the 8th Wisconsin recorded in his diary, "Some one started a fire just at dark, and the City is burning, and although every effort is being made to put out the fire it is spreading, and it looks as though the whole City will be destroyed."[53] While the Union army did labor to prevent fires from threatening residential areas, controlling the flames proved impossible. Oldroyd wrote that "some of the boys went down into the city to view our new possession. It seems ablaze, but I trust only public property is being destroyed, or such as might aid and comfort the enemy here-after."[54] The first Union occupation of Jackson lasted only thirty-six hours, yet reduced invaluable industrial and transportation resources to rubble. When Confederates returned to the capital, then Mississippi governor John Jones Pettus calculated the total cost of the damage at $10 million.[55]

After seizing and eliminating Jackson's capability as a Confederate supply depot, Grant turned his army westward toward his long-sought-after prize, Vicksburg. As the Union columns marched out of the city, Brevet Major Charles Dana Miller recorded that his company "found a hotel here called the 'Confederate House' as the large sign indicated on its front. This had been painted over the words 'United States House.' The boys concluded that it had better close up business under its new title and accordingly applied the torch."[56] Four days after the Federals left, British observer Fremantle entered the city on his three-month tour throughout the South and recorded his impressions: "I saw the ruins of the Roman Catholic church, the priest's house, and the principal hotel, which were still smoking, together with many other buildings which could in no way be identified with the Confederate government. The whole town was a miserable wreck, and presented a deplorable aspect." Fremantle gave great sympathy to the residents, who appear to have suddenly regained their desire to fight the Federal army after it had vacated. He observed, "Nothing could exceed the intense hatred and fury with which its excited citizens speak of the outrages they have undergone—of their desire for a bloody revenge, and of their hope that the Black Flag might be raised." Surveying the wreckage in the city, Fremantle testified that "during the short space of thirty-six hours, in which General Grant occupied the city, his troops had wantonly pillaged nearly all the private houses. They had gutted all the stores, and destroyed what they could not carry away."[57]

Fremantle also chronicled an account of one Jacksonian who protected his house from a mob of looters by sitting next to the front door armed with a loaded double-barreled shotgun. As the spoils-seeking crowd confronted the owner, the man aimed the shotgun at the multitude with the declaration, "No man can die more than once, and I shall never be more ready to die than I am now. There is nothing to prevent your going into this house, except that I shall kill the first two of you who move with this gun. Now then, gentlemen, walk in." Convinced by the threatening invitation, the mass of plunderers, whom curiously Fremantle does not specifically identify as Yankees, left the residence unmolested.[58]

Other citizens were less successful in their attempts to retain personal property. Fremantle described meeting one despairing planter, "mounted on a miserable animal which had been left him by the enemy as not being worth taking away." Fremantle observed that "the small remains of this poor old man's sense had been shattered by the Yankees a few days ago. They cleaned him completely out, taking his horses, mules, cows, and pigs, and stealing his clothes and anything they wanted, destroying what they could not carry away." Embittered as they were, the citizens of Jackson no longer presented a viable threat to the Union and the city would be essentially useless to the South for the rest of the war. In fact, when Federal soldiers vacated and forced local and state authorities to provide for the thousands of refugees and an ever-growing indigent population, the strain on Confederate resources reached the breaking point.[59]

As the Army of the Tennessee drew closer to Vicksburg with each passing day, Lieutenant General John C. Pemberton and the Army of Vicksburg marched out of the fortress for a climatic confrontation. On May 16, Grant decisively defeated Pemberton at the Battle of Champion Hill and drove the Confederate army back in serious disorder. The following day, pursuing Federals routed Pemberton's rear guard at the Battle of the Big Black River Bridge and chased the retreating Rebels into Vicksburg itself. In order to cross the river after fleeing Confederates burned the bridge, Union soldiers confiscated necessary building materials from nearby homes and constructed three temporary bridges. Correspondent Cadwallader noted that the engineering "was done by tearing down the dwelling houses, barns, stables and cotton gins nearest at hand, and flooring the cotton bale and timber floats which were bound together and anchored in the river." By the afternoon of May 18, Grant's men were finally within sight of the Vicksburg defenses.[60]

During the march from Jackson to Vicksburg, the Army of the Tennessee for the first time during the campaign felt the effects of hunger. The Confederate army had stripped this region of most of its edible resources by this point in the war, leaving little for Federal foraging parties to commandeer. Miller remembered that "the troops were short of rations and many went hungry. The country was bare of supplies after two armies had passed over it. It was very difficult especially for the officers to obtain food, and in some instances they paid fifty cents apiece for crackers."[61] Lacking an established supply line, Grant knew he had to reach the Mississippi River before the effects of the short rations began sapping the fighting strength of his army. Osborn Oldroyd wrote on May 17, "We are fighting hard for our *grub*, since we have nothing left but flour, and slapjacks lie too heavy on a soldier's stomach."[62]

For those well-supplied with currency, appetizing food was easier to locate. Cadwallader recalled that during the march he "never paid less than ten dollars in Confederate money for a single meal, although that much was never demanded, and I was quite as willing to give twice that for a satisfactory dinner." As to his generosity, Cadwallader admitted that he "had an abundance of it that cost me nothing, and there was no other way in which I could properly use it."[63]

Even as the army approached the defiant Confederate bastion of Vicksburg, the Federals discovered a surprising amount of Unionist support among local residents. On May 18, while riding with Grant, Cadwallader recorded, "As we approached a tumble-down sort of log cabin near the road a poor sickly looking woman stood at the gate waving a little Union flag." Intrigued, Grant directed a staff officer to investigate the flag bearer's identity, who proved to be the wife of an Illinois river pilot who had moved South before the war, suffered conscription at the hands of Confederate authorities, and at that moment lay extremely ill in the cabin. Grant immediately ordered his staff surgeon to render medical aid to the couple, and then later detached another official to "place a guard to protect the premises; and still another to see that the family was supplied with needful commissary stores. The sick man received daily medical attention till he was able to bear the trip north, when Grant furnished the family free transportation and subsistence as far as Cairo."[64]

Marching at the rear of Grant's army, Sherman's Fifteenth Corps followed behind after completing the destruction of Jackson. When Sherman passed through the small village of Bolton, he located an exceptional souvenir. While enjoying a drink of water mounted on his horse, Sherman stumbled across a discarded book, which upon closer examination he discovered to be Confederate president Jefferson Davis's personal copy of the United States Constitution. Federal soldiers had evidently acquired and discarded the book when ransacking the Davis plantation along the Mississippi River, or had located personal effects of the Confederate president stored inland in vain hopes of protection. Sherman authorized a small unit to inspect Davis's premises, which visited the property and promptly returned with two horses formerly belonging to the southern president's older brother, Joseph Davis.[65]

Until Grant reached the Mississippi River and established a secure supply line with the United States Navy, the growing commissary crisis confronting the Army of the Tennessee continued to worsen. As Grant inspected the Union investment of Vicksburg, his soldiers made their hunger known to the commanding general. Grant later acknowledged in his memoirs, "I remember that in passing around to the left of the line on the 21st, a soldier, recognizing me, said in a rather low voice, but yet so that I heard him, 'Hard tack.' In a moment the cry was taken up all along the line, 'Hard tack! Hard tack!'" Grant quickly explained to his men that rations were forthcoming, and by that night, every soldier in the Army of the Tennessee was fully supplied by the U.S. Government for the first time since they first set foot in Mississippi.[66]

In less than three weeks, from May 1 to May 18, the Army of the Tennessee had marched over two hundred miles, won five engagements with the enemy, conquered and reduced the capital city of Jackson, inflicted nearly eight thousand casualties, destroyed miles of invaluable railroad tracks, divided the opposing Confederate forces, and trapped Pemberton's entire army in Vicksburg. As he traced the ground along Haynes Bluff, where he had endured the worst defeat thus far in his career the previous December at Chickasaw Bayou, Sherman admitted to his friend Grant, "Until this moment, I never thought your expedition a success; I never could see the end clearly till now. But this is a campaign; this is a success if we never take the town." Sherman was correct. In the Vicksburg Campaign, Ulysses S. Grant and the Army of the Tennessee had perfected the punitive policy of "hard war" against southern civilians that Union forces would use to win the war in 1864–65.[67]

Notes

1. William L. Shea and Terrance J. Winschel, *Vicksburg Is the Key: The Struggle for the Mississippi River* (Lincoln: University of Nebraska Press, 2003), 106–16.

2. Mark Grimsley, *The Hard Hand of War: Union Military Policy toward Southern Civilians, 1861–1865* (Cambridge: Cambridge University Press, 1995), 3.

3. Stephen V. Ash, *When the Yankees Came: Conflict and Chaos in the Occupied South, 1861–1865* (Chapel Hill: University of North Carolina Press, 1995), 13–18; Shea and Winschel, *Vicksburg Is the Key*, 106–16.

4. Ulysses S. Grant, *Personal Memoirs of Ulysses S. Grant* (1885; reprint, New York: Barnes & Noble, 2005), 273.

5. Jeffrey L. Patrick, ed., *Three Years with Wallace's Zouaves: The Civil War Memoirs of Thomas Wise Durham* (Macon, Ga.: Mercer University Press, 2003), 151–52.

6. Ira Blanchard, *I Marched with Sherman: Civil War Memoirs of the 20th Illinois Volunteer Infantry* (San Francisco: D. Huff and Co., 1992), 86.

7. Rebecca Blackwell Drake, ed., *A Soldier's Story of the Siege of Vicksburg: From the Diary of Osborn H. I. Oldroyd* (1885; reprint, Raymond, Miss.: Friends of Raymond, 2001), 9.

8. Drake, *Soldier's Story*, 9–10.

9. Mark Grimsley and Todd D. Miller, eds., *The Union Must Stand: The Civil War Diary of John Quincy Adams Campbell, Fifth Iowa Infantry* (Knoxville: University of Tennessee Press, 2000), 92.

10. Terrence J. Winschel, *The Civil War Diary of a Common Soldier: William Wiley of the 77th Illinois Infantry* (Baton Rouge: Louisiana State University Press, 2001), 44.

11. Leo M. Kaiser, ed., "The Civil War Diary of Florison D. Pitts," *Mid-America: An Historical Quarterly* 40, no. 29 (January 1958): 38.

12. Drake, *Soldier's Story*, 13, 16.

13. Grant, *Memoirs*, 275, 276.

14. James R. Arnold, *Grant Wins the War: Decision at Vicksburg* (New York: John Wiley & Sons, 1997), 126.

15. Grant, *Memoirs*, 275, 276.

16. Drake, *Soldier's Story*, 21.

17. Shea and Winschel, *Vicksburg Is the Key*, 106–26.

18. Brooks D. Simpson and Jean V. Berlin, eds., *Sherman's Civil War: Selected Correspondence of William T. Sherman, 1860–1865* (Chapel Hill: University of North Carolina Press, 1999), 468–69.

19. Otto F. Bond, *Under the Flag of the Nation: Diaries and Letters of Owen Johnston Hopkins, a Yankee Volunteer* (Columbus: Ohio State University Press, 1998), 57.

20. Hopkins's reference to "darning" is a pun on the word *darn*, which in the first instance means "to mend," and in the second is a polite synonym of the word *damn*.

21. Bond, *Under the Flag of the Nation*, 57.

22. "Amount of Stock & Property Consumed & taken off by Gen. U. S. Grant's Army, 1863," Miscellaneous Civil War Documents, Mississippi Department of Archives and History, Jackson.

23. Ibid.

24. Simpson and Berlin, *Sherman's Civil War,* 470.

25. John Y. Simon, *The Papers of Ulysses S. Grant,* vol. 8: *April 1–July 6, 1863* (Carbondale: Southern Illinois University Press, 1979), 189.

26. Drake, *Soldier's Story,* 19.

27. Benjamin P. Thomas, ed., *Three Years with Grant: As Recalled by War Correspondent Sylvanus Cadwallader* (New York: Alfred A. Knopf, 1956), 72.

28. Thomas, *Three Years with Grant,* 72.

29. Charles A. Dana, *Recollections of the Civil War: With the Leaders at Washington and in the Field in the Sixties* (reprint, Lincoln: University of Nebraska Press, 1996), 51.

30. Walter Lord, ed., *The Fremantle Diary: Being the Journal of Lieutenant Colonel James Arthur Lyon Fremantle, Coldstream Guards, on His Three Months in the Southern States* (Boston: Little, Brown and Co., 1954), 81.

31. Shea and Winschel, *Vicksburg Is the Key,* 117–24; Terrence J. Winschel, *Vicksburg: Fall of the Confederate Gibraltar* (Abilene, Tex.: McWhiney Foundation Press, 1999), 62–67.

32. Drake, *Soldier's Story,* 24.

33. Ben Wynne, *Mississippi's Civil War: A Narrative History* (Macon, GA: Mercer University Press, 2006); Bond, *Under the Flag of the Nation,* 60.

34. Stewart Bennett and Barbara Tillery, eds., *The Struggle for the Life of the Republic: A Civil War Narrative by Brevet Major Charles Dana Miller, 76th Ohio Volunteer Infantry* (Kent, Ohio: Kent State University Press, 2004), 94.

35. Letitia Dabney Miller, *The Recollections of Letitia Dabney Miller,* Mrs. Cabe Drew Gillespie Collection, Department of Archives and Special Collections, J. D. Williams Library, University of Mississippi, Oxford, quoted in Wynne, *Mississippi's Civil War,* 109.

36. Shea and Winschel, *Vicksburg Is the Key,* 124; Thomas, *Three Years with Grant,* 69.

37. Thomas, *Three Years with Grant,* 69.

38. Shea and Winschel, *Vicksburg Is the Key,* 124–26.

39. Junius Henri Browne, *Four Years in Secessia* (1865; reprint, New York: ARNO & New York Times, 1970), 248.

40. Ibid.

41. Grant, *Memoirs,* 283–84.

42. Ibid.

43. Thomas, *Three Years with Grant,* 74.

44. Michael B. Dougan, "Herrmann Hirsh and the Siege of Jackson," *Journal of Mississippi History* 43 (February 1991): 22–23; Wynne, *Mississippi's Civil War,* 110–11.

45. Thomas, *Three Years with Grant,* 74–75.

46. Dana, *Recollections of the Civil War,* 53.

47. Thomas, *Three Years with Grant,* 74–75.

48. J. W. Greenman Diary, 91–92 (14 May 1863), Manuscript Collection, Mississippi Department of Archives and History, Jackson.

49. Charles A. Wilson, *Reminiscences of a Boy's Service with the 76th Ohio* (Huntington, W.Va.: Blue Acorn Press, 1995), 53.

50. Ibid., 54; Wynne, *Mississippi's Civil War*, 111; Dougan, "Hermann Hirsh and the Siege of Jackson," 22–23.

51. Bennett and Tillery, *The Struggle for the Life of the Republic*, 95.

52. Drake, *Soldier's Story*, 16.

53. Greenman Diary, 91–92.

54. Drake, *Soldier's Story*, 29.

55. Dougan, "Hermann Hirsh and the Siege of Jackson," 23–24; Wynne, *Mississippi's Civil War*, 111.

56. Bennett and Tillery, *The Struggle for the Life of the Republic*, 95.

57. Lord, *The Fremantle Diary*, 87, 88.

58. Ibid., 87.

59. Ibid., 91–92.

60. Thomas, *Three Years with Grant*, 82; Shea and Winschel, *Vicksburg Is the Key*, 142–43.

61. Bennett and Tillery, *The Struggle for the Life of the Republic*, 95.

62. Drake, *Soldier's Story*, 34.

63. Thomas, *Three Years with Grant*, 76.

64. Ibid., 86.

65. Wynne, *Mississippi's Civil War*, 116.

66. Grant, *Memoirs*, 296–97.

67. Quoted in Shea and Winschel, *Vicksburg Is the Key*, 143.

11

POLITICS, POLICY, AND GENERAL GRANT
CLAUSEWITZ ON THE OPERATIONAL ART AS
PRACTICED IN THE VICKSBURG CAMPAIGN

Paul L. Schmelzer

At the highest level, War turns into policy.
—Carl von Clausewitz, *On War*

Familiarity with Clausewitz for many begins (and unfortunately often ends) with a famous definition: "war is a continuation of policy (or politics) by other means." Less a thesis perhaps than an observation, Clausewitz's meaning is clear; in war it is the policy of one entity to attack another, and the policy of another to defend itself. Equally clear is Clausewitz's less well known observation that "political considerations do not determine the posting of guards or the deployment of patrols." In most cases policy "will not extend to operational details." A successful general must not only master and account for a myriad of "technical" details that enable him to defeat his enemy on the battlefield, he must do so in a manner that furthers policy. Multiple accounts exist of Grant's masterful use of "operational details" to defeat his enemy at Vicksburg. Fewer accounts evaluate the equally masterful harmonization of war and policy, demonstrated less by the operations themselves than by the *manner* in which he conducted them. In addition, Grant's actions as commander of an independent department made policy. The effects of those actions reverberated far beyond the Mississippi, driving the subsequent decisions of governments, both North and South.[1]

Grant's application of "Clausewitzian" thinking to the "problem" of Vicksburg was intuitional and largely an outgrowth of his common sense. He could not have been familiar with writings largely unavailable in English (until 1877) and virtually unknown to the military in Grant's time. During Grant's tenure at West Point, the premier military academy in the Western Hemisphere, works on military strategy were conspicuous by their absence from the curriculum. Apart from civil and military engineering, distillations of the works of Baron Antoine-Henri Jomini dominated studies of strategy and tactics.[2]

Grant's time finds Clausewitz "present but not accounted for." Present, in that some of Clausewitz's articles had been translated; not accounted for, in that his ideas remained largely unknown, unexamined, or misunderstood. In our time, Clausewitz forms the basis of modern military doctrine throughout most of the world. Clausewitz wrote extensive works of military history and identified the purpose of theory as "merely" to comprehend history. Clausewitz found history, and especially military history, "incomprehensible" without a theoretical model to order one's thinking. In order to make Grant's dazzling operations through the interior of Mississippi "comprehensible," and to order our thinking, Clausewitz provides the best method.[3]

The Political Context of the Vicksburg Campaign—Criticism of Grant

> He knows he has to do something or off goes his head.
> —Maj. Gen. Cadwallader Washburn

"Nothing is more important in life than finding the right standpoint for seeing and judging events, and then adhering to it." Through this quote, Clausewitz suggests that an understanding of the "probable character and general shape of the war" is essential to formulating military plans. For Grant "the right standpoint" defines, above all, an understanding of the political context in which he operated. Washburn's assertions aside, Grant believed action necessary for the Union cause (as well as his own), and the nature of that action grew out of the political needs of the nation.[4]

Clausewitz's identification of war as extension of policy means little, if confusion exists regarding the definition of the word *policy*. Clausewitz offers a broad "global" definition of the word. Policy extends far beyond the explicit rational intentions of a government and the overt actions devised to carry out that government's purpose. Policy (and therefore war itself) extends far beyond the mere will of the policy makers: "we can only treat policy as representative of all interests of the community." On the battlefield "it is not merely two armies that are facing each other, but two states, two peoples, two nations." Nations drag a myriad of interests with them into war. Many of those interests may not necessarily be known, only revealed (for benefit or detriment) given the pressures and events of the war itself.[5]

The first major interest of the community affecting Grant regarded retention of his command. His first move against Vicksburg in the late fall and early winter of 1862 ended in destruction of his supply base at Holly Springs, effectively derailing his campaign. From that point on Grant found himself under fire from many directions. Skepticism about his suitability for command increased during months of failure to get at the enemy. Critics complained of the sickness and fatigue in Grant's army, as when Cincinnati newspaperman Murat Halstead wrote of "our noble army of the Mississippi . . . wasted by the foolish, drunken, stupid Grant."[6]

Grant exhibited a masterful awareness of his position, the mood of the country and the needs of his superiors through his handling of Secretary Edwin M. Stanton and Abraham Lincoln's "spy," Charles A. Dana. Ostensibly sent as a special commissioner of the War Department investigating the pay service of the armies in the West, Dana's real purpose involved divining the true nature of U. S. Grant and the condition of his troops. Grant's staff resented Dana's mere presence, some suggesting he be thrown in the river upon arrival. Instead Grant chose to be open and accommodating, generating favorable reports to the administration on both Grant's command and the general himself. Grant used Dana as he would any other instrument to further the Union cause. Grant's measures reinforced the administration's trust and provided Lincoln with the means to defend him against charges of drinking and incompetence.[7]

During the early months of 1863, Grant persevered, pursuing seemingly endless schemes to get to Vicksburg and restart his campaign. These improvisations included digging a canal to by-pass Vicksburg's guns (Lincoln's personal favorite) and seeking passage through Yazoo Pass and Lake Providence. All of these operations yielded little except criticisms in the Union press, though "both President Lincoln and General Henry Halleck stood by me to the end of the campaign." Grant's troops also exhibited faith in their commander. Though some of his designs might fail, "he has 37 more plans in his pocket," one of his men confidently announced. Grant's failed schemes yielded positive results in two areas: they kept the Union troops occupied and ultimately baffled the Confederates as to Grant's true intentions. According to early-twentieth-century British army officer and military historian J. F. C. Fuller, Grant converted this "waste of tactical energy into a strategic smoke cloud." As Clausewitz observed, strategy must use the results of the engagement, whether victory or defeat, to serve the aims of war, "even if no actual fighting occurs."[8]

The Political Context II—Northern Politics and Operations

A forward movement to decisive victory was necessary.
—Ulysses S. Grant

The second circumstance conditioning Grant's strategy regarded the relatively fragile nature of the Union home front. Grant appreciated northern social and political divisions, unwanted and revealed only through the course of the war itself. Grant acknowledged that fragility and tailored his strategy to accommodate it, for within "the north there was division if not sedition." Questions of northern political cohesion provide subtext for all of Grant's thinking about the war. The politics of division and sedition determined the nature of the Union war effort as assuredly as did the more rational and overt aspects of Union policy.[9]

The Holly Springs debacle ultimately determined the method of Grant's later operations. Attacking Vicksburg was not enough. *How* Grant approached the city proved of equal importance. Grant refused to go back to Memphis and renew attempts to approach the city east of the river, as Sherman and others advised. To most civilians, retreat signaled defeat, and the country could ill afford another humiliation.

Grant in his memoirs traced the origins of his most admired and hazardous achievement: "The campaign of Vicksburg was suggested and developed by circumstances. The elections of 1862 had gone against the prosecution of the war. Voluntary enlistments had nearly ceased and the draft had been resorted to; this was resisted, and a defeat or backward movement would have made its execution impossible."[10]

Thus in a very real sense, Grant's political insights, conditioned by election results and his evaluation of the mood of the country, determined his methods. Grant's most important, unorthodox, and brilliant campaign, what Fuller called "the most important northern strategic victory of the war," both operationally and strategically, above all required harmonization with the political context. If Grant's subsequent move below Vicksburg contained risk and uncertainty, Grant judged a repeat of the Holly Springs maneuver the greater danger. As historian James M. McPherson has pointed out, even a temporary set-back would have "so adverse an influence on the political situation, as not only to wreck his campaign, but overthrow the Government."[11]

Grant also declined to formulate a suggestion to Sherman to feint at Snyder's Bluff as a positive order. Grant expressed concern that the feint, especially if effective, might be interpreted in the North as a repulse, with both negative effects on the morale of the troops and negative repercussions for Sherman's reputation on the home front. Grant left it up to Sherman to define the method and extent of the demonstration. Sherman believed his troops would understand the purpose of such a move: "I will use troops that I know will trust us and not be humbugged by a repulse." As for the people, Sherman believed "it is none of their business," adding that reports in the newspapers should be treated with scorn. Sherman made the attack and ordered his troops to make "everyman look as numerous as possible," fooling the northern press along with the Rebels as to Grant's true intentions.[12] Grant demonstrated his understanding that he was no mere military technician operating in a vacuum. However desirable "textbook" solutions to military problems might have been and however strong the natural tendency of soldiers to resent what they are sometimes prone to perceive as the intrusion of politics into the difficult business of waging war, Grant understood his purpose. Even winning a battle (or making a successful feint) could derail Union war aims if it adversely affected an administration committed to war and reunion. Grant's understanding of this imperative found its greatest test in his dealings with soldiers whose political utility was seldom matched by any military ability.

Political Soldiers

I can't afford to quarrel with a man whom *I have to command.*
—Ulysses S. Grant (emphasis added)

The understanding of politics driving Grant's operational plan at Vicksburg extended to its execution. The Union war effort depended on the fragile alliance of Republican and Democratic politicians. Effective prosecution of the war required cultivation of soldiers who owed their positions to some special political usefulness, rather than any technical military expertise. Lincoln's use of political soldiers proved necessary, if exasperating to many professionals.

Grant not only understood the realities of Lincoln's situation and the necessity of utilizing political soldiers, he proved adept in their utilization and wrung maximum benefit from their employment. During the Vicksburg Campaign, the troublesome John A. McClernand provided both irritation and opportunity for the professional, Grant. McClernand, perhaps with some justification, felt himself ill-used and manipulated by Halleck and other professionals. He believed he deserved an independent command and resented serving under Grant as a mere corps commander. Surprisingly, Grant detailed McClernand's corps to lead the advance down the west side of the river, seemingly giving the greatest burden to the weakest of his commanders.[13]

Through this action Grant effectively harnessed the political imperatives of the country to his operations. McClernand, unlike most of Grant's subordinates, went on record as being in favor of Grant's proposed move down the river past Vicksburg. Senior to his fellow corps commanders, he was also a friend—of sorts—to Lincoln. Grant commanded McClernand and properly utilized him for what he was: an instrument of his government's policy. In his memoirs, Grant generously acknowledged McClernand's contributions, but Grant remained keenly aware of the political general's wartime efforts to usurp him. "There was no delay in his declaring himself for the Union at all hazards," Grant wrote, "and there was no uncertain sound in his declaration of where he stood in the contest before the country. He also gave up his seat in Congress to take the field in defense of the principles he had proclaimed."[14]

Whatever McClernand's failings as a tactician and administrator, Grant could no more question Lincoln's policy of using McClernand than his policy of using contrabands. If any policy, as Grant stated earlier in his career, proved too odious he could always resign.[15] Grant's difficulties with McClernand during the campaign revealed a complex lesson regarding the nature of political soldiers. Grant tolerated the political general for a long time and acknowledged his contribution to the war effort. Grant found McClernand "highly insubordinate" on occasion, but "I overlooked it, I believed, for the good of the service." Grant's toleration continued until McClernand evidenced moral irresponsibility and demonstrated himself a liability to the service. His claiming of credit for successes not gained, seeking to blame others for defeats, and pushing for Grant's job destroyed his utility to Grant and to the Union. After victory was assured at Vicksburg Grant waited for McClernand "to trip over his own ego one more time," as historian Brooks D. Simpson has aptly described the event, and then relieved him.[16]

In doing so, Grant again harmonized military and political concerns, never losing sight of the fact that his military victory must achieve great and measurable political effects and weighing each of his actions accordingly. Grant accepted all of these political constraints, as he accepted the size of his forces and the abilities of his commanders: each as a "given" quantity harmonized with military actions through the formulation of strategy.[17]

In making these decisions Grant coordinated his operations with domestic politics (the election of 1862 and the effect of Sherman's feint on public opinion); harmonized relations within the army (Grant took his army in hand and carried out his plan against the advice of both his staff and Sherman), and civil-military relations (his recognition of Lincoln's political needs through the use of the president's "friend," McClernand).

Historians and soldiers tend to view all these "constraints" dictated by politics as detriments—at best, necessary evils. While often *true*, it seems wrong to assign too many value judgments to the given reality of the strategic equation. The northern political structure also contributed multiple positive elements. The employment of Grant and Sherman was also "political," and ultimately pushed Grant to the top spot in the army. Grant's ability to master the complexities of northern wartime politics proved as important as his ability to win battles.

Operational Details, Policy, and the Move below Vicksburg

Our belief then is that any kind of interruption, pause, or suspension of activity is inconsistent with the nature of offensive war.

—Clausewitz

You can do a great deal in eight days.

—Grant, explaining his decision to attack Vicksburg before Halleck could recall him

The Vicksburg Campaign and the story leading to its successful conclusion are testimony to Grant's tenacity and simple belief in the correctness of his strategy, his role in its creation, and the single-mindedness with which he carried it out. General in chief Henry Halleck, through abdication, delegated many responsibilities to his commanders in the field. This abdication extended properly to operational and tactical details. Less properly, Halleck's abdications left Grant unable to coordinate himself either with a coherent national strategy or even to deal efficiently with the other side of the Mississippi River. Grant communicated this to Halleck, who, true to form, did nothing.[18]

In the execution of details of the battles leading to the investment of Vicksburg, Grant's contemporary writings exhibit little evidence of systematic and careful planning. The tactics and even larger operational details of the campaign follow circumstance while remaining true to Grant's strategic concept throughout. In his final report, Grant attributed his decision to attack Jackson and invest Vicksburg, rather than aid Nathaniel P. Banks at Port Hudson, to circumstances in the field and his repulse at Grand Gulf.[19]

As early as November 1862, Grant related his evaluation of his position in communications with Sherman, "Of course I can make nothing but independent moves with this command being governed in that by information received from day to day until I am fully informed of when and how all of these other forces are moving so as to make the whole cooperate."[20]

Direction existed neither operationally nor strategically in Grant's department until Grant assumed command of that department himself. The broad outlines of the campaign down the Mississippi existed, perhaps as obvious to all as the move on Forts Henry and Donelson had been, but again the concept mattered little as long as the Union commanders lacked the conviction or direction from above to carry it out. As Grant stated long after the war, "You know the theory of the campaign was to throw myself between Joseph E. Johnston and John C. Pemberton, prevent their union, beat each army separately if I could, and take Vicksburg. It was important to have this movement so far advanced before even the knowledge of it reached Washington that it could not be recalled."[21]

Grant recognized that in pursuing an offensive war, time must accrue to the advantage of the defender. Clausewitz explained some of the reasons for this phenomenon as he saw it. While halting "could make offensive war easier" it would not make its results more certain. The reasons given for halting were "usually [to] camouflage misgivings on the part of the general or vacillation on the part of the government." Grant's actions ensured that misgivings on the part of a general (particularly Halleck, who almost certainly would have counseled caution) or vacillations on the part of a government (Lincoln preferred that Grant join Banks and reduce Port Hudson before tackling Vicksburg) could ruin his plans.[22]

His army crossed the Mississippi below Vicksburg and moved inland. Grant, aware of the unreliability of intelligence, questioned the strength of Johnston's Confederate troops assembling at Jackson and attacked them in order to force the issue. Grant then sent a dispatch to Halleck detailing his move toward Jackson, away from Banks, away from Vicksburg, and away from the river and his supplies. He remarked that a reply from Halleck, presumably a recall order, could not reach him for eight days. Grant short-circuited his chiefs' policy, comfortable in his evaluation of Banks and in spite of his knowledge of Lincoln's and Halleck's preferences. Grant had indeed done "a great deal" in those eight days, committing his army beyond recall.

"Our army was acting as a movable column, without a base," Grant wrote. The Union troops suffered no counterattack, such as had occurred at Belmont and Donelson, no surprise assault, as at Shiloh, and no misfire as at Iuka. Grant mastered no crises on the battlefield in this campaign; instead his troops created them for the enemy. He won five battles, scattered Johnston, wrecked a state capital, and invested Vicksburg. Grant acted as strategist, field commander, and, as in the Mexican American War, quartermaster.[23]

Grant's view of the proper method remained unequivocal: "From the moment of taking command of the 'Army in the Field,' in person, I became satisfied that Vicksburg could only be successfully turned from the South side of the City."[24]

Grant found his operational solution, running Vicksburg's batteries with gunboats and a limited number of supply boats and barges, while marching his troops below on the west bank of the Mississippi. In so doing, Grant found opposition within his own army. Sherman believed the whole move downriver past Vicksburg "unmilitary," and, favoring a return to the central route, attempted to derail Grant's campaign plan. He wrote to John A. Rawlins, Grant's chief of staff, "I would most respectfully suggest, for reasons which I will not name, that General Grant call on his corps commanders for their opinion, concise and positive, on the best general plan of campaign."[25]

Grant sought no advice or council of war to validate or question his judgment. Grant's plan remained solely his risk and responsibility. Sherman's doubt's continued and accompanied him into the field. The fiery general wrote to his brother as operations began, expressing "less confidence" in Grant's moves "than in any similar undertaking of the war." Being a true professional, Sherman expressed his doubts and in spite of them conducted his own operations throughout the campaign as if the plan had been his own.[26]

Grant later explained to staff officer Horace Porter the reasoning behind his methods:

> I will not direct anyone to do what I would not do myself. I never held what might be called councils war and I do not believe in them. They create divided responsibility and at times prevent that unity of action so necessary in the field. Some officers will in all likelihood oppose any plan that is adopted; and when it is put into execution, such officers may, by their arguments in opposition, have so far convinced themselves that the movement will fail that they cannot enter upon it with enthusiasm . . . I believe it is better for a commander to consult his generals informally, get their views and opinions, and then make up his mind what action to take and act accordingly.[27]

If Sherman failed to understand his strategy, Grant could take comfort in the probability that it vexed Pemberton also. The risk and audacity of his campaign, its "unmilitary" character, only increased its shock value as the Confederates tried to divine his true purpose. Owing inspiration to Winfield Scott's 1847 Mexico City Campaign, Grant's plan showed originality in that he relied only partially on a long and tenuous line of communications. It proved the most effective operational innovation in the Civil War. Reminiscent of the French Revolutionary and Napoleonic wars, in which disorganization and poverty forced French abandonment of the depot system, Grant proved the feasibility of armies operating without the degree of support from supply lines that had previously been thought necessary.

Clausewitz contrasted these methods with the old system, finding the new methods of "warfare based on requisition and local sources of supply," so superior to the old depot system that the new armies "no longer seem to be the same instrument." Sherman and Grant refined these methods from this point forward in the war, creating an instrument completely different from the previous Union armies that often floundered on the offensive due to the limitations of formal supply. Given Sherman's reluctance to abandon traditional supply lines before Vicksburg, clearly Grant deserves the title of teacher. While Sherman later evidenced no qualms about cutting his own supply line—not partially, as Grant had done at Vicksburg, but completely—and marching across Georgia and the Carolinas, the seed for this innovation properly belongs to Grant.[28]

Grant's supply methods also brought with them a strategic element aimed directly at secession. Grant ordered his cavalry to live off the country as much as possible, targeting "everything that can be made use of by the enemy in prolonging the war . . . in other words cripple the rebellion in every way."[29]

The Strategic Effects of Grant's Campaign of Rapid Maneuver, North and South

While other commanders obsessed with tactics, interior lines, and lines of communication, Grant thought in campaigns. When Union troops arrived on the Walnut Hills north of Vicksburg, from which the now invested Confederates had slaughtered their attackers in the December 1862 Battle of Chickasaw Bayou, Sherman commented, "Until this moment I never thought your expedition a success. I never could see the end clearly until now, but this is a campaign. This is a success if we never take the town."[30] Lincoln, positively euphoric, concurred, "Whether Gen. Grant shall or shall not consummate the capture of Vicksburg, his campaign form the beginning of this month up to the twenty second day of it, is one of the most brilliant in the world."[31]

Lincoln's rhapsodic musing is understandable. Generally, Confederate leaders such as Thomas J. "Stonewall" Jackson and Robert E. Lee had carried out most of the brilliant campaigns in the current conflict. Grant's example restored Lincoln's morale and demonstrated to the nation progress. Lincoln had "found" a general: "Grant is my man and I am his for the rest of the war." Grant's victory confirmed the North's ability to win the war and Grant's suitability for high command. This confirmation proved invaluable to further Union efforts to achieve success.[32]

Grant always saw the end clearly. The campaign, effective strategically when viewed in isolation in its own theater, generated strategic consequences affecting the conduct of the entire war—all this even "if we never take the town." The effect of one regiment's arrival on another regiment's flank is largely political. Some units break and turn and run at first contact, others turn and fight to the death. The mere arrival of a Union army of investment—approaching from a southerly direction—at the town of Vicksburg generated dismay and disquiet throughout the South.

Grant's move below Vicksburg and the battles accompanying its investment constitute perhaps the greatest example of strategic surprise accomplished in the Civil War. Clausewitz labeled surprise "basically a tactical device," generally limited and transient in its effects. While it is relatively easy to steal a march on the enemy or occupy a road while maneuvering for an advantage, surprise in the strategic realm, surprise that dictates policy, remains a difficult and rare event in military history.[33]

Vicksburg's investment constituted just such an occurrence. Grant arrived on the strategic flank of the Confederacy, and his arrival contributed in a profound way to subsequent Confederate military policy. Surprised Rebels outside Vicksburg pressured Lee to detach troops for its relief. The commander of the Army of Northern Virginia instead responded to the pressure by devising plans for a vigorous attack on northern soil. Lee believed such a move might force the Lincoln administration to detach large forces from Grant and raise the siege. How much of Lee's planning evolved directly from Grant's moves is difficult to say. Lee may have offered this justification for invasion of the North to pacify Secretary of War James Seddon and Jefferson Davis, who both favored direct action aimed at Grant's Army. Rather than detach troops west or go himself and confront Grant, Lee launched his disastrous Gettysburg Campaign, "as a way of drawing Grant from the lower Mississippi Valley." Lee's invasion of the North failed. It did not distract Grant, wreck his strategy, or diminish his numbers, though Lee managed to wreck his own army as a starving Vicksburg surrendered.[34]

War Aims and the Politics of Surrender

The fate of the Confederacy was sealed when Vicksburg fell.
—Grant

Loss of hope is worse than loss of men and land.
—B. H. Liddel-Hart

Just as Grant measured his approach to Vicksburg through the lens of politics, so he viewed its surrender. The manner in which it took place provided the opportunity for him to further the Union's war aims. Grant's famous demand for unconditional surrender at Fort Donelson had fired the imagination of the home front and had made him a hero. It had also won him a promotion and a new moniker, "Unconditional Surrender Grant." Grant proved willing to abandon a previous, successful method and demonstrated his flexibility and commitment to political substance over any empty posturing.

Surrender in and of itself presented a huge technical problem, which Grant adeptly solved to northern political advantage. The logistical requirements of transporting an army of thirty thousand prisoners to northern prison camps, as well as their feeding and housing, represented a great burden on Union resources at a time when Grant wanted to continue pressing the enemy. Grant agreed to parole the prisoners to avoid that burden, assuring that the paroled and demoralized prisoners constituted a drain on increasingly fragile Confederate logistics. Apart from such material considerations, politically the parolees "would scatter to their homes and carry the contagion of defeat with them."[35]

Sherman identified another benefit to Grant's generous surrender terms at Vicksburg: "To me the delicacy with which you have treated a brave but deluded enemy is more eloquent than the most gorgeous oratory of an Everett." Reconciliation comprised the ultimate war aim. Grant wished to destroy armies, but destruction of armies without reconciliation left open the possible renewal of the conflict.[36]

As Clausewitz offered, in war the result is never absolute. "Even the ultimate outcome of a war is not always to be regarded as final. The defeated state often considers the outcome merely as a transitory evil, for which a remedy may still be found in political conditions at some later date."[37]

Grant believed humane treatment essential for permanent reunion and ran the very real risk that some parolees might return to combat before being properly exchanged. That he did not insist on unconditional surrender showed Confederates that flexibility existed that in the future might offer some advantage. If there was no longer hope for victory, perhaps there was hope for acceptable terms of surrender.

Halleck generously evaluated Grant's performance at Vicksburg: "In boldness of plan, rapidity of execution, and brilliancy of results, these operations will compare most favorably with those of Napoleon about Ulm." But he criticized Grant's paroling of the city's garrison. Lincoln replied to Halleck and other unnamed "wiseacres" critical of Grant's policy of parole with a bizarre story of an obnoxious yellow dog, blown to pieces with a fused cartridge by some boys seeking revenge. The dog's owner, named Sykes, looked up, saw the air filled with pieces of yellow dog, and reportedly said, "Well, I guess he'll never be of much account again—as a dog." Lincoln then added for the benefit of any of Grant's detractors missing the point: "Well, I guess Pemberton's forces will never be of much account again—as an army."[38]

Sherman offered another evaluation of the battle, linking it to the evolution of Union war aims: "The value of the capture of Vicksburg, however, was not measured by the list of prisoners, guns and small-arms. . . . the event coincided as to time with another great victory which crowned our arms far away, at Gettysburg. . . . the two occurring at the same moment of time, should have ended the war."[39]

The dual victories of Vicksburg and Gettysburg signaled a great psychological and material blow to the Confederacy, but they failed to stimulate war-winning political change. Vast reserves of political capital remained, given the political will of Davis, the continued existence of the Army of Northern Virginia, and the abilities of Robert E. Lee. Additional targets in the South required identification and destruction. Davis stated his resolve: "The war . . . must go on till the last man of this generation falls in his tracks." Davis was willing to see "every Southern plantation sacked, and every Southern city in flames." The Confederate war aim remained independence, "and that," Davis insisted, "or extermination we will have."[40]

Though the war would continue for another year and nine months, Grant's lightning campaign through Mississippi set the stage and demonstrated the components necessary to win the war. Grant's use of logistical warfare, his mastery of politics, and his partnership with Lincoln all coalesced during the course of the campaign. Grant got possession of Vicksburg and the admiration of a nation. From his wife, Julia, Grant got a new name: "Victor," for victory. Grant's achievement guaranteed further rewards, for as Sherman had prophesied to Halleck, "The man who won the Mississippi would be *the* man."[41]

Notes

1. Carl von Clausewitz, *On War* (Princeton, N.J.: Princeton University Press, 1984), 606.

2. Azar Gat, *Military Thought in the Nineteenth Century* (New York: Oxford University Press, 1992), 18–23. Gat details the influence of Alfred Mahan and of Henry Halleck's translations of Baron Henri Jomini, all of which postdated Grant's tenure at the academy. Gat finds Jomini's influence on all major Civil War generals pervasive, excepting U. S. Grant. James McPherson, *Battle Cry of Freedom* (New York: Oxford University Press, 1988), 331–32, questions the significance of Jominian influence on Civil War strategy, as Grant, "the most successful strategist of the war," never read Jomini. Grady McWhinney and Perry D. Jamieson, *Attack and Die: Civil War Military Tactics and the Southern Heritage* (Tuscaloosa: University of Alabama Press, 1982), 146–53, find the offensive tactics observed during the Mexican American War of more importance than Jomini's writings or the teachings of Mahan at West Point. This debate further illustrates that no common doctrine existed. Bernard Brodie, "The Continuing Relevance of *On War*," in Carl von Clausewitz, *On War* (Princeton, N.J.: Princeton University Press, 1984), 57.

3. Christopher Bassford, *Clausewitz in English* (New York: Oxford University Press, 1994), 35, 51. Halleck lists Clausewitz three times in the chapter bibliographies of his *Elements of Military Art and Science*, without ever identifying Clausewitz's central thesis or any discussion of his main ideas.

4. Clausewitz, *On War*, 606.

5. Ibid, 97, 605–6.

6. Brooks Simpson, *Ulysses S. Grant: Triumph over Adversity, 1822–1865* (New York: Houghton Mifflin, 2000), 177, quotes newspaperman Murat Halstead.

7. Bruce Catton, *Grant Moves South* (Boston: Little, Brown, 1960), 388–90; and Simpson, *Ulysses S. Grant*, 184–85. Both provide good accounts of Dana's mission.

8. Ulysses S. Grant, *Personal Memoirs of U. S. Grant* (New York: Da Capo Press, 1952), 239; Samuel Carter III, *The Final Fortress: The Campaign for Vicksburg, 1862–1863* (New York: St. Martin's Press 1980), 149; J. F. C. Fuller, *The Generalship of Ulysses S. Grant* (London: Da Capo Press, 1929), 184. Clausewitz believed the mere threat of an actual engagement often functions in a manner similar to the engagement itself. Clausewitz, *On War*, 97.

9. Fuller, *Generalship of Grant*, 9.

10. Grant, *Personal Memoirs*, 301.

11. James M. McPherson, *Battle Cry of Freedom* (New York: Oxford University Press, 1988), 637. James R. Arnold, in *Grant Wins the War: Decision at Vicksburg* (New York: Wiley and Sons, 1997), argues the Vicksburg Campaign decided the course of the war. Fuller, *Generalship of Grant*, 28, 128.

12. John Y. Simon, ed., *Papers of Ulysses S. Grant*, 31 vols. (Carbondale: Southern Illinois University Press, 1967–2009), 8:130–31; Herman Hattaway and Archer Jones, *How the North Won: A Military History of the Civil War* (Chicago: University of Illinois Press, 1983), 369.

13. Catton, *Grant Moves South*, 324–40, provides a good account McClernand's views. Adam Badeau, *Military History of U. S. Grant*, 3 vol. (New York: D. Appleton and Co., 1881), 1:183, 616–18.

14. Grant, *Personal Memoirs*, 230.

15. Michael B. Ballard, *U. S. Grant: The Making of a General* (Lanham: Rowman & Littlefield, 2005), 120, suggests that part of Grant's presence might have had something to do with a desire to more closely watch McClernand. Significantly McClernand wrote Grant a letter approving of the plan, and predated it so it would appear that the idea for the move was his. See Simpson, *Ulysses S. Grant*, 183; and Geoffrey Perret, *Ulysses S. Grant: Soldier and President* (New York: Random House, 1997), 240.

16. Brooks D. Simpson, "Lincoln and Grant: A Reappraisal of a Relationship" in Frank J. Williams, William D. Pearson, and Vincent J. Marsala, eds., *Abraham Lincoln: Sources and Style of Leadership* (Westport: Greenwood Press, 1994), 117.

17. Clausewitz, *On War*, 194, 147.

18. Simon., *Papers of Ulysses S. Grant*, 6:199.

19. Ibid., 8:485–508

20. Ibid., 6:263.

21. Ibid., 494. John Russel Young, *Around the World with General Grant*, 2 Vol., (New York: American News Company, 1879), 2:619.

22. Clausewitz, On *War*, 598–99.

23. Young, *Around the World with General Grant*, 624.

24. Simon, *Papers of Ulysses S. Grant*, 8:485.

25. U.S. War Department, *The War of the Rebellion: A Compilation of the Official Records of the Union and Confederate Armies*, 128 vols. (Washington, DC: Government Printing Office, 1880–1901), series 1, vol. 24, pt. 3: 179–80.

26. Rachel Sherman Thorndike, ed., *The Sherman Letters* (New York: Charles Scribner's Sons, 1894), 201.

27. Horace Porter, *Campaigning with Grant* (New York: Century, 1906), 316.

28. Clausewitz, *On War*, 337.

29. Simon, *Papers of Ulysses S. Grant*, 8:160.

30. Carter, *Fortress*, 208.

31. Joseph T. Glatthaar, *Partners in Command: The Relationships Between Leaders in the Civil War* (New York: Free Press, 1994). 194.

32. McPherson, *Battle Cry of Freedom*, 638.

33. Clausewitz, *On War*, 198.

34. Edwin B. Coddington, *The Gettysburg Campaign: A Study in Command* (New York: Scribner, 1968), 5–7. Joseph T. Glatthaar, *Lee's Army: From Victory to Collapse* (New York: Free Press, 2008), 268–69. Archer Jones, *Civil War Command and Strategy: The Process of Victory and Defeat* (New York: Free Press, 1992), 167, finds Lee focused on his own theater despite his statements at the time to the contrary.

35. Grant, *Personal Memoirs of U. S, Grant*, 297–98. McPherson, *Battle Cry of Freedom*, 636.

36. Simon, *Papers of Ulysses S. Grant*, 8:478.

37. Clausewitz, *On War*, 80.

38. Simon, *Papers of Ulysses S. Grant*, 8:532; Grant, *Personal Memoirs*, 299; Catton, *Grant Moves South*, 478–79; Porter, *Campaigning with Grant*, 27–28.

39. William T. Sherman, *Memoirs of William T. Sherman* (New York: Library of America: 1990), 359.

40. McPherson, *Battle Cry of Freedom*, 768.

41. Porter, *Campaigning with Grant*, 285; William T. Sherman, *Home Letters of General Sherman*, ed. M. A. deWolf Howe (New York: Scribner's, 1909), 287. William S. McFeely, *Grant: A Biography* (New York: W. W. Norton, 2002), 81, dates the nickname's origin much earlier and attributes it to Grant's admiration for Victor Emmanuel.

CONTRIBUTORS

INDEX

CONTRIBUTORS

Michael B. Ballard received his PhD in history at Mississippi State University, where he was an archivist in the university library, coordinator of the congressional collection, and associate editor of *The Papers of Ulysses S. Grant*. He retired at the end of 2012. He has published eleven books on the Civil War, among them *Pemberton: A Biography* (1991), which received a nonfiction award from the Mississippi Institute of Arts and Letters, and *Vicksburg: The Campaign That Opened the Mississippi* (2004).

Steven Nathaniel Dossman received both his master's degree and his PhD in history at Texas Christian University, where his dissertation dealt with soldier and civilian interaction during the Vicksburg Campaign. He is the author of *Campaign for Corinth: Blood in Mississippi* (2006).

William B. Feis earned his PhD in military history from the Ohio State University and teaches American history at Buena Vista University in Storm Lake, Iowa. He has written extensively on Civil War military intelligence, including *Grant's Secret Service: The Intelligence War from Belmont to Appomattox* (2002), which was an Editor's Choice of the History Book Club and a finalist for the U.S. Army Historical Foundation Book Award. He is also a coauthor and a coeditor (with Allan R. Millett and Peter Maslowski) of *For the Common Defense: A Military History of the United States from 1607 to 2012* (2012).

Jason M. Frawley received his PhD from Texas Christian University in 2008 and teaches history at Tarrant County College, Northwest Campus. In 2005 he was awarded the George M. Nethken Memorial Fellowship at the George Tyler Moore Center for the Study of the Civil War, and in 2012–13 he was the Thomas W. Smith Post-Doctoral Fellow and Visiting Assistant Professor of Civil War Era Studies at Gettysburg College.

Charles D. Grear received his PhD from Texas Christian University and now teaches at Prairie View A&M University. He has written extensively on the involvement of Texas in the Civil War, including *Why Texans Fought in the Civil War* (2010), and has edited several books, among them *The Chattanooga Campaign* (with Steven E. Woodworth, 2012).

J. Parker Hills retired from the Mississippi Army National Guard with the rank of brigadier general. He is a graduate of the U.S. Army War College and holds a master's degree from Sul Ross State University. In addition to his years of military service and leadership training, he has presided over several historic Civil War battlefield commissions and has authored numerous articles and books on American history and the Civil War. His books include *A Study in Warfighting: Nathan Bedford Forrest and the Battle of Brice's Crossroads* (1995); *The Vicksburg Campaign Driving Tour Guide* (coauthored with the late Warren Grabau, 2008); *Receding Tide: Vicksburg and Gettysburg, the Campaigns That Changed the Civil War* (coauthored with Edwin C. Bearss, 2010); and *Art of Commemoration: Vicksburg National Military Park* (2012).

Gary D. Joiner earned his PhD in history from St. Martin's College, Lancaster University, in the UK. He teaches at Louisiana State University in Shreveport, where he holds the Mary Anne and Leonard Selber Professorship in History. He has written or edited thirteen books, among them *Shiloh and the Western Campaign of 1862* (2009) and *Mr. Lincoln's Brown Water Navy: Mississippi Squadron* (2007).

John R. Lundberg earned his PhD from Texas Christian University and teaches at Collin College in Plano, Texas. He is the author of *The Finishing Stroke: Texans in the 1864 Tennessee Campaign* (2002) and *Granbury's Texas Brigade: Diehard Western Confederates* (2012), as well as numerous articles on Texas and Civil War history.

Paul L. Schmelzer received his PhD in military history from Texas Christian University. Currently, he teaches American history at Colorado State University at Pueblo and military history at Fort Carson.

Timothy B. Smith earned his PhD at Mississippi State University. A veteran of the National Park Service, he teaches history at the University of Tennessee at Martin. He is the author or editor of twelve books on the Civil War, among them *Champion Hill: Decisive Battle for Vicksburg* (2004), *Mississippi in the Civil War: The Home Front* (2010), and *Corinth 1862: Siege, Battle, Occupation* (2012).

Steven E. Woodworth received his PhD from Rice University. He teaches at Texas Christian University and has authored, coauthored, or edited thirty-one books on the Civil War era, among them *Nothing but Victory: The Army of the Tennessee, 1861–1865* (2006) and *Jefferson Davis and His Generals: The Failure of Confederate Command in the West* (1990).

INDEX

Fort Beauregard, South Carolina, 20
Fort Cobun, Mississippi, 16–17, 48, 50, 52
Fort Davis, Texas, 38
Fort Donelson, Battle of, 10, 12, 133–34, 145, 154, 156, 164
Fort Donelson, Tennessee, 220, 221, 224
Fort Henry, Battle of, 133, 154, 156, 164
Fort Henry, Tennessee, 220
Fort Hill, Mississippi, 13, 19
Fort Sheridan, Illinois, 38
Fort Wade, Mississippi, 16–17, 48, 50, 52
Foster, Jacob T., 180–81
Fourteen Mile Creek, 85–88
Fredericksburg, Battle of, 31
Fremantle, Arthur, 202, 208
Frémont, John C., 34
French Revolution, 222
Fuller, J. F. C., 216–17

Galena, Illinois, 131–32
Gardner, Franklin, 70, 73, 76, 78
Garrard, Theophilus Toulmin, 58, 180, 183, 185
Garrott, Isham V., 58, 61
Gates, Elijah, 178–79, 184
Geer, Allen Morgan, 78–79, 81, 83
General Benjamin H. Grierson Society, 39
Gettysburg, Battle of, 20, 32, 153
Gettysburg Campaign, 224–25
Gills Creek, 78, 80
Gist, States Rights, 123
Glasgow, Samuel L., 183
Glover, Danny, 37
Grabau, Warren, 162
Grand Gulf, battle of, 49–51
Grand Gulf, Mississippi, 10–11, 16, 18, 22, 24, 28, 47–54, 61, 67–70, 72, 74, 77–78, 83–84, 145, 147, 157, 159–62, 164, 197–98, 219–20
Grand Gulf batteries, 55
Grant, Fred, 69, 167, 189
Grant, Jesse, 130–32
Grant, Julia, 12, 131, 200, 226
Grant, Ulysses S., 1–13, 15–20, 24–26, 28–32, 37, 39, 43–55, 59–61, 65–85, 87–89, 96–100, 102, 104–7, 110, 112, 117–26, 129–51, 153–69, 173–80, 182, 187–90, 194–95, 197–11, 214–27
Green, Martin Edwin, 55–59, 61, 178, 183–85
Greenman, J. W., 206–7
Greensburg, Louisiana, 73
Greenville, Mississippi, 159
Greenwood, Mississippi, 160
Greer, James A., 12

Gregg, John, 5, 66, 70–74, 76–78, 80–82, 84–88, 96, 98–101, 103–5, 122–26, 147, 165–66, 202
Grenada, Mississippi, 70
Grierson, Benjamin H., 4, 17, 24–39, 71, 74, 76–77, 160, 164
Grierson's Day, 39
Grierson's Raid, 24–25, 28, 30, 33–36, 38, 40, 71, 160
Griffin, Patrick M., 86
Grimsley, Mark, 194
Grindstone Ford, 67
Gunton, Bob, 37

Halleck, Henry W., 18, 68–69, 74, 78, 83–84, 134–42, 145, 151, 155, 167, 216, 218, 220–21, 225–27
Hall's Ferry, 73, 80
Halstead, Murat, 216
Hamer, Thomas, 130
Hankinson's Ferry, 67–68, 70, 72–74, 76–81, 84, 200
Hard Times Landing, 121
Hard Times Plantation, 10, 16–17, 47–49
Hardscrabble Crossroads, 70
Harris, Charles L., 54–55
Harrisonburg, Louisiana, 20
Hatch, Edward, 25, 27, 31, 37
Haynes Bluff, Mississippi, 18–19, 160–61, 210
Hazelhurst, Mississippi, 28–29, 32
Henderson, G. F. R., 72, 76
Hillyer, William S., 69–70, 74–75
Hoadley, Robert, 108–9
Hobbs, Charles A., 54
Hoel, William R., 12, 15–17
Holden, William, 36–37
Holly Springs, Mississippi, 2, 75, 140, 157, 167, 215, 217
Holmes, Samuel A., 101, 104–5
Holmes, Theophilus, 118–19
Hooker, Joseph, 45, 75–76, 81
Hopkins, Owen, 199, 202–3
Hovey, Alvin Peterson, 59, 79
Hurlbut, Stephen A., 69, 74

Illinois State Historical Library, 38
Illinois State Historical Society, 33
Illinois troops: 2nd Artillery, 180, 182; 2nd Cavalry, 73; 3rd Cavalry, 162; 6th Cavalry, 25, 30; 7th Cavalry, 25, 27, 38, 74; 7th Cavalry (Reactivated), 38; 8th Infantry, 99; 20th Infantry, 78; 21st Infantry, 132; 31st Infantry, 106; 47th Infantry, 111; 99th Infantry, 54; Chicago Mercantile Battery, 180, 196

CIVIL WAR CAMPAIGNS IN THE HEARTLAND

The area west of the Appalachian Mountains, known in Civil War parlance as "the West," has always stood in the shadow of the more famous events on the other side of the mountains, the eastern theater, where even today hundreds of thousands visit the storied Virginia battlefields. Nevertheless, a growing number of Civil War historians believe that the outcome of the war was actually decided in the region east of the Mississippi River and west of the watershed between the Atlantic and the Gulf of Mexico.

Modern historians began to rediscover the decisive western theater in the 1960s through the work of the late Thomas Lawrence Connelly, particularly his 1969 book *Army of the Heartland*, in which he analyzed the early years of the Confederacy's largest army in the West. Many able scholars have subsequently contributed to a growing historiography of the war in the West. Despite recent attention to the western theater, less is understood about the truly decisive campaigns of the war than is the case with the dramatic but ultimately indecisive clashes on the east coast.

Several years ago, three of Steven E. Woodworth's graduate students pointed out that the western theater possessed no series of detailed multi-author campaign studies comparable to the excellent and highly acclaimed series Gary W. Gallagher has edited on the campaigns of the eastern theater. Charles D. Grear, Jason M. Frawley, and David Slay joined together in suggesting that Woodworth ought to take the lead in filling the gap. The result is this series, its title a nod of appreciation to Professor Connelly. Its goals are to shed more light on the western campaigns and to spark new scholarship on the western theater.

CIVIL WAR CAMPAIGNS IN THE HEARTLAND SERIES